DICK VITALE'S

LIVING A DREAM

REFLECTIONS ON 25 YEARS SITTING IN
THE BEST SEAT IN THE HOUSE

DICK VITALE

WITH

DICK WEISS

WWW.SPORTSPUBLISHINGLLC.COM

Requests for permission to make copies of any part of this work should be mailed to the following address:

Permissions Department
Sports Publishing L.L.C.
804 North Neil Street
Champaign, IL 61820

Unless otherwise indicated, photos are from Dick Vitale's personal collection. Every reasonable attempt has been made to determine ownership of copyright. Please notify the publisher of any erroneous credits or omissions, and corrections will be made to subsequent editions/future printings.

Director of production: Susan M. Moyer
Developmental editor: Mark E. Zulauf
Book design: Jennifer L. Polson
Project manager: Greg Hickman
Dust jacket design: Joseph T. Brumleve
Copy editors: Holly Birch and Cynthia L. McNew

ISBN: 1-58261-738-4

Printed in the United States.

Where do I start to share my feelings about the importance of Howie Schwab to me throughout my career at ESPN and ABC? Howie is Mr. Dedication. He eats, sleeps, and drinks sports. Believe me, he has been responsible for many of the ideas that I've utilized during my telecasts throughout the years. His research and knowledge have provided me with plenty of information that I have shared with the fans. Much of the data I've used on camera, over the radio waves, through the Internet on ESPN.com, in ESPN the Magazine, and in various other capacities has been imparted to me by Howie. I dedicate this book to Howie Schwab for being so special. He has been invaluable to me in providing any information that I ever request. His quick response to any question I have involving the game of basketball has been remarkable. Yes, Howie Schwab, to put it in Vitalese, you are Awesome, baby, with a capital A. You are without a doubt a three-S man—super, scintillating, and sensational. I thank you so much for all the time and energy you have extended to me throughout my tenure at ESPN.

—Dick Vitale

To Hayden, Madison, Delaney and Griffin Schenker, Hunter Whitlock and Abigail Menear, who keep Joan and me young.

—Dick Weiss

CONTENTS

FOREWORD

Friend. It is the most appropriate word I can think of to describe Dick Vitale. And though I do have a personal relationship with Dick, I mean *friend* in the larger sense of the word.

A 16-year coaching veteran of all levels of the game and one of the most popular—and genuine—television personalities of our generation, Dick has been one of the great assets for basketball, particularly the college game. His impact on our sport has been significant, and through the years, it has spread from coaching to broadcasting. One of college basketball's biggest proponents, Dick has touched millions of lives through the years. The message has always—I repeat always—been positive regarding basketball. He truly has the best interest of the sport in mind, largely because he's been involved in the game in so many different ways.

As a coach, he touched lives in junior high school, high school, college and at the professional level. Not surprisingly, his resume is impressive. Dick led his alma mater, East Rutherford High School in New Jersey, to four sectional and two state championships in the 1960s. From there, he moved on to the college level, first as an assistant at Rutgers and then as the head coach at Detroit University, where he won 78 games, losing just 30 times. He then became head coach of the Detroit Pistons. His love of teaching basketball is still evident in his work. I don't know if Dick has ever really stopped coaching, even though he's not on the sidelines anymore. One thing is certain—he is a friend to all he coached.

Following his successful coaching career, he joined an upstart television initiative called ESPN in 1979 and was actually part of the first college basketball game ever aired by the network. Twenty-five years later, Dick has broadcast more than a thousand games, including many of ours at Duke, and has become a household name for his colorful style and antics, all done because he has a passion for what he does and for whom he reaches. Dick Vitale, simply put, is about people—people from all walks of life, from all levels and all facets of our game. Whether it is his extensive work with charitable causes, touting the next "PTPer" or "Diaper Dandy" on the air, or greeting admiring fans before a game, Dick's exuberance for people is a cornerstone of success in everything he does. He will tell anyone how he feels, on or off the air, and he will mean it. To everyone he touches, he is a friend.

Not only does Dick give us his best on the air every week, he also finds the time to work for so many others through charity—The V. Foundation for Cancer Research and the Boys and Girls Club being the most prominent examples. Dick spends countless hours and devotes so much of his time to great causes such as these, and he does so with the same passion he exudes on your television screen every week. Basketball has given him the opportunity to help others, and he has taken full advantage of that avenue. Again, Dick touches lives. He's a true friend.

His accomplishments are too many to list here. Among the highlights are his election into seven Halls of Fame and earning multiple national media distinctions and awards, including the 2003 National Pathfinder Award, which is given to a person who has demonstrated a commitment to improving the lives of America's youth. Although he has been honored in nearly every way, I still believe the greatest recognition Dick receives is that of "a friend."

Dick has been a great friend to some, but he has never stopped being a friend to many. Mainly, he has been the best friend to the game. To me, that is his impact and legacy in the sport.

—Mike Krzyzewski
Duke University

ACKNOWLEDGMENTS

Before I pay tribute to those at ESPN and ABC who have been vital to my career, I must share a word about the most precious people ever in my life—my mom and dad. My mother and father never had a formal education, but they each had a doctorate of love. They constantly inspired me to always pursue my dreams. I was fortunate to grow up in a home filled with love, which I shared with my mom and dad, my sister Terry and my brother John.

Now that I am beginning to celebrate my Silver Anniversary at ESPN, I want to acknowledge all of the following individuals for the generosity, support, and direction they have given me and a career that has filled me with so much happiness.

My beautiful family, who mean everything to me—my loving wife Lorraine, my daughters Terri and Sherri, my sons-in-law Chris Sforzo and Thomas Krug, and my grandchildren Sydney, Connor and Jake.

In the early days, Scotty Connal believed in me and gave me a golden opportunity. Chet Simmons, our president, put the initial stamp of approval on Scotty's recommendation to use me. And while I've been at ESPN, many former executives such as Bill Grimes, Bill Fitts, and Ellen Beckwith have been essential to my growth. How could I ever not be indebted to Ellen Beckwith, who provided me with all of my assignments.

At ESPN, I want to thank the executives and the administrative staff for their genuine support and, most of all, for their strong belief in my talents. I would like to share a special thank you with executives George Bodenheimer, Mark Shapiro, Steve Bornstein, Howard Katz, Steve Anderson, John Walsh, Al Jaffe, Norby Williamson, Jed Drake, John Wildhack, Dave Miller, Dan Steir, Barry Sacks, Brian Sherriffe, Mo Davenport, Jay Rothman, Tim Corrigan, John Skipper, and Loren Matthews.

Through my numerous years behind the microphone, I have been fortunate that my play-by-play partners have allowed me to operate in a comfort zone and to do what I do best—talk about a game I have such love for.

I have been blessed to work with so many terrific on-air personalities and play-by-play voices, stars who shine, like Mike Patrick, Brad Nessler, Brent Musburger, Keith Jackson, Dan Shulman, Chris Fowler, Bob Ley, Jim Simpson, Digger Phelps, Mike Tirico, Roger Twibell, Linda Cohn, Rece Davis, Mark Jones, Robin Roberts, Jay Bilas, Andy Katz, Brad Daugherty, Michelle Tafoya, Ron Franklin, Bob Carpenter, Dave Sims, and Dave Barnett. It would be impossible to list every *SportsCenter* host whom I've had the pleasure to share moments with in addition to all of those radio hosts at ESPN, but let me tell you, it has been a joy to work with such pros.

Of course, I will never forget the time I had working as part of a trio with John Saunders and Jimmy Valvano. Some of the most special days I enjoyed in my professional life were with those guys. Boy, do I miss Jimmy!

I want to thank all of the producers, directors, graphic operators, and all the people behind the scenes who have been so supportive. Production people like Ray Tipton, Kim Belton, Rob Lemley, Bill Graff, Matt Sandulli, Ed Placey, Larry Holmes, Chip Dean, Scott Johnson, Aaron Owens, Kristi Setaro, Jerry Goodman, Josh Hoffman, Jay Kutlow, Phil Dean, Ken Dennis, Jimmy Moore, Drew Esocoff, Mark Loomis, and Mike Schwab have all been enjoyable to work with and have provided me with professional advice and guidance throughout my career.

ESPN's public relations staff has been very helpful and important over the years. Special thanks to Rosa Gatti, Chris LaPlaca, Mike Soltys, Josh Krulewitz, Rob Tobias, Curt Pires and Dave Nagle. The programming department has had an impact as well—thanks to Dave Brown, Tom Odjakjian, Len DeLuca and Burke Magnus.

I've also had great representation over the years. The individuals at IMG, to me, are the best at what they do. I am so thankful to these representatives, starting with the boss, Barry Frank, his assistant, Sandy Montag, and particularly those who worked with me in the early days, Peter Goldberg, Roy Judelson and, currently, Sue Lipton. I thank them from the bottom of my heart for opening doors that have given me such a fulfilling career. Also, I've been fortunate to be a member of the most prestigious speakers bureau in the world, the Washington Speakers Bureau, and I can't thank enough Harry Rhoads and his staff for all the assistance they have provided me throughout my career.

And where would we be in this business without all of the support people, people who work diligently to take care of all the little things that mean so much? People like Jay Cohen, Heather Behrendt, and a host of others—it would be difficult for me to list them all.

—Dick Vitale

A sincere note of thanks to my wife, Joan Williamson, who was an enormous help working on this manuscript and could have been a great journalist herself; Dick and Lorraine Vitale, who have always been so generous in every way toward Joan and me; their daughters Sherri and Terri and their families; Duke coach Mike Krzyzewski for taking time to do the foreword; my mother Barbara Weiss; my brother Roger; Adam Berkowitz, Leon Carter, Terri Thompson, Roger Rubin, Will Pakuta, Mike O'Keeffe, Wayne Coffey, Delores Thompson, Mitch Lawrence, Kristie Ackert and Bill Price of the *New York Daily News;* Howie Schwab, who has become a good friend through this project and has been a huge reservoir of research information; Josh Krulewitz of ESPN; Mark E. Zulauf and Peter Bannon of Sports Publishing L.L.C., who helped make this happen; Bob Ryan, Steve Wieberg, Brian Morrison, Dan Wetzel, Mike Sheridan, Steve Kirschner, John Feinstein, Mark Blaudschun, Chris Dufresne, Malcolm Moran, Andy Bagnato, Joe Mitch, Herb Gould, Wally Hall, Al Featherston, Bill Brill, Neil Amato, Lennox Rawlings, Bill Cole, Marty Cohen, Caulton Tudor, Phil Chardis, Ken Davis, Mike Waters, Ivan Maisel, Andy Katz, Rob Daniels, Tim Peeler, Mike DeCourcy, Frank Burleson, Lenn Robbins, Jeff Jacobs, Darrell Bird, Allen Cutler, Dick Jerardi, Steve Richardson, Jim O'Connell, Dave Sittler, Tom Shatel, Robyn Norwood, Mark Whicker, Alex Wolff, John Akers, Nanci Donald, Blair Kerkhoff, Josh Barr, Kelly Whiteside, Mary Flannery, Rick Bozich, Pat Forde, Tom Liucci, Gene Wojciechowski, Skip Myslenski, Tony Kornheiser, Mike Wilbon, Lesley Visser, Seth Davis, Dave Jones, Tony Barnhart, Joe Biddle, George Plaster, David Teel, Norb Garrett, Howard Garfinkel, Vahe Gregorian, Clark Francis, Ken Denlinger, Mike Kern, Ray Cella, John Paquette, Jackie MacMullen, Charlie Pierce, Bill Jackson, John Lewandowski, Matt Larson, Diane Weiss, John Jackson, Wayne Coffey, and Rob Daniels—friends in our business who love college sports as much as I do; college coaches and administrators everywhere who feel the same way; Sam Albano and John

Salvo; Joe, Betty Ann, Tyler and Devon Cassidy; Frank and Alma Bonini; Mike Flynn of Blue Star; Rick Troncelliti, Frank Morgan, Pat Plunkett, Jerry McLaughlin, Tom Healy, Gene Whelan, Joe Timony, Allen Rubin, Bobby Jacobs and The Guys.

—Dick Weiss

1

CABLE VISION

Look at me. I'm flying, man.

There I was, flying over the crowd in an Elvis costume on the ESPY Awards show at the MGM Grand in Las Vegas a few years ago.

It wasn't my idea. ESPN was looking for a grand entrance to start the show. And they wanted me involved. I should have known better.

Steve Anderson, one of our senior executives, looked at me and said, "This is going to be great, but I hope you're up for it."

I had no idea. I knew I was really going to kick the ceremony off, but I figured it would be at ground level.

"No," he said, "You're going to go up to the top of the building." They wanted me to be a flying Elvis, like one of those guys who sky-dived out of a plane in that Nicholas Cage movie, *Honeymoon in Vegas*. Man, I don't know how many feet up I was, and they had me strapped into this contraption so they could fly me in on cables.

And then, on top of it, they put me in that suit. It was warm. I mean, it was hot, man. But I'll do anything for ESPN. I love ESPN, baby.

So there I am. I'm flying in. I toss my Elvis wig out to the crowd, where it's caught by Cybill Shepherd.

And I miss the landing.

All throughout rehearsal, the landing had gone as smooth as could be. But this was the real deal now—showtime. I'm gliding down, getting ready to land—all of a sudden, they're pulling me back up again. I'm thinking to myself, "What the hell is this?" Finally, after jerking me back, they bring me onto the stage in a second shot.

Michael Jordan, who was right in front of the stage, just broke up. When I finally got to the stage to start the show, he was nearly in tears from laughing so hard.

There I was, supposedly a grown man, and I'm acting as if I'm about 10.

So what's new?

Welcome to my world. I'm celebrating my Silver Anniversary—25 years at ESPN—and I'm still as crazy as ever. But I'm no longer just that bald-headed, one-eyed wacko who'd gotten the ziggy from the Detroit Pistons.

I'm playing on a bigger stage these days. And enjoying every minute of it, baby.

When I started at ESPN, back in September, 1979, the network operated out of a couple of trailers in Bristol, Connecticut. I was one of their first hires, after Bob Ley and Chris Berman. Using 625 TV cable systems and a satellite for transmission, ESPN initially reached about 20 percent of the nation's viewers.

At first, ESPN focused primarily on more obscure sports such as pistol shooting or the world's strongest man competitions. In fact, the first live event on ESPN was the pro slo-pitch softball world series on September 7, 1979.

Today, ESPN has its own campus, man. It has 28 satellite dishes and currently reaches 86.6 million homes through 26,000 cable providers. It broadcasts in 21 languages worldwide. It has grown from one building to seven; from three satellite dishes to 28; from 78 employees located in Bristol to more than 2,000 worldwide.

And how did I get involved?

Lexington, Kentucky, 1977: The University of Detroit was playing the University of Michigan in the NCAA Sweet 16, the last game I ever coached on the collegiate level.

The Wolverines, coached by Johnny Orr, were No. 1 in the country. They were a group of guys who had lined up the year before against unbeaten Indiana—my favorite team of all time—in the national championship game. Michigan had great players—guys like Phil Hubbard, a great Windex man, and a dynamite guard in Rickey Green, who was as quick as I've ever seen with the ball.

We were good, too. Real good, man. We'd won 21 straight and beaten one of my favorite guys, Al McGuire, who eventually cut down the nets at the championship game with Marquette that year.

My players would salivate at the thought of playing a game against Michigan. They would've died for the chance, but Michigan wouldn't play us. We just couldn't get them on the schedule.

Then, when the NCAA pairings came out, I said, "Oh, oh, all we've got to do is beat Middle Tennessee and we'll play Michigan in the Sweet 16. They can't dodge us any longer."

We lost in the last minute, 86-81. Until my dying day, I will believe that we cost Michigan the national championship because we played them in such an emotional, all-out Maalox Masher that went down to the final minute. We took so much out of them that they didn't have anything left for UNC-Charlotte and Cornbread Maxwell 36 hours later in the regional finals. They lost in a major upset.

Our game was televised by NBC. Curt Gowdy did play-by-play. John Wooden did the color. And I was absolutely in awe of both of them. In those days, the University of Detroit's games didn't get televised. That was our only game of any significance on national TV.

Producing that game was Scotty Connal. I've since found out from Scotty that, while he was there in Lexington for our game, he'd heard me speak at a function and noted to himself, "If I ever become the head of a network and this guy's not tied up, I want to give him a buzz." Well, later on, when he read in transaction reports in the newspapers that the Pistons had given me the ziggy, he did just that.

Not surprisingly, however, when the Pistons decided to fire me, my wife, Lorraine, was the first one to know.

The team had gotten off to a 4-8 start that year, and one night I had been talking to Bill Davidson, the owner, trying to get some things off my chest, some things that had been bothering me since I was hired.

When I hung up, my wife said to me, "Hon, you're getting fired. I heard you talking to Mr. Davidson about decisions that were being made. You just can't do that. You can't talk to an owner like that."

Sure enough, the next morning, while I was getting ready to go in and coach against Dr. J and the Philadelphia 76ers, my administrative assistant, Madelon Hazy, called. She said, "Before you come to practice, Bill Davidson is going to come to your house."

"I'm going to go around the block until the limousine leaves," Lorraine said to me, "but I'm telling you now, prepare yourself. You're getting fired."

I replied, "No way. Everybody knows we've got a team full of young kids. We're rebuilding. But we're creating some excitement and we're getting good fan interest."

Come on, guys, we should all listen to our wives.

Davidson came into the house, and in a low-key way, he said, "Dick, I just made a coaching change."

"Excuse me?" I wondered aloud, "a coaching change?"

"You've been fired."

I couldn't get over it. I'd had such a skyrocketing career, going from teaching sixth grade all the way to coaching the Pistons. And then it was all pulled away from me.

It was tough, man.

Wow, it was embarrassing. The Pistons had started a campaign called the "ReVITALEized" Pistons. They'd made bumper stickers and banners to distribute all over the city to promote the hope that my enthusiasm could turn the team around. I felt bad for letting down so many people, including Madelon Hazy, assistant coaches Mike Brunker, Richie Adubato, Al Menendez, my director of scouting, and many others who had joined me when I was hired. It hurt to know that I'd let them all down.

People always say that I'm the head of the coaches' fraternity, always singing their praises. Well, let me tell you why. If you're fired in the NBA or fired from a major college job, it is just incredibly difficult to get back to that same level. If you were to keep track of the number of guys who got fired, then made it back to the top, the number is very small.

And I'm not one of them.

I started calling people, sending resumes, pleading for people to give me an opportunity. Marketing, public relations, administration—I couldn't get anywhere. Nobody would return my phone calls. I found out, the hard way, that the only people who would call me back were family.

Then, two weeks after I was fired, the phone rang. I heard this voice on the other end of the line say, "My name is Scotty Connal. I'm the head of production for ESPN, and I want you to do our first major college basketball game for this new network."

I'd never heard of it. It sounded like a disease. I mean, ESPN—what is that anyway?

At first, I turned him down. I said, "I can't do a game. I don't know anything about television." (Of course, there are people today who would say that I still don't know anything about television, because I violate every rule of broadcasting—but more on that later.)

But once again, I have to give my wife credit. She said to me, "Rich, all you're doing is sitting around the house." She was right. I was starting to watch soap operas. You know, Luke and Laura, *General Hospital.* I mean, I was embarrassed to go out. I was depressed. I was humiliated. When you're a coach, everybody knows your story. Everybody knows if you're a success or a failure. It's a very difficult life at times.

So when Scotty called me back a couple of days later, I said, "OK, I'll do a game."

It was DePaul and Wisconsin at Chicago. Bill Cofield was the coach of Wisconsin, and they had a great guard, Wes Mathews, out of Connecticut. DePaul was flat-out golden. Those were the Mark Aguirre days, and Hall of Famer Ray Meyer was the coach. He was warm to me, and I felt like a million dollars.

I felt important, felt I'd gotten my self-esteem back.

I went to Chicago the day of the game and checked into the hotel. After I'd gotten some lunch, I figured I'd just mosey around for a while and enjoy the nice day. I had no idea about production meetings.

So I finally strolled into the DePaul Arena about an hour before tipoff. I thought I'd gotten there in plenty of time, but people were frantically running around and everyone kept asking me, "Hey, where have you been? We've been looking for you. We've got a game."

I said, "But I'm early. We've got about an hour and 15 minutes."

They were, like, "Uh-uh, man. We've got to start."

It was a whole new world to me. Guys talking in your ear, "We're going to go to commercial." You're trying to determine when to come in, when to come out.

I worked with a guy named Joe Boyle. He was a hockey guy. I imagine he must have gone crazy after his very first game with Dick Vitale—I haven't seen him since. I hope his career didn't come to an end.

Scotty Connal was also very much into hockey. He was a hockey fanatic. He'd come over from NBC, where he had headed up their college basketball coverage. He was the one who had hired Billy Packer and Al McGuire. He put that team together with Dick Enberg—the best threesome ever.

And he's also responsible for me.

The president of NBC Sports had been Chet Simmons. He came over as the president and the head of ESPN and brought Scotty in as his vice president in charge of production. Then they brought in their first signature hire ever, Jim Simpson, who had called every major event imaginable at NBC—the Orange Bowl, the World Series, the Super Bowl, all the major tennis events—you name an event, he called it. And, let me tell you, he's as classy a pro as you could ever work with. He'd called them all.

Well, after that first game, the phone rang. It was Scotty, who said very bluntly, "Dick, you've got three things we can't teach. You have enthusiasm, candidness and knowledge of the game. What you don't have is any clue on how to get in and get out and anything about the world of television. But that can be taken care of."

He told me that critics were going to rip me about this and that, but not to worry about it. He was just beautiful to me, told me I had a future in TV. He really worked with me.

Scotty called me in several times after that. He told me, "Before you think about getting back into coaching, I want you to know something. You have something special in TV. You connect with the people, whether they agree with you or not."

I didn't know what he meant. I was just thinking that I wanted to get back into coaching.

But I soon began to realize that everywhere I went, people were responding to me.

And not always positively, either. They would say things like, "Dick, I heard what you said last night—I don't agree with you, man."

That's when it dawned on me that I'd hit a nerve.

The first time that happened to me was when Houston played North Carolina State in the NCAA finals in 1983. Now, Houston had a freshman point guard, Alvin Franklin, and North Carolina State had two seniors—Sidney Lowe and Dereck Whittenburg—in the backcourt.

I came out and said, "You're not going to win the national title with a freshman guard."

And the next day, Reid Gettys, one of the Houston guards, was quoted all over saying, "Well, you know, opinions are like butts. Everyone has one."

I thought, "Wow, I must be making an impact because that was the first Final Four I went to for ESPN and all these Houston fans were coming up, saying, 'We're going to show you, Dickie V.'"

I told myself, "My God, I must be connecting."

That's when it started to kick in that maybe I'd found a career. It was four years after I'd started. And maybe I didn't want to get back into coaching.

I will never, ever forget the time I did the Pistons caravan with Will Robinson—who's 90-some years old, coached Spencer Haywood in high school, and was the first African American Division I college coach. At Illinois State, he coached Doug Collins, who would go on to become a star with the 76ers. Will is still going strong, scouting for the Pistons.

We were trying to excite people with the caravan, trying to get people to come and buy tickets and follow us. So every day, I'd go to a section of Michigan and Will would go with me. I'd speak at a breakfast. I'd speak at a lunch. I'd do evening banquets. I was just trying to drum up some enthusiasm for the program.

One day in the car, Will turns to me and says, "You're wasting your time in coaching. And I don't mean this to be critical. You should be in TV. You've got so many stories. I've been listening to you. Every banquet, you've got another story going."

Now, every time he sees me, he says, "I told you this 30 years ago, man. You should have listened to me."

And he's probably right. But back then, I just didn't know.

When I first started at ESPN, I felt I was really making an impact with the coaches because we'd all been in that locker room, fighting and scraping for survival. I could empathize with them and they could empathize with me.

Well, most of them could.

When I was working in television and Digger Phelps was still coaching at Notre Dame, I would call him to try to get as much information for the game as possible. I always try to get that from the coaches, their assistants, and the media. Digger was the only guy in America who never called me back. I'd leave a message; he wouldn't call back.

Then one day, I ran into my buddy Eddie Broderick from New York, who is a Notre Dame grad and a basketball junkie. He teased me: "Hey, I know you called Digger and Digger didn't return the call."

I said, "Yeah, I know. I'm still waiting for him to call me back."

"Yeah, I heard him tell a bunch of people, 'I don't call those *cable* guys. I only call McGuire and Packer.'"

Well, in 2002, my guy Digger was one of the roasters for "Roastin' Dickie V," a benefit for the Life Treatment Centers of South

Bend, Indiana. The event raised dollars for those battling drug and alcohol problems. It was held in front of a packed house in the hockey arena portion of the Joyce Athletic and Convocation Center. I was happy to allow those on the dais to have a chance to rip on me for such a great cause.

After Digger was finished, I got up and turned to him and said, "Hey, Digger, I know I would call you, man, trying to get information on your team and you couldn't call me back. Do you see where your check comes from today? *Cable*. ESPN, baby. You're one of us, man."

Then, just to needle him a bit more, I turned to Muffett McGraw, the women's coach at Notre Dame, and asked to borrow her national championship ring. I said, "Take a look at this national championship ring. This is something you weren't able to bring here in 30 years."

Another way I knew I'd started making an impact was by the kind of contract I had. When I started, I was making around $350, $500, then $700 a game. I don't know the numbers. Forty to 50 games a year. That's not a lot of cash, man.

Then, all of a sudden, things began to change. ESPN is now owned by Disney, and I can tell you that my favorite guy is Mickey Mouse. I love that mouse, baby. It's not $350 a game any more.

I would drive Ellen Beckwith, who did the game assignments, completely bananas. Wow, did I get a thrill out of seeing that light on the camera and doing those games. She would schedule me for two or three games a week. I'd call her up to say, "I want more than that; give me four or five." I'd drive her nuts because I'd want a game almost every night.

I just fell in love with the gig.

It changed my life. My whole personality changed. I felt uplifted. I became high-spirited; I became excited again. I'd found something I really loved.

It was giving me visibility, too—except in my own household. My daughters told me I was a big fraud. They'd tell their mother, "I don't know why dad keeps saying he's on TV. We keep watching TV, and we never see him." That's because we never had cable where we lived in West Bloomfield, a suburb of Detroit.

Eventually, I realized that going to ESPN was the best decision I'd ever made in my life.

College basketball was the first sport to be associated with ESPN. There were so many great games out there, and initially the only network that was doing them was NBC, which was then the home for the NCAA Tournament. They had an extensive regular-season schedule, but it was all on the weekends.

The weekday games were just sitting there. They were either on local TV or not televised at all.

So ESPN stepped up to fill the void.

The Big East was the first major conference to jump on board with regularly scheduled games. They were still members of the Eastern College Athletic Conference, so they were under contract to play an ECAC Game of the Week on Saturdays. But Big East commissioner Dave Gavitt wanted more exposure, so he negotiated a deal in 1982 for us to televise one of their games on Monday night prime time, playing off what the NFL had done with Monday night football.

ESPN called it Big Monday. It gave the Big East a huge advantage. It certainly didn't hurt, either, that the conference had players like Patrick Ewing of Georgetown and Chris Mullin of St. John's. Their games were being televised all over the country. You don't think that helps in recruiting? Coaches were on the phone telling prospects, "Hey, man, we're on ESPN." Now there are so many networks, you expect everybody to be on. But back then it was a novel idea.

Pretty soon other conferences lined up, too, and they got their own nights. Today, Big Monday includes games with the Big East, the Big 12 and the Mountain West. The Big Ten and the SEC are on Tuesday. The ACC is on Wednesday, and on Saturday, there is a mixture of ACC, Atlantic 10, Big Ten, Big East and Conference USA.

The difference between college basketball and other sports is that in basketball, everybody plays twice in conference, home and home. In 1985, for example, CBS carried the Georgetown-St. John's game when they were ranked No. 1 and 2. But ESPN had the rematch at the Garden—the famous sweater game where Lou Carnesecca wore his lucky sweater and big John Thompson showed up wearing a wild sweater of his own. That game reached 2.9 million homes and drew an 8.0 rating, the best ever for a college basketball game on the network.

ESPN also had another big advantage in those early years. They were smart enough to purchase the rights to the early rounds of the NCAA Tournament. At one time, they had them all the way through the regional semifinals. They had that great regional semi in 1981 where Danny Ainge raced the length of the floor in the final moments to score the winning basket against Notre Dame in a 51-50 victory for BYU.

When ESPN had the first-round games from 1980 through 1990, CBS, which in 1982 had been awarded the TV rights previously held by NBC, would usually carry one late-night game. ESPN had the rest. They would carry 15 of 16 games in each of the first two days of the tournament. Six of them would be live, noon through midnight, and the rest would be on tape delay. It was a basketball orgy for the sports junkie and an insomniac's dream.

ESPN got in on the ground floor of other unique concepts, too, like the Big East–ACC challenge, which ran for four straight nights in December, and the Great Eight, which started in 1994 and went through 1999 and involved inviting the Final Eight teams from the year before. They also did midnight games. Late-night basketball was actually started by the Ohio Valley Conference, which was desperate for some weekend exposure. The games were done strictly on a volunteer basis.

After a while, teams like UMass, which was looking for some added exposure when John Calipari was trying to build his program up there, asked in. UMass loved the idea so much that they volunteered to continue the tradition, even after they got to be nationally ranked.

Then there was Championship Week.

It started innocently enough in 1986, when the MAAC and the Altantic 10 played a championship doubleheader on a Monday night in the Meadowlands. Tom Odjakjian purchased the rights from a local syndicator. As soon as the Missouri Valley Conference heard about it, they called and asked if they could be scheduled on Tuesday. The schedule became so crowded after a while that the Sun Belt actually offered to move its championship game up a week so it wouldn't bump up against the big boys.

ESPN has also reached out in the past to cover the Division II, III and NAIA Tournament championship games.

We've done some crazy events, too, like that President's Day game between George Washington and James Madison in 1992. And we even covered a game with no fans in the stands—back in 1989, the North Atlantic basketball tournament was played under quarantine conditions because of a measles epidemic in the conference. Everyone from the network who was under 35 and was assigned to do that championship game between Siena and Boston U in Hartford had to be inoculated.

ESPN has always been on the cutting edge. We have all four major league sports: football, baseball, basketball and hockey. We do college football and men's and women's college basketball. It's all sports 24/7. We also took the NCAA Tournament to another level when we did the first- and second-round games.

CBS eventually bought the rights to the entire tournament for $6 billion. But during the regular season, there's no bigger player than ESPN, with all the games and the variety of teams you can see play. Monday, Tuesday, Wednesday, Thursday and Saturday, we've got games.

Last year, we televised 287 men's season games and 23 conference championship games with automatic bids to the NCAA Tournament, including the Big East and the ACC. We have selection shows for both the Division I men's and women's pairings each March. We did the Coaches vs. Cancer, preseason NIT, the NIT and women's Final Four.

We have given so many kids a chance for exposure. We've set the table. We have made soap opera stars of coaches like Rick Pitino, Jimmy Boeheim, Mike Krzyzewski, John Chaney, Tom Izzo, Tubby Smith and Roy Williams. These guys are on regularly.

Almost as often as I am.

Let's face it, I'm a hot dog. I'm mustard. I'm all that jazz. But that's me. I've always been that way, not just for television. People who want to know what I'm all about only have to ask my friends. I had a '55 red and white Ford convertible with leather seats in high school. I loved the flashy car, the pizzazz.

And I always liked to be everybody's friend. I was looking at my high school yearbook the other day. I know people aren't going to believe this—I had hair, man. I had hair. And the label underneath my picture reads, "Everybody's buddy."

That phrase has always summarized my personality.

You've seen it in the studio.

Like the time Austin Peay played Illinois in the 1987 NCAA Tournament. We're doing cutaways to different games. Bob Ley was there, along with producer Steve Anderson. And we're all trying to have a little fun in the studio. I felt like Austin Peay had no shot, and I said so: "I'm going to tell you now. Austin Peay has no shot.

"This is a total M&Mer," I said. "If they win, I'll stand on my head."

And then the score comes in. Man, the phones started ringing off the hook—"He'd better stand on his head."

Well, I'd said I would, hadn't I? So I let the guys stand me on my head on the desk in front of the camera. It was a riot.

Hey, I did it again at Austin Peay later on, when they invited me to be the keynote speaker at their basketball banquet.

I was amazed. They let loose on me with this cheer: "Let's go, Peay. Let's go, Peay—On Vitale. On Vitale."

But they probably didn't realize that, as I was standing there listening to them razz me, I was getting paid for that visit to Clarksville, Tennessee. Hey, sometimes schools razz me like that, but you know what? Sometimes they buy me lunch.

I got all over Colorado State in 2001 for scheduling teams like Gardner Webb.

I came on ESPN and said, "Colorado State—they're loaded up with cupcakes. Take a look at their preseason schedule." I pointed out that Gardner Webb had once been a junior college.

Well, Rick Scruggs, the coach down there, used that as a promotional tool. When Colorado State traveled to Boiling Springs, North Carolina to play them early that season, the townspeople held a cupcake day—they baked thousands of cupcakes and gave them to their fans.

Guess what? Gardner Webb upset Colorado State, 56-54. Rick Scruggs sent a dozen cupcakes to my house in Florida via FedEx the next day.

Man, were they good, too. I took a picture with the cupcakes and sent it back with a note, telling Rick that I was glad he'd taken my comments in good fun and thanking him for a delicious afternoon snack.

Speaking of cupcakes, Michigan once scheduled so many easy opponents that I told my buddy Bill Frieder, the coach there at the time, "You're playing so many cupcakes, I'm going to call your schedule 'The Hostess Classic.'"

I've had some wacky moments at ESPN. I sometimes go to my room and wonder, "Why don't I grow up?"

I've done some crazy things over the years.

One time in 1989, I was in the studio when Georgetown was playing Princeton in a first-round NCAA Tournament game at Providence. Georgetown had just won the Big East, and they were a huge favorite. It was like a 1-16 matchup.

But nobody had bothered to tell Pete Carril's team.

At one point, Tom Odjakjian—I call him O.J.; he was in college programming at the time and had worked at Princeton as the assistant sports information director and then as the assistant commissioner of the ECAC before coming to ESPN—gave me a Princeton sweatshirt to wear in the studio during the second half. I remember putting it on and cheering for the Tigers—I've always been a believer in rooting for the little guy. Hey, man, all of us little guys have to stick together, right?

I even said on the air that if Princeton were to win, I would hitchhike to Providence and join the Princeton cheerleaders in their next round.

And was it ever a knee knocker, baby.

Luckily for me, though, Alonzo Mourning—the human eraser—blocked a shot at the end, and Georgetown hung on to win by a mere point.

And as it turned out, that game might have saved the automatic bids for the smaller conferences because there was a push by bigtime leagues to eliminate automatic berths for the little guys.

Another time, we were all singing in the studio during a commercial break—John Saunders, the late Jimmy Valvano and me. We started dancing up a storm and having the time of our lives. So we all agreed that the three of us were going to come back from the break in unison and do a Temptations dance routine. It would've been awesome, baby—if not for one little detail. When the red light came on, the two of them sat down. I was left out there by myself, dancing like an idiot—and having a blast.

You might have seen that one, but not all of the wacky times make it to your TV screen.

We have this little room at ESPN where we gather to watch all the first- and second-round games in the tournament. We call it our Green Room, just like the ones Letterman and Leno have. Everybody gathers there during March Madness. We have a number of monitors on and we'll watch games as they're played all over the country. Man, we'll have every game in the nation on.

And we have this little ritual.

Jim Valvano started it years ago. When a team would get into a bit of trouble, he would take a fork and throw it at the monitor: "Stick a fork in them, man. They're done. Get your watch and go home."

Then the guys would all tease me. Like this past year—Digger Phelps got on camera and said to me, "Oh, by the way, Dick, you don't know anything about the NCAA watches because you don't have any. But I've got about 20 of them—maybe you'd like me to send you one?"

I mean, they bust my chops. I take it regularly from Phelps, Chris Fowler, our producers—the whole gang. It's all in good fun, though.

We have all kinds of guys in there, cheering. Howie Schwab, a coordinating producer who's my main research guy, is a big St. John's guy and he's wearing his Red Storm hat and his Red Storm jacket. We got UConn fanatics, dressed in their blue and white, UConn colors. We got Syracuse guys in their orange.

Then there's the front row.

You have to be there years to earn a seat there. Andy Katz, the college basketball writer for ESPN.com, tried to sit in the front row, and we all jumped on him. We said, "Wait a minute, Andy. You're a diaper dandy. You haven't earned the right. The front row is for veterans." Jay Bilas, a Dukie, and Katz are both workaholics and extremely knowledgeable—but they've still got to work years before they get the privilege of sitting in our front row. Chris Fowler's now sitting up there with Digger and me.

See, that's the beauty of what I do at ESPN. It's just flat-out fun.

Besides, what other job would let me create my own dictionary?

It all started in the locker room when I was a coach. Players would say "Coach, I didn't get any PT. Coach, they didn't give me the rock." I just transferred all that over to TV.

Over the years I think those sayings have become commonplace playground lingo. Just recently, a guy came up to me at the Broken Egg, which is a restaurant on Siesta Key in Sarasota, Florida. Usually when I'm at home, I'll start my day with breakfast at the Broken Egg, which is kinda like my office away from home. I'll have papers spread all over my table. My cell phone will be ringing like crazy with all of my various basketball contacts. And I'll be reading articles that my daughter, Sherri, pulls off of different websites for me—articles from writers like our own Andy Katz, Dan Wetzel of CBS SportsLine.com, Mike DeCourcy of SportingNews.com or Frank Burleson, formerly of FoxSports.com.

This guy came up to my table and said, "Hey, Dickie V, my nine-year-old son was playing in the yard with his friend and I overheard him saying, 'You better get a TO, baby. You better get a TO.'"

Man, I can't believe it—what have I started?

Phrases like that have become common lingo to basketball fans. It just makes it fun. And that's what the game is, fun. And I've tried to fit my personality to the game.

ESPN has been involved in so many creative commercials to promote college basketball. One year they did a whole series in which I played a guy named Hoops Malone. And George Gervin, a former star in the ABA and NBA, was one of my buddies. The spots ran the whole season.

People started calling me Hoops. ESPN got big banners and posters promoting it everywhere. I had a blast doing it.

It was almost like a sitcom. They had me doing all kinds of things—dancing, shooting the rock, arguing with George Gervin. They involved guys like Tom Izzo, head coach of Michigan State, and Steve Wojciechowski, an assistant coach at Duke. I talked about players, the recruiting wars, about what goes on in the game.

They were just 30-second segments, but they had people believing it was a real series. *Hoops Malone.* People would come up to me and ask, "Hey, when can we see *Hoops Malone?*" They really thought it was a sitcom.

"Hey Dickie V, I saw you in a sitcom. *Hoops Malone,* man."

I'm thinking to myself, "You didn't see me playing in any sitcom. Fooled you."

I actually was asked to do a sitcom, though. A group flew my wife, Lorraine, and me out to Hollywood. We met with some studio executives, and they told my agent they'd seen other guys in the sports world make the transition to entertainment—Bob Uecker, Alex Karras. They said, "Dick, we really think we can put something together that you can be proud of. We'll make you a coach and put you with some quality actors and make it work. We'll even film a lot of it in Orlando."

It was flattering. But I looked at Lorraine. She looked at me. And I said, "That's not me, man. I want to do games. I want to stay with my games, do basketball, do what I'm comfortable with."

Like most broadcasters, though, I occasionally come in for my share of criticism. I mean, you can't keep everybody happy. No way. Rudy Martzke, an influential TV critic from *USA Today*, is always trying to play me off against Billy Packer of CBS. But our job descriptions are so different. Packer does one game nationally for CBS a week, and then he has ACC games he does regionally for Jefferson-Pilot.

But at ESPN, I'm not just an analyst. We have all kinds of remote hookups where they come to us for *SportsCenter* hits. I do ESPN radio, ESPN news and my own website. So ESPN creates a forum where I'm giving a lot of opinions.

They want my opinion when Roy Williams leaves Kansas for North Carolina, or when the rules change. So it's not just the Xs and Os of the game. That's just one part of the job description.

I feel I bring passion, enthusiasm and preparation to a game. Now, I've had critics who've ripped me for being too loud and talking too much. You don't have to go to Harvard to pick up on that. But in 24 years, no one has ever accused me of not being prepared or not knowing my subject matter.

As far as styles go, there are some people who like upbeat guys and some people who like downbeat guys. That's why you have Chevys and Buicks, blondes and brunettes, chocolate and vanilla ice cream. You have choices.

And I've made mine.

Jim Simpson, the legendary play-by-play guy—and a real favorite of mine—who was one of my first partners, once told me that every game he did was the most important game in the world to those kids playing, to their families, to their coaches, to their alumni and to their fans.

One night, a long time ago, he and I were doing a game—a so-so game. Somebody came up to me and asked, "What game do you guys have coming up?" I turned to the guy and said, "Aw, it's just another game, man, just another game."

Jim grabbed me and said, "There is no such thing as just another game."

He was right. That's why, since that moment, I've always treated every one like it's the national championship game.

Unfortunately, in our business, there are a lot of guys who do good jobs, but when the telecast is over, it's a forgotten show and nobody knows they were on. That's why I have such admiration for John Madden and Chris Berman. Why? Because they have a great enthusiasm for every game they do.

I've said so many times I feel like a kid at heart, making a living on college campuses, hanging with all the young people. And I think they've helped to keep that youthful spirit alive in me.

Some of them have even started helping from day one.

ESPN was shooting a commercial spot for the ESPY Awards, and they decided that I would announce my new diaper dandies from a Sarasota hospital. We're going to do several tapes. So here I am, in front of the maternity ward with these newborn babies who are crying their eyes out.

I'm there, looking at them, talking on the air, saying, "We're going to talk about my diaper dandies, man, the best new players in college basketball—and how about these diaper dandies?"

The babies are screaming. They're crying. They're hysterical.

A nurse comes down and says, "Gee, thanks a lot, Dickie V. You woke them all up."

Hey, it's never too early to meet fans.

Passing me through the stands has been a regular ritual at Duke. The first time it happened, I was a little stunned and a little worried. Now, as I've gotten a bit older, I've started to worry a little more about my back. I tell them ahead of time, "Now, remember, I'm not a young kid any more."

But I don't know if they believe that.

I remember going to Duke one time and all the students on one side started chanting "Bald," and the students on the other side responded with "Head"—"Bald . . . Head, Bald . . . Head." It was all in good fun, so I took out a comb and pretended I was combing my hair.

You can really feel the excitement of those Cameron Crazies.

One time in 1994, I was in Cincinnati for Midnight Madness, and ESPN brought a kid out and offered to pay his tuition if he could make a halfcourt shot. And I told him, "Son, if you make this shot, ESPN's paying for your room and board and I'll pay for your books."

I came on with Robin Roberts, the host of the show, and started whipping the crowd into a frenzy. I am so proud that I had a chance to work with Robin, who has now become a big star on *Good Morning America* with Diane Sawyer and Charles Gibson. Man, that night we had more than 12,000 going bananas at the Shoemaker Center in Cincinnati.

Well, this kid, Cory Clouse, he just let it fly. I mean, he nailed it and the place just turned into pandemonium. He and I started dancing, jumping with joy.

I'll tell you this, man. I've looked him up I don't know how many times. I've made calls because I want to write him that check.

I've spoken to him and his wife. But for some reason, the guy doesn't come through and present me with the bill for the books.

I'm starting to wonder, "Hey, man, did you finish school?" Please, this is your last shot, Cory—give me a buzz; send me the bill. I want to make good on my promise.

Let me tell you, I've met so many quality people during my time at ESPN.

For one, there's Freddie Gaudelli. He's one of the guys who was once assigned, as part of his responsibilities, to be my driver. Now he's one of the most powerful sports producers in the country. He produces *Monday Night Football*, the biggest sporting event on television, and he has won numerous awards for his production talents. He also served for a number of years as the producer of the ESPY Awards show, which honors the best athletes in the business.

And, of course, there's the first guy ESPN hired to pick me up at the airport—one day, all of a sudden I had a driver, baby. When I'd fly in, he'd pick me up and get me all my papers—I'm a paper fanatic. I read every paper I can get my hands on. This guy also worked in the mail room and the video library.

His name was George Bodenheimer. He was constantly telling me, "You know, I go to a great college, Denison University, which is a highly rated liberal arts school, and look what I'm doing. Here I am, working in the mail room. Where am I going?"

There was something about him, though. I knew he was a winner. You could spot it right away. You talk to him a couple of times, and you just know that this guy's got it.

I told him, "George, someday, you're going to make it. Someday, you're going to be big."

Well, how big is he now?

Wow, talk about a superstar—my guy George has not only become the president of ESPN, he's been appointed the president of ABC Sports as well.

I remember picking up the paper a couple of years ago and reading the headline, "Named the President of ESPN: George Bodenheimer." I called up his office and got on his voice mail and I said, "Mr. Bodenheimer, I'm calling because I just want you to know, man, I'm your buddy. I'm Dickie V. I'm getting older. Please don't forget me. I'm the guy you drove around way back when. I'm the guy you'd get papers for in the morning.

"Remember how you would tell me you were going nowhere and I'd tell you, 'George, someday you're going to make it and make it big.' Think about it. You're the president of ESPN. Don't give me a wristwatch when I reach 65. Give me a new contract."

I love all parts of the sports world, but I feel like I would be making a major mistake to try broadcasting another sport. Sometimes I see announcers trying to do that. I'm not talking about play-by-play guys. They are versatile. I'm talking about guys who are analysts and experts in their given areas. That's why I love John Madden. He knows football and does what he does in a positive way with a lot of spirit and passion.

I've also noticed that when you have a unique personality, it helps in TV. Let's face it. I didn't come from any school of communication. I probably violate all the rules they teach. But there's one thing that I've always had—my enthusiasm. Since I was a little kid, I've always been energetic and enthusiastic. And I know that when that leaves me, the party's over. When the juices stop flowing and I don't feel the adrenaline of going to do a game, then I know it's over. Nobody's going to have to tell me.

It'll be the end of Dickie V.

You know, I was never called Dick back in my old neighborhood. It was Richie with my family, and even today my sister Terry and my brother John still refer to me as Rich. And all my intimate friends back in New Jersey, guys I grew up with, Tommy Longo, Lou Ravettine, Bob Stolarz, Tom Ramsden, Tony Comeleo, Ken Kurnath, and Charles Alberta still call me Rich or Richie. And my wife never, ever calls me Dick. A lot of times she'd probably like to call me worse—but never Dick.

When I got fired by the Pistons in 1979, I had a lot of free time. We had a basket in the back yard, so every day after my daughters came home from school, I worked with them on layup drills, right- and left-handed ones. Bob Lanier—the Big Fellow, a Hall of Famer who played for me with the Pistons—would stop by the house and work with my kids as well. And, man, I thought they were really enjoying playing.

At the time, they were elementary school girls. So we signed them up with the CYO. If you put my girls in layup drills and watched them shoot, you'd say, "Wow. They're pretty good."

But when the games began, they had absolutely no idea how to get free, and they couldn't handle people getting in their faces guarding them. Finally, they came home one day and they told my wife, "Mom, we're afraid to tell Dad, but we really don't want to play basketball. We don't like basketball."

My wife came to me and said, "Rich, I want you to understand something. Terri and Sherri don't want to play basketball, and there's no use trying to get them to be players."

I finally looked at her and said, "You're 100 percent right."

I grabbed them and said, "You don't have to play basketball because of me. All I want you to do is find something in your life that you like—swimming, dancing, music, softball, tennis, anything—and attack it with the best of your ability."

That's when they got their first taste of tennis—they couldn't wait to go out the next day and hit the ball, man.

They just fell in love with it and it became part of their lives. How much a part of their lives? They ended up earning tennis scholarships to Notre Dame after winning several state championships in Florida. I have to give my wife credit. She handled it so well with them. She never put pressure on them. She made it a positive experience, helped them keep their goals realistic. They weren't saying, "I'm going to be the next Chris Evert."

They knew what their limitations were, and it's helped them in their tennis and their lives.

I would advise any parent that way.

We all dream of success, and you want nothing but the best for your kids. There's nothing wrong with that. But you must understand they are kids.

My mother would say to me all the time, "Richie, Richie, Richie. Basketball, basketball, basketball. That's all you're doing, chasing guys who wear shorts. When are you going to study?" If there's one regret I have in my life, it's that I probably never applied myself like I should have academically.

I was sitting in the back of the classroom one day and reading Dick Young's column in the *Daily News*. That was a must read. I loved his *dot . . . dot . . . dot* with all the notes, everything going on in sports in the New York area and nationally.

And I remember the teacher yelling at me, "You got a brain but you never want to use it. Sports, sports, sports. Where's sports going to take you in life?"

Oh, man, as I tell people, you should see where it's taken me.

It comes down to loving what you do and doing what you love.

By the way, that first game: December 5, 1979. DePaul won, 90-77.

They were terrific.

2

SOUNDING OFF

I hope this doesn't come as a shock, but after 24 years on TV, I have a few opinions on college basketball. And in honor of my upcoming Silver Anniversary at ESPN, I'm going to share them with you.

First things first. A word of advice for college coaches: If an NBA general manager calls and offers you big cash, think twice. No, better yet, just hang up.

The NBA is not for you.

I know the league went through a period when it was trendy for a pro team to jump on a big-profile college coach to turn their franchise around.

I saw it with Rick Pitino when the Boston Celtics came calling in 1997, right after he had coached Kentucky to a second straight Final Four and threw out a 10-year deal worth $50 million. As far as I was concerned, Pitino was the Lee Iococca of coaching. I mean, this guy was an entrepreneur. He was a sharp tactician. He had that special stature; success was just written all over his chest. He had the entire package, man—personality, teaching ability, motivation—and there was no doubt he was going to be hunted down by the NBA. He looked like he was on the verge of a dynasty after coaching the Cats to three Final Fours in five years.

But he left.

I saw it again when the Nets grabbed up John Calipari from UMass after he got to the Final Four in 1996.

The Chicago Bulls became enamored with Tim Floyd of Iowa State when Michael Jordan retired for the second time and Phil Jackson left in a huff after a championship season in 1998. The Washington Wizards wooed Mike Jarvis of St. John's, then offered the job to Leonard Hamilton of the University of Miami in 1999. The Atlanta Hawks went after Lon Kruger of Illinois in 2000 after Tom Izzo—whose Michigan State team had just made their trip to the Final Four—turned them down.

We saw how it all worked out—or, rather, how it didn't.

Pitino lasted three and a half years and never made the playoffs before he resigned in the middle of the 2001 season with a 102-146 record. He took over a team that was in total disarray. They were dreaming, man—could you blame them?—of winning the lottery and getting Tim Duncan with the first pick in the 1997 draft. But it just didn't happen. In the NBA, sometimes it's a question of being lucky. And Pitino wasn't lucky. He'd promised he would leave at the end of that season if Boston didn't make it. He was true to his word, walking away from the rest of a 10-year deal and $27 million when he felt he couldn't deliver after a 12-22 start.

Floyd, Calipari, Hamilton and Kruger were all pushed out the door, too.

Floyd and Chicago GM Jerry Krause were fishing buddies. But Floyd was stuck in a major rebuilding project with young players and had a 49-190 record in three-plus seasons before resigning on Christmas Eve, 2001—after a 4-21 start.

Calipari's Nets actually made the playoffs in 1998, but his overall record in two-plus years was 72-112 before he was let go midway through March of 1999.

Kruger had a 69-122 record in two and a half years with the Hawks. Before his final year, the Hawks' owners, who had just traded for forward Glenn Robinson, guaranteed the team would make the playoffs and promised season ticket holders a $125 rebate if they didn't. Kruger was out December 27, 2002.

Hamilton resigned after just one year and a 15-67 record.

Heard enough?

Most of them never had a shot. A lot of college guys take over bad NBA jobs. And I don't know why, man.

First of all, a college coach wouldn't get the job if it wasn't a bad situation. Very few great NBA jobs are going to open up.

Pitino, Calipari and Hamilton are back in college where they belong. Pitino returned to the Bluegrass State and signed on with Louisville. I mean, could you have blamed him for being excited about that job? Sure, he could have gone to Michigan, but his wife, Joanne, loved the Kentucky area. And Rick felt very comfortable with that situation. He was really excited about working for Tom Jurich, the AD there. To me, there was no doubt Louisville would be the winner over the Wolverines.

The one concern Rick had—he shared it on the phone with me—was how the Kentucky fans would react. And in fact, he was viewed as a traitor by some longtime Kentucky fans. One guy even went so far as to say that when his father died, he'd been buried with a basketball that was autographed by Pitino—and now he was thinking about exhuming the body just to get rid of the ball. How sick is that? But when push came to shove, Pitino wasn't going to allow any of that to enter into the equation.

"The NBA was a business, and I didn't have fun at that business," Pitino admitted. "Now I think it's fun again. I enjoy it when we're at .500 as well as winning championships. People say it's winning and losing. But Pat Riley, I guess, was right in his analysis. 'At the NBA level,' he was quoted as saying, 'you either win and are smiling or lose and you're in misery.' Here it's different. I mean, you can be 19-13 and still go to the NIT and have a good time."

He has it going at the 'Ville, filling those seats in Freedom Hall to capacity and taking the Cardinals to the NCAA Tournament in only his second year there. He may be only a couple of players away from the Final Four.

Calipari has Memphis up and running, too. Of course, it didn't hurt that he got DaJuan Wagner to sign with the Tigers his second year. Wagner led Memphis to the NIT title in his only year there, and Calipari coached the Tigers to the NCAA Tournament last year.

And watch out for Leonard Hamilton at Florida State. That guy always could recruit. Just check out the results he had as an assistant at Kentucky, head coach at Oklahoma State and Miami. Look at the class he brought in this year—6'5" forward Vakeaton Wafer from Heritage Christian in Cleveland, Texas; 6'7" Antonio Griffin from Scottsdale Junior College in Arizona; and 6'10" Diego Romero of Lon Morris JC in Texas. That's one of the top five recruiting classes in the country, according to Clark Francis of *The Hoop Scoop*.

You can count on it, as I've said several times on TV, Florida State will be in the first division of the ACC within three years.

Floyd just got the New Orleans Hornets job after spending two years in limbo. Kruger, who got the ziggy at midseason, took an assistant's job with the Knicks.

Another thing: You can't get back to the top of the mountain in the NBA as quickly as you can in college. Look at Bob Knight and Rick Pitino at their new schools. In college, you can change things quickly through the recruiting scene. But you can't do that in the NBA with the salary cap.

In the pros, your hands are tied. Many times you're left with the personnel you inherit. Okay, okay, you're praying, hoping, you'll win the lottery like Cleveland and get a LeBron James. Sometimes you're lucky.

And sometimes you're not.

All those guys who came up the coaching ladder from high school through college to the pros have that incredible work ethic, but they aren't able to practice it in the pros. I couldn't adjust to that. When I was coaching the Pistons, I still remember my All-Star center, Bob Lanier, telling me, over and over, "You can't run these practices like you did in college. You can't run these two and a half-hour practices. Players can't handle that *and* playing three or four nights a week."

Why would college guys want to coach in the NBA, anyway? Why leave a great situation where you're the man like Mike Krzyzewski is at Duke or Roy Williams is at North Carolina?

By the same token, I think it's very difficult for a former great NBA player to go in and coach on the college level because of the recruiting rules, the alumni functions, all the academic restrictions and many other problems they're not used to dealing with. It's a totally different world. On the other hand, the best NBA coaches today are ex-players who understand what the league is all about.

And here's my two cents on contracts with "out" clauses.

Now, I'm all for coaches getting multiyear deals and getting big guarantees. I believe—hey, we live in America—you should get what you can while you're on top of the world, as long as you do it legitimately. But when a school gives a coach a six- or seven-year extension, the AD should be able to look into his eyes and say, "Look, I want to extend your contract. I love you. I care about you. I know you're great for our program. But I'm going to tell you now—you sign that contract, there's no out."

Otherwise, what's the purpose of the seven-, eight-, nine-year deal? It becomes a joke. It's essentially meaningless. In many cases, coaches have contracts with these out clauses that allow them to simply move on whenever they want. It's a one-sided deal—and I don't think it's right. I don't blame the coaches if they can get that, of course—but, man, that is not the way I would do business if I were an AD.

Look at me. I'm on a roll.

While I'm on my soap box, here are some other opinions I want to lay on you, baby.

ESPN kicked into high gear in September, 1979. Since then, there has been a dazzling group of guys who have been very influential in changing the landscape of college basketball.

I call them my VIPs (Vitale's Influential People), and I've listed them in order of the impact they've had.

1. Dave Gavitt

He was the architect behind the Big East, which gave Eastern schools a chance for national visibility and an opportunity to compete for the national title. When it was first formed in 1979, it was magical. Syracuse versus Georgetown at the Carrier Dome with 30,000-plus. Later, the Big East Tournament at the Garden. He had the big stars going head to head. That was always special. Dave Gavitt wanted coaches who were major names, and it was exciting to see the battles between John Thompson, Rollie Massimino, Louie Carnesecca, Jim Boeheim and company.

Gavitt was a visionary. He was way ahead of his time in the way he negotiated TV deals with CBS, ABC and ESPN to get his teams more national exposure. The ultimate prize for him came in 1985 when three Big East teams—Georgetown, Villanova and St. John's—made it to the Final Four. And Villanova won it all.

Gavitt and Mike Tranghese, the current commissioner of the Big East, have poured their hearts and souls into being the architects of the Big East. It has to be extremely frustrating for Gavitt as he watches his buddy Tranghese attempting to keep the conference intact. Indications are that the Big East will become two separate conferences—one for basketball and one for football.

2. Chet Simmons, Scotty Connal and Tom Odjakjian, ESPN

One had the vision. Another was a production genius. And the third made the matchups. When Simmons and Connal came over to ESPN from NBC, they brought instant credibility to ESPN, a young network, because they were giants in their field. At the time, there were still doubters out there because cable was so new and people had only so much vision. O.J. gave it creativity. Together they formed the nucleus for ESPN college basketball.

ESPN wanted to be known as the network of football, skiing, billiards and college basketball—all sports.

Today, ESPN has all four major league sports. Mission accomplished.

3. John Thompson

He had the same stature as the mayor of D.C. when he coached Georgetown—and no wonder. Thompson is a Hall of Famer. He was one of the first African American coaches hired in Division I and is credited with opening so many doors for other African American coaches like John Chaney of Temple and Nolan Richardson of Arkansas because of his success.

There are some in the college basketball fraternity who feel John Thompson had the same effect for African American coaches that Jackie Robinson had when he was the first African American player in major league baseball. I mean, that could be a little bit of a stretch, but there's no doubt about it—he had a big-time impact.

Thompson transformed Georgetown into a dominant force on the national scene when he took the Hoyas to the NCAA Final Four three of four years—in 1982, 1984 and 1985—during the Patrick Ewing era. He became the first African American coach to win the national title in 1984. He developed a reputation for recruiting celebrated big men—like Patrick Ewing, Dikembe Mutombo and Alonzo Mourning—and for playing disciplined, intense basketball, particularly on the defensive end.

He was also a spokesman for the rights of minority players, once walking off the court to protest the variations of Proposition 48—more on this in a bit—because he felt it discriminated against economically deprived kids.

4. Dean Smith

Hey, man, just think about this number—879.

Smith was head coach at North Carolina for 36 years and set the record for career victories—879—before he retired in 1997.

When you think about the history of basketball, what Smith accomplished at North Carolina has to rank as Numero Uno. Think about it. Not only did the school win national championships in 1982 and 1993, not only did the Tar Heels make all those journeys to the Final Four, but there was never a hint of any impropriety, never a hint of any NCAA violation. You can't say that about too many other programs.

And check out these numbers, too—23 straight NCAA berths, 27 straight 20-win seasons, 33 straight 1-2-3 finishes in the ACC.

Smith was one of the most innovative coaches in the history of the sport. Who can ever forget his Four Corners with Phil Ford? Who can ever forget how he utilized the clock in the final minutes? Who can forget his team-first concept? He imparted a lot of that knowledge to Larry Brown and Roy Williams, who are two of the best minds in the game today.

You know, we once played North Carolina when I was at Detroit. Dean said, "Hey, I want to come up because Tom LaGarde,"—one of his star players—"went to Detroit Central Catholic and I want to give him a homecoming."

I was elated. My alums were going to go nuts over the fact that Carolina was coming up. Only there was one catch—Dean said, "You've got to come down here twice." I knew I had no problem because I wasn't going to be at Detroit in two years. Aha. Only kidding, man. But you know what? It ended up that way. I never did get to make that journey to Chapel Hill as a coach.

5. Bob Knight

He coached Indiana University for 29 years, from 1971 to 2000, before leaving that program and eventually moving on to Texas Tech. He *was* Hoosier basketball, baby. He dominated the Big Ten during that period. He won three national championships in 1976, 1981 and 1987. He also won a gold medal in the 1979 Pan Am games and the 1984 Olympics.

The guy is an absolute genius as a coach. He believes he can beat anybody with almost any players if they'll play together as a unit.

And he's probably right.

He is such a perfectionist. And a purist. He's a linear descendant of Hank Iba and Pete Newell. He's got a chance to be the first guy to crack the 900-win mark for career victories.

Nobody's condoning his throwing a chair and screaming and yelling at the media, of course. That's a no-no. But he's never been accused of cheating, and his graduation rates are always exceptional.

6. Mike Krzyzewski

He's become the voice for the current group of coaches. He's like E.F. Hutton. Whenever he speaks—says something about college basketball—people listen because he cares so much about the sport.

And they respect him.

Look at what he's accomplished at Duke, winning three national championships, in 1991, 1992 and 2001, and going to the Final Four nine times. It's truly amazing in this day and age.

Mike has built a model program down in Durham.

I occasionally hear about Duke players in the NBA, that they don't perform as well as they did on the college level. But Mike Krzyzewski's job is to put the best possible team on the floor, to get the most out of his players and get them to perform. Whatever else happens later, that's out of his hands, man.

Duke gets great kids, the best of the best. When you're talking Shane Battier, Grant Hill, Johnny Dawkins, Jason Williams, Michael Dunleavy, Danny Ferry, you're talking about kids who have the total package, academically and athletically. And Mike refines them, gets the most out of their abilities.

What makes a great coach, to me, is the ability to get the maximum out of every athlete. If you get that 100 percent, you've done a phenomenal job in the coaching profession. That's what Mike can sell.

Mike is also turning out head coaches from his staff on a regular basis—young guys who are in major programs like Tommy Amaker at Michigan, Mike Brey at Notre Dame, and Quin Snyder at Missouri. Plus he was involved in international basketball as an assistant on the 1992 Dream Team.

Coach K played for Bobby Knight at West Point and then coached under him at Indiana before he got his big break. The two of them had a falling-out after Duke beat Indiana in the 1992 Final Four. But Mike had enough class to realize who'd given him his start—and his philosophy—in this business. He invited Knight to introduce him when he was inducted into the Hall of Fame in 2001.

7. Dick Enberg, Billy Packer and Al McGuire

They were the greatest threesome ever to step into a college basketball broadcasting booth for NBC. Dick was the maestro, the award-winning play-by-play man. Billy was the main analyst with all the opinions. And Al was the street-smart, wisecracking ex-coach who was a great storyteller.

They played beautiful music together.

That group helped to popularize the game. They also get credit for doing the Magic-Bird national championship game in 1979, when the status of the Final Four was elevated from just an event to a Super Bowl. Billy's since gone on to do 21 NCAA championship games for CBS.

I have done zero.

I'm often asked, "Aren't you really envious of the fact that Billy gets to sit at courtside for all these bigger games and yet, throughout your career, you will never do one national championship game?"

"Give me a break," I tell them. "I've been so lucky just to be involved with the game I love, and, believe me, we have such a strong presence at the Final Four. During the week we are analyzing the teams involved, interviewing the coaches who are chasing their dreams of cutting the nets down, and having a ball mingling with all the beautiful fans who are present."

There are a lot of things we all wish for. Man, if I could live in a perfect world, I'd love to have the looks of a Tom Cruise, the body of an Arnold Schwarzenegger, the cash of a Bill Gates, the smoothness of a Bob Costas on the tube, and the potential, which is unlimited, of a guy like our own Mike Tirico—but I've learned to deal with the cards I've been dealt in life. I'm just a simple, ugly guy having a blast making a living doing something that I love—talking hoops.

And the trio of Enberg, Packer, and McGuire certainly influenced me in that respect. When I got into broadcasting, I wanted to be a little bit of Packer, because of his knowledge of the Xs and Os, and a little bit of Al, because of his sense of humor.

8. C.M. Newton

He was a pioneer in race relations in the Deep South, first at Alabama, where he signed Wendell Hudson, the school's first African American player, in 1969. Newton coached the Tide to three SEC championships, in 1974, 1975 and 1976, two NCAA Tournaments and four NIT appearances. Later on, he coached Vanderbilt to the Tournament in 1988 and 1989. He was selected SEC Coach of the Year in 1972, 1976, 1988 and 1989 before taking the AD job at Kentucky.

Newton deserves credit for bringing in Rick Pitino in 1989 after the program had just gotten hammered by the NCAA. Kentucky won a title in 1996. When Pitino left for the NBA, Newton had the vision to hire Tubby Smith as head coach in 1997. Smith was the first African American men's coach at a school that had been vilified by some as an outpost for racism when Adolph Rupp was there. Smith won a national championship in 1998, his first year in the Bluegrass, securing both his and C.M.'s legacies.

C.M. also hired Bernadette Maddox from Rick's staff to coach the women's basketball team in 1995. She was Kentucky's first African American women's coach.

For those reasons alone—not to mention all the work he's done with the Olympic Committee and the NCAA Selection Committee—C.M. has earned the right to be enshrined in Springfield as a contributor to the game of basketball.

9. Ed Steitz

You may not know his name, but he was the head of the NCAA Rules Committee when college basketball was going through a major evolution. He made two huge changes in 1985 that altered the game forever. He put in a shot clock, and then he instituted the three-point shot.

Before the shot clock, there was always the fear of slow-down games. No more of that, with the 35-second clock. Teams could still take their time, but they couldn't stall.

As for the three, it changed the way the game was played. College basketball had previously been dominated by the low-post big man. Now it could be affected more by the shooters, who could get an extra point if they made that shot from 19-9.

I was really surprised that some coaches were very stubbornly against the use of the three-point shot early on. Guys like Denny Crum and Bobby Knight—other than when it was available for Steve Alford.

Knight was old-school. He believed in the value of high-percentage shots and of making that extra pass. We were talking about it one time because it was driving him bananas. He said, "That's not what the game is about. I've learned the game from the best of the best—Pete Newell and Clair Bee. And it was all about teaching kids to respect the ball and not turn it over, taking the high-percentage shot."

Then you started to see teams letting it fly from all over—especially in the ACC the year they actually went to a 19-foot line. That wasn't healthy for the game. Even now, when I see teams shooting the ball 30-35 times out of their 60 shots, I'm disturbed.

But I thought Rick Pitino was the first to do a fantastic job of screening and spreading the court and making good use of the trifecta when he was at Providence. Then people started emulating it, and now it's used all over. It's part of everybody's offensive sets. I mean, J.J. Redick of Duke hits three of those shots, and it gets the place going bananas.

10. Sonny Vaccaro

I first got to know Sonny at the Dapper Dan Game in Pittsburgh when he was putting together a special All-American game, which would also raise huge dollars for charities in the Pittsburgh area. Now Sonny's the head of grass roots for Adidas, running the ABCD camp and the Big Time Tournament in Vegas and the EA All-American game. He convinced both Kobe Bryant and Tracy McGrady to go with his shoe company when they came out of high school.

Hey, he made his biggest impact when he worked for Nike. Sonny played a big role in Nike signing up Michael Jordan when he realized Jordan could become a great marketing icon. Sonny's also the guy who created the concept of paying out big cash to coaches who would wear Nike shoes. In fact, many in the coaching fraternity should give this guy a big hug every time they see him, because he's largely responsible for the willingness of shoe companies to sign many of them to lucrative, multiyear deals. He became Phil Knight's first lieutenant, and Sonny's contact and influence with the coaches paid big, big dividends. I remember, when I was coaching at Detroit, how I would jump for joy when Donnis Butcher, the former Knickerbocker who worked for Converse, would come in and lay a free pair of shoes on me. Then all of a sudden, guys were making mega-dollars for signing shoe deals.

11. Phil Knight and George Raveling

Nike CEO Phil Knight is the big gun in the shoe wars. Think about it. I guess if you have a bag of cash like he does, you can get in the door with many teams. Nobody can deny the power he's brought to the table. Nike has ties to many of the major programs like Duke, North Carolina and Michigan.

When Sonny left Nike, George Raveling came on board and the beat went on. George brings a wealth of experience to the world of basketball, having coached on every level, first as an assistant at Villanova and Maryland, then as a head coach at Washington State, Iowa, and Southern California. He was always known as a great recruiter—and he must have had the golden touch with LeBron James. I'm sure George had a big smile on his face when he found out he'd be able to give a pile of George Washingtons—to the tune of $90 million—to the kid. That certainly helps win a lot of recruiting battles.

12. Howard Garfinkel

The Super Garf. I know ABCD and Nike control the camps today; but in the '60s, '70s and '80s, Five Star was king of the hill. It's still the best teaching camp out there with big-time lecturers. Garf was so instrumental in getting guys started in coaching. Hubie Brown, still coaching at age 70 with the Memphis Grizzlies, will be the first to tell you how Mr. Garfinkel gave him a chance and helped him get an assistant's job at Duke. He also played a role in the lives of Rick Pitino, Mike Fratello, John Calipari.

And yours truly.

The Super Garf has never allowed me to forget he had enough influence to get me an interview with Dick Lloyd of Rutgers, which launched my college coaching career.

Garf always had the great ones, the five pluses.

He tells a story about a kid from Laney High School in Wilmington, North Carolina, who went to the Pittsburgh session of his camp in 1980. Garf sees this kid in a workout. He's watching. He's on the committee to pick the Street and Smith All-America team. And he couldn't believe what he was seeing.

He calls up Dave Krider, who picked the team. And Garf says, "Stop the presses. You want to look good, you'd better get this guy on your first team, because trust me, he's better than all those guys you got selected."

Bottom line, Krider called back the next day and said there was nothing he could do. The magazine had already been put to bed.

They missed on Michael Jordan.

But Dean Smith didn't.

Everybody wants to be the man. Coaches will be the first ones to tell you how important recruiting is. I did a speaking engagement in the corporate world recently and we got to talking about sales.

I told that group, "You think your job is tough? There's no worse feeling in this world than walking into the home of a 17-year-old kid and knowing that this teenager's controlling your life. If you sign him, you go on to the promised land, you get that multiyear extension, you become a superstar. If he says no, you're applying for jobs at Wal-Mart or the local Ford or General Motors dealerships and everywhere else."

The great player has the advantage because schools will wait for him. They'll do anything he desires. He's the crème de la crème. He controls the whole deal. He's got the coach just hanging there.

But some are definitely worth it, man.

If I could pick one player to coach, it would be Magic Johnson. Why? Because he was a joy. Plus he could play anywhere. Who can forget that magic day during his rookie season with the Lakers in 1980?

Magic once shared with my wife and me the story about the night the Lakers flew to Philadelphia to play the 76ers in Game 6 of the 1980 NBA finals without Kareem. We were sitting with him at Magic's Roundball Classic—formerly known as the Dapper Dan and currently named the EA Sports Roundball Classic—and he said to me, "Dickie V, I simply told the guys we were going to win; I was going to play in the post."

So what did he do? He went off for 42. He just dominated. And the Lakers won the world title.

He's one of those guys you just dream of having because he really was an extension of the coach. He had the mind of a coach. All he wanted to do was win, win, win. Guys like Magic never seem to get enough of what they do, and they do it with such joy and jubilation.

Actually, we tried to recruit him when I was at the University of Detroit. But we had no shot. I told my assistant, David "Smokey"

Gaines, "We're wasting our time. He's from Lansing, and Michigan State is located right around the corner in East Lansing. We're not getting him out of that area." He was so loved there, and he was close to his family, there was no way of getting involved. But believe me, we tried.

He stayed only two years before leaving for the NBA, but that was long enough for the Spartans to cut down the nets in 1979.

That's why I've always been a big advocate of the student athlete and allowing him as much freedom of choice as possible. If I were a great player, I wouldn't sign a national letter of intent. I would verbally commit instead. That way, if a coach decides to take another job, I'm not locked in to a school.

That's what happened with 6'9" Charlie Villanueva from Blair Academy, one of the top five prospects in the country. Charlie committed to Illinois in the fall of 2002, but never signed, saying he wanted to keep his options open in case he wanted to declare for the NBA.

As it turned out, it's a good thing he did.

Bill Self left Illinois for Kansas the next spring, and Villanueva was suddenly free to explore new opportunities. He declared for the draft, but never signed with an agent—how smart that decision was, because there's no way that he would have been drafted high enough to warrant coming out of the scholastic ranks. By going to Connecticut and playing for Jim Calhoun, he will have a chance to really improve his stock.

Same thing happened with two Kentucky recruits.

Shagari Alleyne, the 7'4" giant from Rice High School in Manhattan, originally committed to Rutgers but never signed. He'd become disenchanted with the program over the winter and started to search out higher-profile programs.

When Kentucky lost 6'8" junior Marquis Estill to the NBA draft, Tubby began searching for a big man. Alleyne is a prospect, but he'll be wearing the Big Blue uniform. So will 7'2" Lukas Obrzut, the big Polish import who attended Bridgeton Academy. Obrzut originally committed to Fordham, but after Bob Hill decided to step down after a 2-25 season, he opened up to being recruited. And Kentucky was right there.

The more I think about it, the more I feel that we should forget about the early commitment. I mean, signing early is an absolutely meaningless gesture. Why? Because, in most cases, the kids have not met the necessary standards or they end up changing their minds anyway. Nevertheless, as soon as they sign, the alumni and boosters immediately get excited about a class that may not become a reality. And when it doesn't happen, everyone gets embarrassed—the kid, the school, the coaches. It just doesn't make sense.

When Duke signed 6'9", 245-pound forward Kris Humphries from Hopkins High in Minneapolis in November, they thought they were getting a McDonald's All-American who could give them some much needed power inside. Humphries averaged 25 points and 14 rebounds his senior year and appeared to be a perfect fit.

But it didn't work out. Humphries—who was concerned about PT—asked out of his national letter of intent and opted for Minnesota. Humphries's father played for the University of Minnesota in football and is an active booster there. Obviously, that helped with his decision to stay home.

Ordinarily, the NCAA makes any student who reneges after signing a national letter of intent sit out for a year, but Humphries's family filed an appeal for a waiver with the National Letter of Intent Committee.

And there have been exceptions in the past. Take Allan Houston, for example. He signed with Louisville; he'd always wanted to go there. His father, Wade, was an assistant to Denny Crum. But when Wade got a job at Tennessee in 1989, Louisville released Allan, and the National Letter of Intent Committee issued a waiver so he could play right away for his dad.

Personally, I feel if Duke wants to release Humphries—which they did—he should be allowed to play immediately.

Case closed. No debate. Lucky for Humphries that the committee felt the same way and ruled that he will be able to wear the Golden Gophers' uniform during the 2003-04 season.

A kid should be allowed to transfer and not have to sit out a year if he goes with the blessing of the coach. If a coach doesn't want him to go, though, and he goes anyway, then that kid should sit out a year. But if the eighth, ninth, 10th man wants to go and the coach gives him his okay, he should be allowed to play right away.

In non-revenue sports, any kid who transfers is eligible to play immediately, so why should basketball players be treated differently?

I also feel strongly about Proposition 48.

Originally, the NCAA established eligibility standards in 1973, requiring all student athletes to graduate from high school with a 2.0 GPA. The college presidents raised the bar in 1986, requiring a minimum of 700 on the SAT or 17 on the ACT and a 2.0 GPA in 11 core courses. That was Prop. 48.

In 1992, the presidents raised the standards again, requiring a 2.5 GPA in 13 core courses. Finally, in 1996, a sliding scale was instituted, which is based on a combination of board scores and GPA.

At first, the NCAA would make all Prop. 48 non-qualifiers sit out a year, meaning that they could not even practice with the team. That, to me, was pure nonsense—anyone who thought those kids weren't going to find somewhere else to play hoops had to be kidding themselves. Why not allow them to at least practice in a structured environment? I'm glad they've since modified that rule. Now, a partial qualifier—who has the score but not the core, or vice versa—can practice. If he's on target to get his degree in four years, he can get back a lost year of eligibility.

Having coached at the University of Detroit and dealt with inner city players, I've always believed in giving kids opportunities.

I'm in good company since John Thompson and John Chaney agree with me.

Thompson, like a lot of black educators, has always felt that the SATs and the ACTs were culturally biased against blacks.

Back in 1989, legislation was passed that actually threatened to take Prop. 48 to a further extreme by stopping schools from admitting Prop. 48 athletes altogether. It was called Prop. 42.

Thompson felt the new rule would hurt the lowest socioeconomic segment of society. He was so upset about it that he announced he would walk off the court in protest when his team played a game against Boston College on January 14. He said he was staging the walk-out to bring attention to a tremendous tragedy.

Just before tipoff, Thompson got out of his chair and walked toward the locker room to the applause of the crowd at the Cap Centre in Landover, Maryland. Thompson left the building, got into his car and drove around the city, listening to the radio broadcast of the game. Thompson also boycotted the Hoyas' next game at Providence.

He made a statement—loud and clear—about how he felt about a kid being labeled with a number: "There's nothing more frustrating than to think we labeled a kid as a number, as a 48."

It wasn't long before his protest drew a reaction from the NCAA. A day after the Providence game, Albert Witte, the president of the NCAA, and Martin Massengale, the chairman of the Presidents' Committee, said they would recommend legislation that would postpone any changes to Prop. 48.

So now we're back to square one.

Whenever you factor SATs into the mix as a means of determining eligibility, those who have finanical means have a distinct advantage. I mean, some parents are able to enroll their children in programs like the Princeton Review, which will help them improve their board scores. Most kids in the inner city don't have that opportunity, but that doesn't mean they shouldn't be given a chance to succeed.

I remember Rumeal Robinson, the kid from Boston who was a star on Michigan's national championship team and was a non-projector as a freshman. He came from a tough situation. He was left on the steps of a family in Cambridge who wound up raising him, guiding and directing him.

I remember him telling me one day how much he despised and hated that label. He said that every time he read about himself, it would always say "Rumeal Robinson sat out last year because he was a Prop. 48."

He said that when he would go into a classroom, all the kids would look at him like they were thinking, "That's the kid. That's the kid who's ineligible." That's a tough thing to live with, because what it's saying is you're not bright.

But he knew he was smart. He felt if somebody gave him a chance, he could do it. And how did he do it? He graduated in three years. He went on to play in the NBA and eventually took some graduate courses at Harvard.

Now, let's say we didn't give this kid a chance because of a cold-blooded number—I think that would have been a crime. Hey, here's a kid who wound up being a heckuva basketball player *and* a student who proved he could do the work.

So I propose that a school should base admission on what a kid does in the classroom; base it on his potential, on what he does in his core curriculum rather than on the results of a standardized test.

Now, there's no question that every school should have the right to decide who gets admitted. After all, every school's mission isn't exactly the same as all the others. But the fundamental goal of every school should be to graduate its students. Nobody wants a kid to play four years at a school and wind up with zilch in terms of a degree.

These days, coaches are taking a lot of heat over graduation rates. It's so unfair, especially when we see the way graduation rates are determined. A player transfers, and a coach is penalized. It's like he didn't graduate a player. A guy leaves early for the pros—Elton Brand leaves early, Corey Maggette, William Avery—and a coach is going to get penalized for that. Cincinnati has had a number of kids who have left early; and the school has taken a lot of junior college transfers. Even if those kids graduate, it doesn't count.

Where's the logic? Where's the sense of reality?

Every school is different. Every one is unique. I think the graduation rate for athletes should be compared to the university's overall graduation rate. Look at what the graduation rate is for the non-athlete student body and then see how close to that the graduation rate for basketball players falls.

Mike Krzyzewski stopped me in my tracks once when I congratulated him about his graduation rates in the past. He said, "Why shouldn't they graduate at Duke? We're getting the better student, getting a kid who values academics, who has gotten a head start in life. Obviously, Duke is fortunate to get the type of student athlete who combines an academic drive with the talent to be a superstar in the world of hoops."

At a lot of places, though, you can tell a kid that academics means a lot, but you've got to work to convince that kid of its importance.

Sometimes, I get a big kick when I go to campuses and the head coach says, "I've assigned one of my assistants to make sure the player gets up early, goes to class."

I walk away, shake my head, and ask myself, "Is that what college is supposed to be? Is the coach supposed to be a babysitter? Is he supposed to take the athlete by the hand, make sure he goes to class? I'd like the student athlete to understand that it's one of *his* main responsibilities to go to class."

If the NCAA really wanted to solve the problem of graduation rates, they'd make freshmen ineligible. But that will never happen because it's too logical, has too much common sense. Administrators spout a lot of rhetoric. They form a lot of committees. They have all these seminars about how they're going to change this, how they're going to change that. But it's really all about one thing, man—the chase of the dollar.

One thing I get a big kick out of is administrators having all these meetings, all these sessions. And we hear about saving money. We hear about how athletics has to save money. But when administrators go to all these conventions, they're never at Motel 6. They're at the greatest resorts in the world, at the Ritz Carlton, Amelia Island, Laguna Beach. Always the best of the best—and they're complaining about budgets and money? Why not stay at a Motel 6?

The other thing is, guys are always talking about making new rules and regulations when they've never even been to a kid's home. They've never been out on the streets to know what it is to recruit. They've never experienced the pressure of what it's like in the inner city. They've never seen some of the lives these poor kids have to endure.

Let me tell you, some of these kids are like beautiful flowers. They blossom when they're given a chance.

I know what I've experienced as a coach, and I feel for that guy in the locker room. I feel for what a kid is going through. Especially with the increased pressure to make the NCAA Tournament.

Some coaches are pushing to expand the number again—from the current 65—so that making the field doesn't become such a pass/ fail situation.

I really hope and pray we don't see any more expansion, though. Some people have been lobbying to get everybody in Division I in. Well, in essence, we really do let them all in, because other than the Ivy League, we have postseason play in all conferences, and that gives everybody that one last opportunity to step forward in championship week and earn an automatic bid by winning their conference tournament.

Being in a conference tournament is the last shot.

I love the jubilation of those mid-major schools that win their conference tournaments. It's so special to them. In a way, that's their NCAA championship. But not everyone agrees with me.

Lute Olson of Arizona and Mike Montgomery of Stanford came out against the Pac-10 conference tournament last year.

I was against their reasoning, even though I can understand it from their standpoint. Because they're likely to be in the NCAA Tournament every year, they feel that the conference tournament becomes more of a burden than a pleasure. I know they're talking about academics, about missed class time.

But I believe if a kid really wants to be a student, he'll find the time.

It reminds me of old times with Bobby Knight. I'd come into Bloomington to do games for ESPN, and he'd be screaming and yelling about 9:00 P.M. starts: "The players don't get in until 12 midnight, after showering, and the next day, they've got to be up for class."

I'd say, "Come on, Bobby, let's get real. If we were doing this every day, you'd have an argument. But we're asking you to do this once, twice a year. Come on, now, give me a break."

My point is this: just walk into any dorm, man. You think those kids are sitting in a library at 10, 11 at night? Some kids in those dorms are up till three, four in the morning—and not necessarily studying. So I don't buy that academic dilemma argument.

Another thing I don't buy is that the NCAA is in favor of wiping out early-season tournaments—like Maui, the Great Alaskan Shootout, the Preseason NIT. That would be a disaster. It would eliminate mid-major teams like Ball State, who beat Kansas and UCLA in 2001 to get to the finals in the Maui Classic, playing the biggies on a neutral court. The NCAA appealed a ruling that would have allowed these tournaments to continue, and the courts ruled in favor of the NCAA. Who knows how this complicated scenario will eventually turn out?

Eliminating the tournaments will certainly hurt the student athletes

This gets down to control, man. Power. This is about administrators from major conferences wanting more control of the revenue generated by these tournaments. They'd rather have their teams play on three home courts so they can keep all the cash.

There are so many positives to these games. Players get a chance to develop a competitive spirit against kids they normally don't play against. They also get to travel, to see places they may not have seen.

I know when teams come to New York, it becomes an educational experience for them. They take in the city. They visit Wall Street.

It also gives teams a chance to eliminate a lot of the bargain-basement goodies, the cupcakes, on their schedule.

Hey, remember we were talking earlier about the institution of the three-point shot? Did you know that the Rules Committee is considering pushing the three-point shot back from 19-9 to the international distance of 20-6 and adding a trapezoid lane?

They've put off a final decision until 2004, but hey, at least they don't plan to remain status quo. I mean, if the changes are going to make the game better, why not tweak the rules a little?

The current three-point shot has changed the game, largely for the good, but also for the bad. For the good, obviously, it gives a team a chance to come back. It gives a team the opportunity to spring that upset when there's a team on fire with a guy who can knock down the trifecta.

Pitino was the first to take advantage of it. He did it back in 1986 and in 1987 when he got to the Final Four with Billy Donovan and company. Certainly Indiana used it with Alford. But Pitino's kids, they really let it fly. Then he took advantage of it down at Kentucky as well—The Bombinos.

But there are times when I think the shot is used too much.

I've done games when I was sitting there, totally bored out of my mind. A team is down 15, 16, and everything I've ever preached about the game, everything I've ever learned about the game—from hearing the Wizard of Westwood speak, from listening to Knight and Dean Smith—is being violated. Sometimes I ask myself, what has happened to shot selection? Teams are just coming down the court and going for the trifecta. The high-percentage shot just gets taken away. I'm for moving the line back just to reduce the number of shots.

I think pushing the three-point line back a little is okay. I don't want to push it back to the NBA line, or it'll be a heave. Of course, there will still be players with great range like J.J. Redick of Duke, who can drill shots from anywhere.

As for the trapezoid lane, I've always felt that widening the lane could create more exciting basketball because it will move the big guy away from the three-second area. It will bring about, just as C.M. Newton has said, a situation where there'll be more activity from the players on the perimeter. It will help to create better opportunities for the little guy.

Some of the rules have certainly changed the game tremendously. The shot clock has been an enormous plus. Too many teams were playing in slow motion.

The game that highlighted the problem was the nationally televised ACC championship matchup between Virginia and North Carolina in 1982. Those two teams had all that talent with Michael Jordan, James Worthy and Ralph Sampson playing against one another—and the final score was North Carolina 47, Virginia 44.

But you know, the crazy thing was that North Carolina had a 44-43 lead with six minutes to play and refused to shoot unless Sampson and his team came out of the zone they were playing. Virginia had committed just one personal, and they let almost five minutes run off the clock before they started fouling. Finally, with 28 seconds left, they put Carolina in the bonus. Matt Doherty made one of two free throws, and Virginia got the ball. But they never got off the last shot. Carolina had just one personal, and they kept fouling before Virginia could shoot. It got so frustrating that Virginia finally turned the ball over with three seconds to play.

It made for bad TV, man.

You had all those guys just standing around, not playing. That's when I knew things had to change.

The only negative now is that the clock limits the chances of the little guy springing that major upset. Before the clock, the little guy had a great opportunity to spread the court, get a great ball handler who could milk the clock and shorten the game. The more you shorten the game, the better chance you've got of reducing the power of the stronger team.

But it was a wise decision going to the clock.

I'd like to see one more rule change. I hate the alternating possession rule. Over the years, I've been involved in a number of games in which a player has made a great defensive play, tying up the ball late in the game, yet I have to look across the floor to an arrow to determine who gets possession. Let the refs throw the ball up in the air. Then coaches would have to develop strategies to create opportunities in jump ball situations.

Even Hall of Famers—and those who should be.

One thing I love about the Basketball Hall of Fame in Springfield, Massachusetts, is that it has put people like John Chaney of

Temple, Lute Olson of Arizona, Mike Krzyzewski of Duke, Bobby Knight of Indiana, Dean Smith of North Carolina, Denny Crum of Louisville and Louie Carnesecca of St. John's in there while they're alive and can enjoy the thrill of it with their families. What bothers me is that some of these places wait to honor people after they're long gone, when they can never get to feel the excitement of that moment. What greater feeling is there than to strut around and see your bust up there with the greatest in the world?

That's why I think the Hall of Fame should open the doors for Jimmy Boeheim. There are a couple of more guys in the East—Jim Calhoun of Connecticut and Gary Williams of Maryland—who also deserve to be enshrined.

I mean, when you thought about UConn years ago, you were talking about a regional program. Calhoun's changed that, put the school in the top 10, top 15 in the country on a regular basis. His record might be even better if he played more of his games on campus. If I were him, I'd play all my home games at Gampel Pavilion instead of playing some of them at Hartford Civic Center. Gampel is the New England version of Cameron Indoor Stadium. The fans are right on top of you, and the noise level is incredible.

I know if I were there, I'd say to their AD, "Hey, don't worry about the dollars you can get at that other place, I want to win 'em all."

And Williams has turned Maryland into one of the top three teams in the ACC. He won it all in 2002. And he did it without any McDonald's All-Americans on his roster. He turned Maryland into one of the top teams in the ACC recently, coaching the Terps to the Final Four in 2001 and increasing the popularity of the sport at his school to a point where athletic officials have built a new 18,000-seat on-campus arena that is always full.

Let me tell you another guy who deserves consideration—Lefty Driesell, who just retired at Georgia State, but made his reputation at

Maryland. As soon as Lefty showed up in College Park in 1969, he said, "We want to be the UCLA of the East." He invented Midnight Madness.

He was a recruiting genius. I remember visiting him. George Raveling and the late Jim Maloney—his assistants at the time—had stacks and stacks of magazines and newspapers from around the country so they could read about every prospect in America.

He won 786 games in 41 years, 384 of them at Maryland. He also won at least 100 games at Davidson, James Madison and Georgia State, becoming the only coach to do that at four different schools.

Unfortunately, some of his best teams at Maryland never got a chance to play in the Tournament because back then, the NCAA would invite only one team per conference. That one team—in 1974—that had Tom McMillen, Len Elmore, Mo Howard, John Lucas and Jim O'Brien—was good enough to win it most years, but they lost to NC State with David Thompson, 103-100, in that incredible overtime game in the ACC Tournament finals.

Eddie Sutton certainly deserves consideration, too. Look at the job he's done at Oklahoma State, taking them to the Final Four in 1995 and turning them into a top 20 team in the Big 12. He's also taken Creighton, Arkansas and Kentucky to the NCAA Tournament.

Oh, and one more thing.

Let me tell you what I'm going to do this year. Many people may not agree with me. In fact, I know I'm going to get heat on this. But I believe it, baby. Next October, November, I'm going to start screaming on TV that at Indiana, they ought to rename the court at Assembly Hall "The Bob Knight Center."

Come on, man. When you look at what he did at IU—raising money for the library, doing all the fundraising, making sure his kids graduated, running a clean program and coaching the Hoosiers to three national championships—it's the right thing to do.

I know I'm going to hear it from all the Myles Brand people, screaming and yelling and going crazy about it. But I don't care. The reason I don't care is that I've always believed promoting that which is right.

And the bottom line is there's nobody who's done more for that school than the General.

Yes, I have my share of opinions.

America, baby, consider yourself warned.

3

LeBRON MANIA

All right, let's go to Cleveland, 2003. LeBron Mania is coming on strong at the home of the Rock and Roll Museum. Start me up, baby.

The Cavaliers won the NBA draft lottery, and it didn't take their owner, Gordon Gund, long to decide whom he was going to select. LeBron James. Or King James to you, according to the T-shirt he wore to a couple of summer camps after his junior year.

LeBronski is taking his show to the big time, and he will have them dancing in the aisles and doing high fives, because this kid has the whole package. He's a three-S man—super, scintillating and sensational—and he's a Rolls Roycer, a PTPer.

Gordon Gund was jumping for joy after those ping pong balls stopped bouncing. I'm telling you, you talk about a city that needed a bump, that needed juice—well, they're getting it now, big time. Cleveland: new uniforms, new logo, and now they have, as they say, the new kid on the block—the future star of the Cavaliers organization—LeBron James. Yes, America, get ready. LeBron Mania will have the city of Cleveland going absolutely bananas.

I can already hear the box office cash registers going ring-a-ling-ding-ding with all those season ticket sales pouring in.

Hey, I want to call for tickets myself. I want to see LeBron. Who wouldn't?

This guy is the real deal. He's 6'8", 240 pounds. He averaged 30.4 points, 9.7 rebounds, 4.9 assists and 2.9 steals as a senior at St. Vincent-St. Mary High School, just 40 miles down the road in Akron, Ohio. They won the mythical national high school championship. He won every conceivable national Player of the Year award.

His fan appeal is incredible. He's just got it: that certain presence, those specific movie-star looks. He's got the whole package, man. But the biggest thing he's got is that he's going to back it up on the floor. The kid flies.

I read a quote from Danny Ainge, who is now the head of basketball operations for the Boston Celtics. Danny said, "He's the best high school player I've ever seen in my life." Man, that is something else. He went on to say, "I've seen Magic Johnson, Gene Banks, Jonathan Bender, Tracy McGrady, Lamar Odom, Kobe Bryant, and he's better than all those guys." And that's a quote from Danny Ainge, who knows a little something about the game. Danny says he loves LeBron because he has the great body, the great vision and the great instincts.

I have to tell you, based on my time at ESPN—so that excludes guys like Magic, Moses, Kareem and Wilt, guys prior to 1979—LeBron is the best high school player I have ever laid eyes on. He's the truth, the whole truth, and nothing but the truth.

Nike must agree. They've locked him up to a blockbuster sneaker and personal apparel contract, a seven-year deal worth more than $90 million. It's the largest initial deal ever given to an unproven player and almost matches the five-year, $100 million contract Tiger Woods signed with Nike in 2000.

Ninety million?

Does it blow my mind? Yeah, it blows my mind—especially when I think back. I'll never forget the stir caused years ago by the thought of player endorsements. Everybody said, "Oh my God, they're paying $100,000 for Joe DiMaggio and Ted Williams." It was unbelievable: $100,000. Can you imagine what they'd get today? They would own the franchises.

When I was coaching at the University of Detroit, the Converse guy would come along and maybe give you a pair of Chuck Taylors and a sweatsuit—and you'd think you were in hog heaven.

But shoe contracts have come a long way in the last few years. Shaquille O'Neal signed a $3 million deal with Reebok in 1992. Four years later, 17-year-old Kobe Bryant got $5 million to sign with Adidas. Allen Iverson signed a $50 million lifetime contract with Reebok in 1996, and Tracy McGrady signed a six-year deal worth $12 million with Adidas in 1997.

Nike even gave Freddie Adu, a 13-year-old soccer sensation who came to the United States from Nigeria and who is considered the best young American soccer talent ever, $1 million for his endorsement. The next thing you know, shoe companies will be going into the maternity wards, trying to sign up the diaper dandies.

Anyway, that's small change to what LeBron was making before he ever played his first NBA game.

Oh yeah, the guy also reportedly got a $1 million signing bonus and a five-year, $5 million deal when he inked up with Upper Deck cards.

Guys say he should go to school? He could buy a college, man.

Nike came out the big-time winner. Bob Ley did an *Outside the Lines* show on ESPN with Sonny Vaccaro of Adidas and Dan Wetzel of *CBS Sportsline*. Bob Ley said it came down to a two-team race, a battle between the pockets of Phil Knight and the pockets of Reebok.

Sonny'd made a bid with Adidas, which tried to romance James with billboards and messages on buses in his hometown. "My heart was in it. I love the kid," Sonny said, "but I couldn't play in that league in terms of the dollars that were involved."

Reebok actually offered more dough, but LeBron liked Nike's presentation better. They flew his agent, Aaron Goodwin, his mother, Gloria James, and LeBron out to their corporate headquarters in Beaverton, Oregon, to make a final pitch. Nike said they would give LeBron some creative input into the design of his sneaker model.

Nike is playing for big stakes—an $8 billion market for athletic shoes in the U.S. If LeBron helps Nike preserve just one percent of the market share—if he sells 900,000 pairs of LeBron shoes over the length of the contract, the company breaks even.

Why did Phil Knight give him that much cash? Well, let me tell you something. In the world of the athletic shoe business, the magical word is "connection." Can you connect as a player in the world of marketing? Can you get others to want to wear that shoe? Can you project that image of "street cred," man? Especially in the teenage market, where the 13-, 14-, 15-, 16-year-old kid is willing to buy the $150 shoe, where they're eager to lay out that kind of cash.

And you'd better believe that Nike wouldn't have given this kid $90 million unless they think they can get it back. I mean, Phil Knight was not born yesterday, man. He's a business machine. He knows how to make cash.

When Nike signed Michael Jordan in 1984 for $2.5 million over five years, he was a bargain. By the time he retired for the first time in 1993, Nike had turned him into a brand name and had already sold hundreds of millions of dollars' worth of Air Jordan shoes.

They anticipate that LeBron will be that attractive because, first of all, he's one of those special personalities with charisma galore, so he'll connect with the young teenager.

It's something that hasn't happened for Kobe Bryant or Shaquille O'Neal. Think about Kobe. Oh man, this guy has been so special. I was shocked at the news of Kobe's arrest for an alleged sexual assault while he was in Eagle County, Colorado for surgery to correct a knee problem. Man, this is one guy I have never believed could ever find himself in a situation like this. I mean, he's handled himself with such distinction during his seven years with the Lakers. And let me tell you this about his playing ability—Kobe has been a flat-out superstar. In fact, in 10 years, we may be arguing about who's the greatest ever to play the game—Michael or Kobe.

But the kid just did not sell shoes in his deal with Adidas. He recently signed a $40 million, five-year endorsement deal with Nike— well below the amount they've given to LeBron. And now, no matter what comes of his arrest, Kobe's marketability will be limited even more.

It's going to be more than just a shoe deal with LeBron. It's going to be a fashion statement, with clothing and all kinds of good- ies.

And let me tell you, it all has to relate to how he plays on the floor. Look at Allen Iverson. He is one player who has connected with the kids. Kids in the inner city love the little guy, and they flock to the stores to buy shoes from Reebok.

Well, let me tell you, they're really going to flock to buy LeBron's shoes, because he's the real deal.

Yes, LeBron is going to be a marketing machine.

I remember Sonny Vaccaro telling me, "Trust me, he's got that magical personality that will connect with the populace."

LeBron was big long before I met him. He was on the cover of *Sports Illustrated* when he was a junior in high school. They were call- ing him "The Chosen One." He's been on the front of *ESPN the Magazine*. In the last two years, *The Akron Beacon Journal* had more coverage on LeBron than it had on the Cavs.

Early last season, I did one of his games. I just had to see the phenomenon for myself. ESPN had signed on to do LeBron's game against Oak Hill Academy at Cleveland State's Convocation Center. It was the first time ESPN had carried a high school game since 1988.

I'll be honest with you. I was a little apprehensive about doing that game. The first time my boss, Dan Steir, who is in charge of college basketball at ESPN, called me about it, I was a little hesitant. I just didn't think we wanted to make this kid, who is so young, this big. I felt we might be treating this kid and this game bigger than any college game. I thought, "Wow, think about it—Bill Walton, Dan Shulman, Dick Vitale, Jay Bilas, all of us at this game. We don't even put a cast like that on an NBA or a college game, and now we're going to do it for a high school game?"

I said maybe it would be better to let Bill Walton, the Big Redhead, do the game and I could just simply watch. I felt Bill would be ideal because he was the number one talent for our NBA coverage and because LeBron was obviously headed for the pros. But ESPN execs felt LeBron had become a national news story worth sharing with the rest of the country. They were planning to do the game as a lead-in to a special program about the next wave of potential superstar athletes.

I know Billy Packer came out in *USA Today* and said that he wouldn't have done it. He claimed that if he were in my situation, he would have refused to do that high school game. Well, I don't feel like that. I'm a loyal team player, so I'll do whatever my team wants me to do. And, hey, are you kidding me? Do you think I wanted to get fired and give up the best job in the world? Plus, I guess I'm just not as big as Billy.

When we arrived, there were 14, 15 TV trucks and spotlights all over. And there must have been 100 media guys there to chronicle the event. The scene was like a rock concert. It was like, here comes

Bruce Springsteen, here comes P. Diddy or Madonna, ready to rock the place—except it was LeBron's concert, his big coming-out party. He was on national television and he was getting rivers and rivers of ink. Tickets had been sold for $10 to $35, but scalpers were getting $100 for courtside seats.

LeBron truly was like a rock star walking into the arena, man. He even had a bodyguard. You could feel this electricity in the air, like this awesome performance was about to take place. He had everybody in the palm of his hand.

And then it happened—the house lights went down and the stage lights came on. He went off for 31 points, 13 rebounds and six assists. He made spectacular dunks and executed no-look and behind-the-back passes while leading St. Vincent-St. Mary to a 65-46 upset victory. It was like he was straight out of an old Timex commercial—he kept ticking and ticking and never took a licking.

It was a rare experience for me. I didn't care that he missed his first few jump shots. I just saw that body, that ball-handling ability, and that explosiveness. And, man, what great vision. He had unbelievable instincts.

The game pulled a stunning 2.0 overnight rating in large markets and an audience of about 2.5 million viewers. It was the largest audience for a regularly scheduled ESPN 2 show in the channel's nine-year history.

But this was about so much more than basketball. We had never been on the air together before, so I met Bill Walton before the game and we shared our game plan. We decided to address just about every issue voiced by critics who believed the game should not have been aired.

We talked about money and about pressure. We talked about the team's ambitious road schedules and gave both sides of the story. We also talked about whether or not LeBron—who was then still a 17-year-old high school student—was being exploited.

I mean, take a look at the money this kid generates.

St. Vincent-St. Mary played on ESPN twice. They played their home games at the 5,292-seat University of Akron Arena, where the school had sold 3,000 season tickets. Reportedly, they got $15,000 plus travel expenses for road games and had a 10-game pay-per-view package on Time-Warner in northeast Ohio. And on eBay, a LeBron James autograph went for $104 and a LeBron James bobblehead doll sold for $16.50.

We've heard a lot about exploitation, and that worries me because there is a lot of that going on here. People are already scheming about how they can make money, in an unsavory manner, off this teenager.

"This is the world we've created," Walton observed.

LeBron is the exception to every rule, although it looks like the NBA is getting younger every year. I tried to be careful to present the flip side, offering a list of kids who have left high school to turn pro early only to come away with nothing—nothing but shattered dreams and a questionable future.

Then I asked Bill the big question: "What would you do if you'd had the opportunity to be selected No. 1 in the NBA draft and pick up a $25 million sneaker contract when you graduated from high school?"

At that time, it was rumored that James could get that much from the shoe companies. Who'd have ever thought it would balloon to $90 million? Well, I pushed the Big Redhead over and over about his decision to go to UCLA if he'd had all those dollars being dangled in front of him.

"Dick," he responded, "you obviously don't know me. I would not have taken the money. It all depends on what you value in life. I dreamed of being a college student athlete. But our world has changed. Do kids today still value education? Do they still value knowledge? Do they still value hard work?"

"Come on, Bill. It's easy to say you would have gone to UCLA because you weren't looking at those kind of dollars," I answered. "Well, I don't agree. We don't know what you'd have done because you're not in his situation looking at millions of dollars for your shoe deal and being the first pick in the draft. It's a whole different ballgame, the dollars then and the dollars now. It's as different as night and day."

I do respect his conviction, though.

I'll never forget that after the game, I got a big hug from LeBron. He said, "I want to thank you for coming out to my game." Those were his exact words. And I said to him, "Just make certain you surround yourself with good people who worry about you, who give a damn about you. Get advice from those who have been there—like Tracy McGracy or Kevin Garnett—and follow their pattern, because obviously whatever they're doing is working."

The kid came across as being so sincere. I felt he liked his teammates, liked his school, liked being in school. I'll tell you what told me a lot about him as a kid—his sophomore year, he made All-State in football as a wide receiver. His junior year, he decided he wasn't going to play football because everybody talked him out of it. They said that he couldn't risk an injury that could ruin his chances in basketball.

Early in the season, though, he was watching the football team lose a game. He said to the coach, "Coach, I've got to play." And he came back out. To me, that showed unselfishness, that he cared about his teammates.

If only this were a fairy tale.

The Oak Hill game was played on a Thursday. It didn't take long for the earthquake to hit. That Sunday, ESPN, which has won numerous awards for its *Outside the Lines* program, did one devoted to LeBron. It was hosted by my buddy Bob Ley, who played a vital role in teaching me during the early part of my career how to respond in a studio setting. Also part of the program, via remote camera from each of our homes, were Billy Packer and myself. There were immediate sparks.

Billy ripped me for working the game and lumped me among the unsavory characters who participate in exploitation and misuse of the game. He also included himself in that group, as well as his network and the sneaker companies.

"Any of us who thought this was positive for the game is crazy," he said. "That's not the message we want to go out, in a healthy game, to millions of kids."

Packer's claim was this: "If CBS was doing that game, I would refuse to do it. Get somebody else. I don't think it was the right thing."

I didn't like the term *unsavory*. I don't think of either of us as unsavory—that word has a sleazy, under-handed connotation to it.

Billy can believe what he wants. But I'll tell you this—I know I'd never do anything unless my heart was in the right place.

For example, on that show, I suggested that maybe we should eliminate freshman eligibility. That might solve some of the problems of graduation rates. But Billy immediately made it sound like I was an idiot for making that claim. I also stated that until we have a meeting of the minds between people like NBA commissioner David Stern, new executive director of the NCAA Myles Brand, and Billy Hunter of the Players' Association, we will never be able to solve the dilemma that's been created for everyone involved in the game by the active recruitment of younger players. I praised Stern for his passion for the NBA game and the amazing marketing job he's done.

Well, Billy criticized me for praising David Stern. And he jumped all over Stern, claming he's done nothing for the NBA. I do think Stern definitely cares about the NBA, though. Deep down, I really believe him when he says setting the minimum age at which a player can declare for the draft at 20 is good for the college game.

As for the controversy over doing that game, here's my take.

There was a deal brokered between ESPN, the promoter and the school. It ended up positive, all around. People talk about LeBron being exploited. They say he became a marketing tool with the kind of exposure he received, but I disagree. LeBron benefited from the PR, and the school benefited from the dollars they made.

St. Vincent-St. Mary played to sold-out arenas in Philly, Pittsburgh, Columbus, Greensboro, L.A. and Trenton. Reportedly, the school made over $1 million during their road trip. They were awarded an Adidas contract.

Whenever I take on a project, I do research to see where the money is going and to find out how many school days a player is missing. With LeBron, I found out that there was very little class time being missed with his traveling. I found out the money was coming back to the school's general fund, not to its athletic department. All of that made me feel a little less apprehensive about the situation than I had originally felt.

But back to LeBron's memorable year.

I remember watching on TV the game from Trenton when he got 52 on Westchester High of Los Angeles, a West Coast power. Here is this high school kid, right, and he doesn't just do it against cupcake city. Westchester is an L.A. power, and they had this kid, Trevor Ariza, who's going to UCLA. And LeBron put on a show.

He had them dancing in the aisles, baby.

I was watching *SportsCenter*. I called to Lorraine, saying, "Look at this. Look at that." I thought I was watching Jordan, Michael the Magnificent at his best. He was a human highlight film.

Even Lorraine, who doesn't know much about basketball, was impressed: "You can't be serious. This kid is in high school?"

But, hey, it wasn't all one big party for the kid.

LeBron didn't do himself much good from a PR standpoint when, in January 2003, he started driving around Akron in a new Hummer H2, the same vehicle all the pros drive. Those babies go for $50,000, minimum. And this one came fully loaded with three TVs and a hookup for video games.

His mother, Gloria, said she obtained a bank loan to finance the vehicle as a present for LeBron on his 18th birthday. The Ohio High School Athletic Association investigated and eventually cleared LeBron of any wrongdoing. But I thought it was an absolute disaster.

LeBron should have waited until at least after graduation. To me, by driving that Hummer while still in high school, all he was doing was highlighting how far he'd made it. So many people are lying in wait to take shots whenever someone else makes it to the top. And all his mom did by allowing him to have that kind of vehicle at such a young age was to expose him to critics big time. Why not wait until after graduation? But it reaches a point where everybody's afraid to say *no* because nobody wants to get on the wrong side of what this kid is about—dollars, man, dollars.

Then, less than a month later, the OHSAA was knocking on LeBron's door again. This time, it was because he had accepted a pair of Retro jerseys worth $845 from a store in Cleveland. LeBron was declared ineligible for the rest of the season, but a judge overturned the decision, ruling that he could return to play after sitting out two games.

He dropped 52 in his first game back.

Immediately afterwards, a Vegas online sports book began taking bets on which shoe company would land James as an endorser. Nike was tabbed as the favorite, going off at 1:2 odds; Adidas was 3:2, and other companies were a 3:1 bet.

Eventually, LeBron led his team to a third state title, then won MVP awards at the McDonald's All-American game, the Jordan Capital Classic in Washington D.C. and the EA Sports Roundball Classic in Chicago.

His jersey's already been shipped off to the Basketball Hall of Fame, but you can get a replica—not autographed, of course—for $100 on eBay.

Now it's on to the pros for him. In LeBron's case, it's the right thing for him to do—how can he possibly pass up those dollars just to risk injuring himself in college, which would end it all for him?

But too many others try to make that leap before they've had a chance to fully develop as a player and as a person. And the system itself is totally wacky. Unless the NBA and the NCAA get together with the Players' Association and recognize the need to put into place a rule setting the minimum age for declaring for the NBA draft at 20, we'll continue to see a lot of kids get hurt.

Pro basketball has been infatuated with high school players ever since center Moses Malone of Petersburg, Virginia, who had signed with Maryland in 1972, decided to skip college and sign with the ABA's Utah Jazz. Center Darryl Dawkins of Orlando, Florida, and Bill Willoughby of Englewood, New Jersey, each made the quantum leap in 1975, signing with the NBA's Philadelphia 76ers and the Atlanta Hawks, respectively.

But it wasn't until 1995 when the league—much to the chagrin of college coaches—began seriously looking at the prep talent pool, opening the floodgates for younger players like forward Kevin Garnett of Chicago Farragut to declare that year. Then guard Kobe Bryant of Lower Merion High in Pennsylvania declared in 1996, and forward Tracy McGrady of Mt. Zion Academy in Durham, North Carolina followed suit in '97.

Garnett, Bryant and McGrady have all been feel-good success stories, developing into three of the top 10 players in the league and backing up the theory espoused by NBA director of scouting Marty

Blake: gifted young players develop quicker in a pro atmosphere than in college.

But not everyone has made a smooth transition.

Forward Leon Smith of Chicago King was drafted first by San Antonio in 1999 and then traded to Dallas. He was a discipline problem with the Mavericks, had a series of run-ins with the law in his hometown, and then attempted to commit suicide by swallowing more than 200 aspirin tablets. The 6'11" Smith got his act together long enough to lead the CBA in rebounding this season with the Gary Steelheads. Atlanta offered him a rare second chance in March, signing him for the rest of the season.

Guard DeShawn Stevenson, who was selected first by Utah in the 2000 draft, has had to deal with a misdemeanor charge of statutory rape that resulted in probation.

In 2002, Amare Stoudemire, a 6'9", 260-pound man-child from Cypress Creek, Florida, put his name into the 2002 draft and was taken by Phoenix with the ninth pick. He was the league's Rookie of the Year.

It's the Stoudemires who make it that we all hear about, but nobody ever talks about the rest—like McDonald's All-Americans 6'9" D'Angelo Collins of L.A. and 6'6" Lenny Cooke of Brooklyn—who don't make it, who listened to people on the streets filling their heads up with delusions of grandeur.

Collins lost his college eligibility by declaring for the draft—and wasn't drafted.

Cooke was the bomb before LeBron. He ruled ABCD as a sophomore before LeBron took over. He led La Salle to the CHSAA city championship as a sophomore and was the MVP of the Entertainers' League at Rucker Park after his junior year—he was arguably the most talented high school prospect in the New York Metropolitan area.

He thought about playing for Mike Jarvis at St. John's, but he made the controversial decision to bypass college and declare for the pros in January 2003.

Cooke signed with an agent—Mike Harrison of Immortal Sports in Santa Monica—moved to Southern California and began working out at Dorsey High School.

Given the fact that NBA teams selected four high school prospects—centers Kwame Brown, Tyson Chandler, Eddy Curry and DeSagana Diop—with the first eight picks in the previous year, Cooke was hoping to catch a ride on the same bandwagon. But he was injured in the Chicago pre-draft camp and never heard his name called. The last I heard, he had a new agent and was getting his act together with a USBL team in Brooklyn.

Besides LeBron, five other high school stars declared for the NBA last spring: 6'10" center Ndudi Ebi of Westbury Christian in Houston, Texas; forward Charlie Villanueva of Blair Academy in New Jersey; 6'10", 360-pound center James Lang of Central Park Christian in Birmingham, Alabama; 6'10" Kendrick Perkins of Beaumont, Texas; 6'9" forward Travis Outlaw of Starkville High in Mississipi. They all wanted to test the waters.

Originally, Villanueva had verbally committed to Illinois, Ebi signed with Arizona, Perkins signed with Memphis, Outlaw signed with Mississippi State, and Lang signed with an agent.

Only Villanueva had the common sense to pull out, opting to go to UConn.

I know Portland chose Outlaw at 23 in the first round, and Minnesota, who previously drafted Garnett, took Ebi at 26. Memphis took Perkins at 27, then traded him to Boston, and New Orleans took Lang at 48. But these kids could have done better a year from now. They were impatient. They should have gone to college for at least a year or two.

Please, somebody tell them to get real and get to campus; enjoy life as a student athlete. Play for the great ones—like Jim Calhoun, John Calipari, Lute Olson. All three have coached in the Final Four, and Calhoun and Olson are sporting championship rings.

Here's my advice: Develop your potential; improve yourself so you'll be a lock for the lottery. Think what college did for the stock of guys like scoring sensation Carmelo Anthony of Syracuse, forward Chris Bosh of Georgia Tech and guard T.J. Ford of Texas. Where would they be if they were drafted out of high school? No way would they be top 10 selections.

Now think about this: It's not just these five high school kids going pro. Five? I mean, look at baseball and hockey. There are hundreds and hundreds of kids who come out of the high school ranks and sign professional contracts.

This has created an environment where kids want to be listed in the draft just as an ego trip. They throw their name in just to feel good, and then maybe pull their name out when they realize they're going to sit the pine or they're not going to be a first-round choice. Some college kids do the same thing merely for ego gratification, too.

I was recently talking to an NFL player on the golf course, and he said something that blew me away. I don't know how accurate the claim is, but he said, "There's a report out that says five years after guys are done playing professional football, a high percentage of them go bankrupt, get involved with drugs and alcohol, or get really messed up, because they're so used to living in the fast lane that they can't adjust."

One thing I try to stress to kids is that college can help them to gain the skills and abilities that are essential in making the transition from the basketball arena out into the real world. Remember, college isn't just about developing a jump shot. It's about developing as a total person—learning discipline, learning how to manage time, learning how to get along with other kinds of people.

Here's a cautionary tale—one of the sad stories in my life. It leaves me feeling very empty, even today.

I once had a player like LeBron.

His name was Leslie Cason, he was 6'10", and I coached him at East Rutherford High School in New Jersey. Now there is no one who goes out and lectures about staying away from the drug and alcohol scene more than I do. Speech after speech after speech. I did it back then, too. And I haven't changed much. But some of the decisions Leslie made just started to crush me.

I was just like any other coach out there, always trying to find a way to keep Leslie eligible. Sometimes, as many of us will, you make excuses, give alibis as you try to do all you can to get them to reach their full potential. Sometimes when I look back, I don't have regret because I thought basketball was his only savior. I thought basketball would be the thing that might have been able to bring out the success that people expected of him, the thing that helped build his self-esteem.

Leslie was a terrific talent. His sophomore and junior years, he was just incredible. But then, his senior year, his abilities diminished. We dominated only because the competition wasn't up to the level of the rest of our team. We managed to finish 29-0 and win the state championship for Group I schools, which were the smallest schools in terms of enrollment.

But Leslie's game had disappeared so much that he was a major disappointment at the Dapper Dan game for Sonny Vaccaro. This was the game where he would get a chance to compete against America's premier high school superstars. Man, he was a bust. He didn't do anything. I felt humiliated for him as I sat there and watched.

I remember going to Sonny after the game. He looked at me in bewilderment, as if to say, "This was the worst performance by any kid that I've ever had at the Dapper."

And, man, that hurt.

After that game, I sat with Leslie and told him, "You're no longer the player you once were. You have a problem off the court. You're not being honest with yourself, and you're not being honest with me."

Then he looked at me and said, "Coach, you've always been in my corner. Believe me, Coach, I'm not messing around."

I simply said to him, "Leslie, we can't solve your problem until you admit that you have one. The bottom line is that you are not the same player or person that I once knew."

Well, Leslie did mess around, and he lost his life at the early age of 43.

Ian O' Connor, who now writes for *USA Today* and is an outstanding columnist, wrote a detailed article in the *New York Daily News* about Leslie Cason in 1996. That's the year Rick Pitino guided Kentucky to the national title. The fact that the finals were being held at the Meadowlands in East Rutherford, N.J.—the home of Cason and the place where I coached on the scholastic level—provided the impetus for O'Connor's story. I happened across it one morning as I was in New York City getting ready for the national semifinals. On the back page of the *Daily News* was this big article about Leslie. It was all about his tragic journey through life after basketball.

It noted that he was living in an apartment in the Bowery. O'Connor had gone down there and interviewed him. Leslie had no money, no furniture. He sent me a message through the article. Leslie said, "I only wish I would have listened to Coach because Coach was in my corner, but I didn't listen, and that's sad when I think about other kids like me out there."

Leslie had thought life was going to be all easy for him. People on the street were filling his head with junk. I once asked him, "Where were they when you were in the ninth, 10th grade, these people you're starting to listen to? They start playing that same song: 'Well, your coach is just a white dude, trying to use you, man, trying to use you to get a job.'"

I kept telling him, "I won't be going with you as a package deal. I'll be going somewhere where somebody gives me a chance. I've got a chance at Rutgers."

He went off to junior college. We got him into San Jacinto down in Texas.

He was so talented. I remember when Willis Reed looked at him one time and said, "My God, I can't believe his skill for a big kid playing on the perimeter." He wasn't a bad kid, but he followed everyone. He followed the wrong people.

It crushes me. I mean, 43—he lost his life at such an early age. He should have been like two other superstars who came out of high school at the same time—John Shumate of Elizabeth and Gary Brokaw of New Brunswick—who both went to Notre Dame. Instead, he became a part-time player at Rutgers when Tom Young tried to help him after he came out of San Jac.

And I tried to help him at the end.

I will never forget getting a letter from George Ibach, the pastor of the Bowery Mission. He told me all about Leslie's plight and how his life had been destroyed by the drug scene.

I still have the letters Leslie wrote me near the end of his life, telling me, "I wish I would have listened."

And then he got mad at me. He wrote me this letter: "Coach, I've never asked you for money"—and he never did—"but I'm really struggling in the Bowery. I'm living in this apartment. I have no furniture, no clothing, nothing. Could you just help me with something?"

I felt very bad.

I immediately wrote him and said, "Without a doubt."

That's when I contacted Pastor Ibach, who was meeting with Leslie on a regular basis. I then wrote to Leslie, "I'll send money regularly to the priest and he'll distribute it to you for anything you need in the way of clothing or food."

He got furious.

He wrote me back, saying, "You don't trust me. You're going to send it to them. They're going to steal the money. You got to send *me* the money." Well, you know where the money was going to go.

I sent the money to Ibach, who went out and bought Leslie a lot of stuff. But then one day the pastor returned the money I'd just sent.

Leslie had died April 27, 1997, from AIDS. He had been addicted to heroin and contracted the disease through an infected needle. Prior to his death, his body had withered to 103 pounds and he had been confined to a wheelchair.

I will always remember Leslie as this young kid with a world of potential who had been known as Pee-Wee when he was in elementary school. To this day, it crushes me. I feel like I was a failure at helping him to become what he should have become.

Those are the kind of coaching stories that tear your insides apart. I firmly believe, and I've said it on numerous occasions, that if I had stayed in coaching, rather than coming to work in TV, I would have never made it past the age of 50 because I gave my heart and soul to everyone whom I was ever involved with.

I saw what Lefty Driesell went through with Lenny Bias. He told me, "You do all you can to help a kid because you love them, but you can't hold a kid's hand, man, and walk with them 24 hours a day."

How true that is.

At the time, I was too wrapped up with Leslie because I was trying to help him. Or was I? Certain people were turning to me and saying that I was trying to help myself.

Obviously, as a coach, you want to do well, but you also want to get the most out of your players.

I say a prayer for Leslie every night, but I still feel so sad because this kid never became what I thought he could have become.

He would have been like a Danny Manning, who was Mr. Versatility, an inside-outside player. At 6'10" he was so graceful. Leslie was Manning before Manning, of course, but he was that type of player. He could have led a club, could have carried a club.

Here was this kid, I thought—when he was real young, I never had to worry about where he was. I knew where to find him every time—the Clinton playground. Lights would be on and he'd be playing hour after hour as an eighth-, ninth-, 10th-grade player. Then, his senior year, we couldn't find him any more. He was with all the wrong people, out on the streets living life in the fast lane.

That's how fast it changes.

That's what I tried to tell LeBron. "Everybody wants a little piece of little LeBron, and you know why. The cash register is going to go ring-a-ling, ding, ding, and it's going to ring and ring and ring and some people are smelling those dollars. You've got to be so concerned about the type of people you keep around you. Get the leeches out of your life and deal with those who genuinely love you. Make good decisions. If you ever need any help, any advice, give me a buzz."

I read some quotes from Jermaine O'Neal, the young star of the Indiana Pacers who turned pro right out of high school. He said LeBron was set up to fail because of the unbelievable expectations placed on him. O'Neal said, "I read where he's the next Michael Jordan or the next Magic Johnson. What a bull's-eye this kid's going to have on his back from the day he puts on an NBA uniform."

He's right.

But let me tell you something. The kid's been involved in so many incidents throughout his senior year—the Hummer, the suspension, games played all over America—and he's responded positively to all of them.

Now, whether or not he can take it from high school to the level of Kobe Bryant and Kevin Garnett is the big question. What

LeBron has over Kobe and Kevin, on the high school level, is that body. That body is chiseled. He has great stamina. And I'll tell you something else. He possesses the ability to endure the kind of evaluation, scrutiny, and pressure to perform in the public eye that he'll face every day. And has faced every day.

How soon before LeBron makes his presence felt in the NBA?

He'll make his mark by the end of the first quarter of his first regular-season game.

LeBron has already made a dazzling start to his professional career. In his NBA debut on July 9, 2003, he scored 14 points against the Orlando Magic in a 40-minute summer league game. He also had six assists and grabbed seven rebounds in front of a crowded TD Waterhouse Centre. 15,123 people had each paid the $5 ticket price to see whether James is the real deal. Let me tell you, LeBron is every bit as good as Amare Stoudemire, the 2003 Rookie of the Year. Trust me, baby, he will be the bomb.

He's going to be an impact player, especially if he's surrounded by people who can finish plays. That is going to be the key. Remember, in Kobe's case, he got placed in a great environment in L.A. If LeBron can get in an environment where he has people who can finish, he'll be a star. Just like Magic, man, he has that rare ability to make people better because of his passing and his vision.

But if he doesn't have people who can make the play, he could make the mistake of trying to do it all himself, which can lead to bad shot selection. In high school, he can take bad shots and still come back with an immediate offensive rebound, but not at the NBA level.

Remember, he has to keep his peers happy. If he starts to take bad shots, it will tick off his teammates, and obviously, that will lead to major frustration. LeBron has never suffered the losing he'll likely suffer early in his career. With Cleveland, he'll be with a team needing more than LeBron to help them jump out of the basement.

And what a young cast he'll have around him in Cleveland. I hope people realize that and don't let their expectations run wild. I hope people remember that in Patrick Ewing's first year with the Knicks—and he was the No. 1 pick in the draft—they won 23 games. Twenty-three, my friends. Keep that in mind.

There are a lot of young players in Cleveland who are also learning how to play, including forward Darius Miles, who jumped out of high school, and DaJuan Wagner from Camden, a kid with talent who left Memphis after one year.

But in this league you need some structure, you need some experience, and you need people who know how to win. It all starts with leadership. It will be interesting to see how Paul Silas, the new coach, does, but I believe Gordon Gund and Jim Paxson made a great choice going for a veteran coach who played in the NBA and has a great relationship with players.

Yes, Cleveland is heading in the right direction. Don't doubt that Gordon Gund is smiling, big time—and he has a right to be-cause it has been a long, cold wintry night in basketball the last two years there. Things will heat up and it will be sunny sunshine like you cannot believe, even on the coldest night, when the Cavaliers take the floor.

Of course, with this kind of hype being generated, it hasn't taken long for folks to start looking for the next LeBron.

After LaShawn and Mark Walker sent Reebok a videotape of their three-year-old son, Mark Jr., hitting 18 straight baskets on an eight-foot hoop in their driveway, the shoe company signed the kid for an undisclosed amount of money and began using him in a national marketing campaign.

I guess they wanted to get a head start on Nike.

4

MICHAEL AND THE PTPers

I couldn't do a book about my career at ESPN without mentioning the top players, the PTPers, that I've covered. And I couldn't do a book without devoting some time to Michael Jordan.

Michael the Magnificent.

One time, I did a speaking engagement at the Magic Johnson Roundball Classic in Detroit—Sonny Vaccaro's game.

Someone asked me whom I think is the greatest player ever.

I didn't even have to think about it, man. "You kidding me? Michael Jordan. He's in another world. When he was at his peak, nobody could emulate what he did."

The crowd was like, "Now wait a minute—this is Magic's turf."

Maybe so, but even Magic would be the first to tell you this guy was special. It wasn't just Jordan's offense. It was his defensive ability—playing the passing lanes, rebounding—coupled with his ability to make the big shot, the way he created momentum with the dunk, how he continually improved the range on his shot.

He had such great respect for the game and always played to win. He hated losing. He won six NBA titles with the Chicago Bulls and one NCAA title in 1982 when he was a freshman at North Carolina and was part of that great trio that included Sam Perkins and James Worthy.

I hear this one-liner all the time—and I still laugh when I hear it—"Hey, the only person who's ever been able to stop Michael Jordan has been Dean Smith."

Jordan never averaged 20 points in college, but he certainly made a huge impact. He led the ACC in scoring as a junior with 19.4 points per game and was named national Player of the Year. He was also the leading scorer on the 1983 Pan American team and the 1984 U.S. Olympic team—both won gold medals.

But really, Dean Smith laid the foundation for Jordan's success, because he taught him how to be a complete player. He taught the young athlete what a good shot is, taught him how to play within a team framework, gave him the confidence to take big shots.

When Jordan was a freshman, North Carolina played Georgetown in the NCAA championship game in New Orleans. The game came down to one play.

Georgetown led, 62-61, but Carolina had the ball and Dean Smith called a timeout. He knew John Thompson would probably focus on James Worthy—his best player—and ignore Michael—his youngest. So he called his team together and told Michael to knock it down. Jordan drained an 18-footer from the corner with 17 seconds left to give Dean Smith his first national championship.

That was only the beginning.

The great ones never have a fear of failure. There are so many athletes who run away from pressure late in the game—they disappear; they don't want the ball; they find ways to get away from the action. To be successful, you can't be afraid to fail.

I got to witness Michael's greatness the next two years when I did his games in college. Michael began pulling off miracle finishes on a regular basis. He came out of nowhere to pick up a loose ball and make an area code J from 24 feet at the buzzer to force Tulane into OT. Then he caught up with Lefty Driesell's son, Chucky, and swatted away a potential game-winning layup against Maryland.

But the game I remember most was North Carolina-Virginia in 1983 at the old Carmichael Auditorium. Virginia had 7'4" Ralph Sampson, who was the reigning national Player of the Year. They had been to the Final Four the year before. The Carolina-Virginia games had all been classics since Ralph had arrived at the school.

That year, Carolina won the first game, 101-95, in Charlottesville, to break Virginia's 34-game home-court winning streak. Virginia looked like it was out for some revenge in the rematch. They had a 10-point lead with four minutes to play.

But North Carolina wouldn't go away. They cut the lead to 63-60 in the final minute. Then Michael took over. After Ralph missed the front end of a one-and-one, Michael tipped in a missed shot. Then he stole the ball from Rick Carlisle and drove the length of the floor for a dunk that gave Carolina a 64-63 victory.

The place went bonkers.

"Pound for pound, the best player in the country," I start screaming. "Michael 'the Magnificent' Jordan."

The Virginia writers made a big deal of it. The headlines in the papers the next day read, "Vitale says Jordan's the best."

The next time I did a Virginia game in Charlottesville, Sampson gave me the cold shoulder. I could feel the chill when he said, "Well, Al McGuire thinks I'm No. 1."

He got over it, though. And I never changed my opinion.

Later on I was doing one of Michael's games in Chapel Hill, and this lady comes down to the press room and says, "Hi, I want to say hello to you," and proceeds to plant a big kiss on me.

I'm going, "Who is this?"

"I'm Michael Jordan's mother."

I found that very touching.

You've seen what Michael's done since then. I guess the only people who couldn't see his potential were the GMs at Houston and Portland when Michael declared for the pros after his junior year. They had the first two picks in the draft that year. Houston took Hakeem Olajuwon. Portland took Sam Bowie of Kentucky. It was Rod Thorn of Chicago who selected Jordan.

Playing in the North Carolina system was such a plus for the kid. Maybe it limited him statistically, but he learned how to play the game and took it to the next level in the NBA.

It was just a matter of time before Jordan busted out once he got the freedom he wanted. He dominated the NBA; Jordan ripped it up from 1985 through 1993.

Then he left to pursue a major league baseball career.

I got to know him well when he was trying to make the White Sox. He lived in my subdivision in Sarasota during training camp. I remember talking to him about whether he missed basketball, and he told me, "I haven't touched a ball in about a year and a half."

"Michael, I'm just curious," I said. "If you had to play tonight— go into the locker room, put a uniform on and go out—what could you do?"

"Well, I know I'd get 20."

"Twenty?" I asked. "With not having played in so long?"

And he replied, "What's so difficult about getting five points a quarter? That means I get one breakaway layup, hit one jumper and make one foul shot."

Most people would say, "Oh my God, 20 points? Are you kidding? Do you know how special that is?" To this guy, it was like it was nothing.

And he was right. He probably could have even stepped out and gotten 30.

The thought process of a great athlete is simply amazing. I talked to Alex Rodriguez of the Texas Rangers one time about hitting 40 homers. He said to me, "You break it down into months—you mean to tell me April, May, June, July, August, and September, I can't go out and get seven a month?"

Great players think on a different level, man.

I remember once when Michael and I were in the White Sox trainer's room and he had just gotten crucified in *Sports Illustrated* for wasting his time in baseball—"No shot. Give it up. You're not going to make it."

And, man, you could see the fire in him. I can still remember his words. "Dick, what is the guy talking about? I've already made it in baseball. You know why? I learned as a youngster, a long time ago, that if you can look in the mirror and know you've given it your best shot, you're a winner. I could be on every golf course in America right now, relaxing. But I'm here. This is no gimmick. I'm in the batting cage, 6:30, 7:00 in the morning. Look at my hands—blisters all over. I'm giving it my all. Now, I may not make it to the major leagues, but nobody can tell me I haven't given it my best shot."

He would work religiously. Walt Hriniak, the batting instructor, said, "Michael is trying to do in several weeks what guys have been doing for years."

In my eyes, what made Michael very special was that he was willing to put his neck on the line—to be scrutinized in the batting cage, to face the likes of Roger Clemens. Yet he wasn't worried about that. He accepted that challenge.

Eventually, he left baseball, came back to the Bulls and won three more championships before retiring again in 1998. His last game, he scored 45 points—and made the deciding shot—as Chicago beat

Utah on the road to win it all again. Then he came back one more time with Washington.

He finally retired for good in the spring of 2003. He was 40. Obviously, for every player, there comes a moment when he's got to stand at the podium. It's just a matter of when. I don't care how great he is. The only thing I feel bad about is that Michael didn't go out in a blaze of glory. But he came back and proved he could still play, even if the Wizards didn't make the playoffs.

I think he was frustrated with the work ethic of some of the young players because he's a guy who knows what it takes to win. I think he realized that the tank was finally on empty and it was time to get out before he started humiliating himself.

A week after the season ended, the Wizards severed their ties with Jordan. He wanted to stay on in the front office after he sold out all those games for them, but they no longer wanted him around. It ended on a negative note. It hurt to see him pulling away in his car that way. It was just really sad. I didn't like to see Michael Jordan given the ziggy, given the ax. I'd have liked to see him calling the shots.

But his legacy is firmly in place.

And—who knows?—he may even add to his legend yet.

I really believe that somewhere down the line, we'll see him accept the challenge of playing on the Senior PGA Tour. I wouldn't put it past him.

Michael has to go down as the best player I've covered in my 24 years at ESPN. But there have been other special performers, so I thought I'd celebrate the best of the best since I've been on the tube.

My All-Rolls Royce teams. My top 25 players. I divided them into gold, silver and bronze. Since I'm a big believer in kids staying in school, I restricted these teams to guys who stayed in college at least three years. Sorry, Isiah. Sorry, Allen Iverson and Jason Kidd. You were all great, but you left for the NBA after only two seasons.

Before you say anything, 14 of the 25 players I picked are from the Atlantic Coast Conference. But I'm not apologizing. Hey, the conference won seven national titles during my era and had a team in the Final Four every year but two from 1988 through 2003.

My Gold Medal team—my Super Seven—looks like this:
- Michael Jordan, 6'6" guard, North Carolina (1982-84)
- Christian Laettner, 6'11" center, Duke (1989-92)
- Danny Manning, 6'10" forward, Kansas (1985-88)
- Patrick Ewing, 7' center, Georgetown (1982-85)
- Steve Alford, 6'2" guard, Indiana (1984-87)
- David Robinson, 7'1" center, Navy (1984-87)
- Chris Mullin, 6'5"guard, St. John's (1982-85)

You know how I feel about **Michael Jordan**. He is the greatest player of all time. Before he came along, I thought Magic, Oscar Robertson, and Jerry West were the best players ever, but this guy changed my opinion. He defies description.

He's the only person I know who could fly on his own.

Here are the rest.

Christian Laettner was just a tremendous—to me, he's the consummate—college player, a consensus All-American and the national Player of the Year his senior year. He made more big shots than anyone in the history of the NCAA Tournament. He helped lead Duke to back-to-back NCAA championships in 1991 and 1992. Certainly, most people remember the shot he made against Kentucky, but what about the jumper he nailed to beat UConn at the buzzer of the 1990 Eastern Regionals?

He was a little moody, had up-and-down swings; personality-wise, he could get into the faces of some of his teammates. But he had that drive, man; he hated to lose, and he'd let you know about it.

He's probably best known for his performance in the 1992 NCAA Eastern Regional finals when he scored 31 points against Kentucky, shooting 10 for 10 from the field and making 10 of 10 free throws. One of those shots was a dramatic jumper at the buzzer for the 103-102 win in OT.

It was an ESPN instant classic.

I didn't think Duke had a prayer after Sean Woods made that driving shot to put Kentucky ahead with 2.3 seconds left. Mike Krzyzewski called a timeout. I was surprised that Kentucky didn't put anybody on the ball during the inbounds play. I'm not second-guessing here, but I've always believed in taking away vision so a guy can't make that pass. But I can understand the logic of trying to play five on four. Rick Pitino wanted a safety. But it was a perfect pass, a perfect play, a perfect moment.

Danny Manning single-handedly carried an average Kansas team to the 1988 national championship, beating powerful Big 8 rival Oklahoma in the title game.

I mean, 1988: Kansas is 12-8 and they're struggling. Larry Brown's club is thinking NIT, man. NIT, NIT, NIT.

And here comes Danny and The Miracles, and they go on a run; he absolutely carries them on his back—Danny carries four other guys and leads them to the national title.

He is the all-time leading scorer in Kansas history, and he was a unanimous first-team All-American in 1987 and 1988.

Manning averaged 27.2 points and 9.3 rebounds in the Tournament. He had 31 when the Jayhawks defeated Oklahoma, in that All-Big 12 final in Kansas City. It was just an incredible performance in every way possible. The one thing that characterized his game was versatility—inside, outside, wing player, ball handler.

Patrick Ewing was the first big-time star of the Big East—and the league's best player ever. He epitomized John Thompson's suffocating defensive style of play with his fierce intensity.

Patrick Ewing was a three-time first-team All-American, in 1983, 1984 and 1985. He was a modern-day Bill Russell, who led Georgetown to the 1984 national title and two other championship games in 1982 and 1985.

He set the tone for those great Hoya teams because he came out and played so fiercely. He really owned the lane. His First Commandment was: Thou shalt not enter the lane.

Just ask North Carolina—when Ewing was a freshman and Georgetown was playing the Tar Heels for the championship, he goaltended their first four shots of the game just to send that message.

He was like a goalie in hockey. He just protected the basket, and opposing teams were in major trouble because they couldn't get the ball inside. Defensively, Georgetown had guards like Gene Smith, who would really pressure the ball, and the Hoyas could gamble and take chances with Patrick as The Protector.

I remember getting all over his coach, John Thompson, one time on TV. I'd gone to D.C. to do one of their games. I felt that Ewing had to work a little more on his drop-step moves, on his offensive moves. Afterwards, I go into the locker room, and there's Big John standing there, so I tell him, "Hey, John, great win today."

"I want you to come with me," he says. "Come over here."

He takes me over to Patrick's locker.

"Hey, Patrick," he says, "this is the guy who says you've got no footwork, you've got no ability to drop-step, you don't post up inside."

"Oh great," I'm thinking. "Wow, am I going to get eaten alive, now, man. This is going to be really interesting."

Then John says, "I want you to listen to him now."

What a relief that was. I ended up having a great conversation with Patrick.

Steve Alford was the best pure shooter I've ever covered. He'd wanted to play for Indiana from the time he was a sophomore at New Castle High in Indiana. And he went on to become the epitome of a Knight player.

Over the years, I have watched the game evolve. One of the lost arts is moving without the ball. When the game gets rolling and it's five on five and it becomes a halfcourt game—like many of the tournament games are—and a coach needs execution to be efficient, a lot of players are limited because they can't get free for their shot.

Well, Alford was an absolute artist in getting free for the shot. He did a phenomenal job as part of the Indiana passing game, and he had a great knack of reading the defense. Once he got free, he had one of the most devastating jump shots I've ever seen.

He was a two-time first-team All-American, in 1986 and 1987, and the best shooter ever to play for the General, Bobby Knight, at Indiana. He shot 53.3 percent from the floor and 89.8 percent from the line.

Bobby was tough on him. The one thing about the General is that if you are a star, you probably get more heat than any of the players who are coming off the bench. At practice he's in your face all the time. He suspended Alford for a game as a sophomore because he didn't think he was living up to expectations, and he was all over him when the NCAA suspended the kid for the Kentucky game after he posed for a sorority charity calendar that helped to raise money for handicapped kids. (Just think about how ludicrous a rule like that is to penalize a kid who's only trying to help others in need and not receiving a single penny in return.)

I remember being at an Indiana practice session one time when Bobby was all over Alford, and I asked Steve, "How tough is that to take?"

"As long as we're winning and I get my PT, I have no problems with it," he said.

And Indiana won big his senior year. Won it all.

I often tease the General when I see him. "You are supposed to be a genius, you're a Hall of Famer, you've got the best shooter in America. And who takes the last shot in the championship game against Syracuse?" It was Keith Smart, taking a fall-away jumper on the baseline behind the basket. If any other coach had done that and Smart had missed the shot, people would have screamed. But it went down and tickled the twine, and Indiana cut down the nets.

I can really get into a great performance, baby. When I go to rock concerts and watch Tina Turner or Lionel Richie, I jump out of my seat. Same with Tim McGraw and Faith Hill.

I got that same feeling when I watched **David Robinson** play—mainly because his stardom was so unexpected. Robinson is the perfect example of the student athlete. He came to the Naval Academy at Annapolis as a skinny 6'6" freshman from Osbourn Park, Virginia, where he scored 1320 on his SATs and was better known for his knowledge of computers than for his basketball abilities. But he grew several inches and became the best player in the country his senior year, taking a military academy that had a limited talent pool and height restrictions for its applicants—and no real basketball tradition—straight to national prominence.

Now, I've got to give a plug to Pete Herrmann, who was formerly the coach at Navy and is now an assistant at Georgia. Pete helped Robinson big time when the kid first got to the Naval Academy. Robinson learned how to play in the post, how to use the drop step, how to get free in the lane.

And Robinson just kept getting better and better.

I was there when he put on a show against Kentucky. Navy going to play Kentucky at Rupp—you don't give them much of a shot.

But Robinson had an amazing game: 45 points, 20 rebounds and 10 blocked shots, a triple double. All of a sudden came whistles out of the blue—this kid had fouled out. I jumped out of my seat. My partner, Keith Jackson—yes, that's right, Mr. "Whoa Nellie" of college football fame—looked at me like I was wacky. But I gave Robinson a standing ovation. I thought he warranted it, man. I violated all the rules of journalism by cheering. But that's how I felt at the moment.

In fact, I've done it only one other time, and that was just recently, during the 2003 season, when Nick Collison scored 24 points and grabbed 23 rebounds in a victory over Texas.

If I had it to do over, I'd stand again, baby. I'm just like the fans, and I appreciate a great effort.

And I don't think anyone knew Robinson would be this good. Check out his senior season when he won all kinds of national Player of the Year awards. He averaged 28.2 points, 11.8 rebounds and 4.6 blocked shots.

I will never forget sitting on the dais at the Naismith Awards ceremony in Atlanta in 1987. I was the featured speaker, and Bobby Knight was there to receive the national Coach of the Year award. There were over a thousand people in attendance. Robinson was wearing his Navy blues. He looked like a million bucks. They turned out the lights and put the spotlight on him, and he talked about how he wanted to thank his mom and dad, who'd taught him more about life than just basketball. He said they taught him about getting along with people, about how it's important to have diversity in life. He wanted to thank them for getting him involved with computers.

I was sitting next to Bobby. He looked at me and said, "How would you like to coach that kid?"

So when Knight was called on to receive his award, he had the spotlight shine on David Robinson again and told all the youngsters in the crowd, "I want you to look at this young man, because he represents all that is good in America. He represents everything we want our student athletes to be."

If there was one player who could match Alford shot for shot, it was **Chris Mullin**. He once beat Alford in a national Elks Club foul-shooting contest.

He was 10.

Later, Mullin was a consensus first-team All-American in 1984 and 1985 and a Wooden Award winner his senior year when St. John's reached the NCAA Final Four. He was a lefty guard, and he could really stroke it.

He was from Brooklyn, a CYO legend who led Xaverian to the state championship and was the perfect star for St. John's, a commuter school in Queens. Mullin played for Louie Carnesecca and became St. John's all-time leading scorer and the first guy to score more than 2,000 points in his career. If Patrick Ewing was the best ever to play in the Big East, this guy was 1-A.

Mullin said he would have gone to Duke if it hadn't been for the Big East. He turned out to be the most popular player in the history of St. John's and the second best player in the history of the Big East. Mullin provided the perfect foil for Patrick Ewing during the league's glory days when marketing was important. He helped create that Washington D.C.-versus-New York rivalry because Georgetown and St. John's were ranked either No. 1 or 2 during the 1985 season.

Mullin wasn't the fastest guy in the world, or the best athlete, but his work ethic was incredible. Once, he and his friends sneaked into a locked CYO gym and spent the weekend playing basketball during a snowstorm. And he had his own key to Alumni Hall, just so he could work on his jumper.

He was a self-made player who wound up becoming the star of the most talented St. John's team ever—the one with Bill Wennington,

Mark Jackson, Walter Berry and Ron Rowan—that reached the NCAA
Final Four his senior year.

Here's my Silver Medal team, my Elite Eight:
• Grant Hill, 6'8" forward, Duke (1991-94)
• Ralph Sampson, 7'4" center, Virginia (1980-83)
• Len Bias, 6'8" forward, Maryland (1983-86)
• Tim Duncan, 7' center, Wake Forest (1994-97)
• Hakeem Olajuwon, 7' center, Houston (1982-84)
• James Worthy, 6'9" forward, North Carolina (1980-82)
• Darrell Griffith, 6'4" guard, Louisville (1977-80)
• Jason Williams, 6'3" guard, Duke (2000-02)

Grant Hill was the most unselfish superstar I've ever watched.
A lot of that comes from his family, I'm sure.

Hill was a unanimous first-team All-American as a senior in
1994 when he averaged 17.4 points and 6.9 rebounds and led Duke
to the NCAA championship game.

He was the fifth leading scorer and second leading rebounder as
a freshman and second leading scorer and third leading rebounder as
a sophomore for teams that won back-to-back national championships in 1991 and 1992.

What a classy kid. What a classy family. His father, Calvin, went
to Yale. His mom was a college roomie of Hillary Clinton at Wellesley.

When he was 13 years old—just a young guy, a quarterback on
the junior high team—he told his father, a Hall of Fame running
back from the Dallas Cowboys, that he wanted to drop football in
order to concentrate on hoops.

Obviously, he made the right choice.

At 7'4", **Ralph Sampson** was a towering force of nature who
took Virginia out of the shadows of North Carolina and showed the

basketball world that there was more than one national contender in the ACC.

He was selected national Player of the Year by AP and UPI in 1981, 1982 and 1983. He won the Naismith Award three times and the Wooden Award twice, in his junior and senior years.

Sampson was known for his unselfish play and averaged just 15 points and 12 rebounds his final year. But Virginia basketball thrived with him in the middle, winning the NIT his freshman year, reaching the Final Four his sophomore year and the Elite Eight his senior season. I wish he'd had a little more hunger, a little more intensity. But he was a laid-back guy. He was a dominator in the lane.

I still get sad when I think about **Len Bias**. He was the best player ever to play for Maryland.

He was the ACC Player of the Year twice, led the league in scoring twice, and was one of the league's best players ever. He made every All-America team as a senior after averaging 23.2 points and 7.0 rebounds and shooting 54.2 percent from the floor and 86.4 from the line, and he was the second pick in the 1986 NBA draft.

The Celtics took him. He was supposed to step into Larry Bird's shoes. Less than 24 hours later, he overdosed on cocaine at a private party in a dorm on campus and died.

He was bigger than life when he played for the Left-Hander—Lefty Driesell—though.

I made the mistake of putting him on my second-team All-America roster in preseason before his senior year. Toward the end of the season, during a pregame warmup before a Maryland game, Bias came up to me and asked, "Dickie V, you can't be serious. I'm not on your first team?" Who can ever forget the 35 points he scored in a win for Maryland at the Smith Center. Late in overtime, he stole an inbounds pass and converted it into a dunk, then blocked Kenny Smith's driving shot at the other end to seal the deal.

Tim Duncan was the ultimate sleeper. No one knew he would become the most dominant player in the ACC when he arrived from St. Croix in the Virgin Islands. He was actually a swimmer when he was younger. A friend of Dave Odom spotted him in a pickup game on a dirt court and told the coach about him. Wake Forest signed him without much competition; the only other school he visited was Central State in Ohio.

He led Wake to back-to-back ACC tournament titles. Duncan was a two-time ACC Player of the Year and was selected a first-team All-American in 1997.

And now he's the best player in the NBA. When the San Antonio Spurs defeated the New Jersey Nets, 88-76, in Game 6 of the 2003 finals to win the championship, he had 21 points, 20 rebounds, 10 assists and eight blocked shots—a near quadruple double.

Hakeem Olajuwon was discovered playing soccer by a friend of Guy V. Lewis who happened to be doing Peace Corps work in Nigeria. (To this day, it amazes me that Lewis hasn't received the kind of credit others have for the amazing job he did in building a powerhouse with Houston.) Olajuwon picked up on basketball quickly and led Houston to three straight Final Fours. Once that happened, schools began freeing up their recruiting budgets to travel overseas in search of the next great foreign import.

Olajuwon was the first big international star I covered. I will never forget laying his nickname on him. The first time I ever saw him was down in New Orleans his freshman year at the Final Four. I said, "Hey, 'Akeem the Dream.' The dream, man. Someday you are going to be special." He laughed in his own unique way and said, "Thank you, thank you." He was a first-team All-American his junior year when he averaged 16.8 points and led the country in rebounding and blocked shots.

He was never able to get that gold trophy, but it wasn't his fault.

James Worthy was the best player on the floor when North Carolina defeated Georgetown to win the 1982 national championship. Worthy scored 28 points, made that now-famous pick off a bad pass by Freddie Brown in the final seconds as Dean Smith finally got the monkey off his back to win his first national title after six other trips to the Final Four.

Dean Smith knew about James Worthy when the kid came to his camp as an eighth grader and started dominating the 11th and 12th graders. He played three years for Carolina and made second-team All-America as a junior when he averaged 15.6 points and 6.3 rebounds on that 1982 team.

Worthy was from Gastonia, North Carolina, the same hometown as Sleepy Floyd, who played for Georgetown. Both of them were All-Americans and played against each other in the NCAA finals. Worthy got the best of Floyd in his last college game, going off for 28 points and getting selected the Most Outstanding Player in the Tournament. Then he went to the Lakers, where he became a Hall of Famer, playing on those Showtime teams with Magic and Kareem.

I chose **Darrell Griffith** because he was the star of those exciting, high-rising teams at Louisville that were constantly making a run at the NCAA title. He was able to sustain the excitement surrounding the national championship game that had been generated the previous year, which had featured a 1979 matchup of a Larry Bird-led Indiana State team and Magic Johnson's Michigan State squad. Griffith was the team leader on the 1980 Louisville national championship team. The Cardinals were known as the Doctors of Dunk, and Griffith's nickname was Dr. Dunkenstein.

He was a consensus first-team All American and Wooden Award winner his senior year when he averaged 22.5 points.

Griffith was a local kid who really epitomized what Louisville was doing in those days. They had guys who could attack the basket, who could really come after you on the offensive boards and would cut your heart out with a 2-2-1 press that Denny Crum learned from John Wooden when he was an assistant at UCLA.

Griffith led the Cardinals to four straight NCAA Tournaments and the 1980 national championship and was the first player to surpass 2,000 points in U of L history.

Jason Williams was the most explosive scoring point guard I've ever seen. He was the consensus national Player of the Year as a junior, averaging 21.5 points. He was one of the most creative scoring threats in Duke history during his career, one of only three ACC players to finish with more than 2,000 points and 600 assists.

You should have seen him in the 2001 Jimmy V Classic against Kentucky. Hey, man, Duke was in trouble. Coach K pulled the starting five at the start of the second half. He was upset. Kentucky was putting the hurt on them. Rashaad Carruth was having the game of his life. The crowd was going crazy at the Meadowlands. And all of a sudden, Coach K sends the first five back in and Williams goes off. Jumper, top of the key, steal, jumper. One special play after another. The kid carried the team the rest of the game. I told him afterwards, he could have scored whenever he wanted to. He scored 23 of Duke's final 31 points in regulation and helped them wipe out a 12-point deficit. Williams finished with 38, and Duke won in OT.

He played only three years for Duke. Too bad. But his parents arranged for him to take extra summer school courses so he could earn a degree in three years and then enter the NBA draft. Williams was selected by Chicago with the second pick in the draft in 2002. Jason was a second-team All-Rookie selection.

Unfortunately, he slammed his week-old motorcycle into a telephone pole on the north side of Chicago in late June 2003. He landed 10 feet away from his bike, and a witness said he told paramedics he had no feeling in his legs. I was heartbroken hearing reports that there was a broken pelvis and severe ligament damage to one knee. Those injuries will keep him out of the 2003-04 season.

I can only imagine what his mom and dad must have felt like when they got that phone call. That family is so close. I saw them at Duke games all the time. I've got to believe that they couldn't have been happy when Jason purchased that motorcycle. But then, it's so easy to second-guess—why, why? We all feel invincible.

Jason has so much going for him. He has a family that provides him with loads of love, plus a Duke family that's in his corner and the genuine support of the Bulls organization. With his determination and the outstanding medical team that's helping him, don't bet against this kid putting on a uniform again. Believe me, he is absolutely one of the most special people to play this game during my tenure at ESPN and ABC.

Now a few words about my Bronze Medal team—I call them my Terrific Ten:
- Alonzo Mourning, 6'10" center, Georgetown (1989-1992)
- Johnny Dawkins, 6'2" guard, Duke (1983-86)
- Bobby Hurley Jr., 6' guard, Duke (1990-93)
- Ray Allen, 6'5" guard, UConn (1994-96)
- Shane Battier, 6'8" forward, Duke (1988-2001)
- Juan Dixon, 6'3" guard, Maryland (1999-2002)
- Sean Elliott, 6'8" forward, Arizona (1986-89)
- Dwayne Washington, 6'2" guard, Syracuse (1984-86)
- Antawn Jamison, 6'8" forward, North Carolina (1996-98)
- Danny Ferry, 6'9" forward, Duke (1986-89)

Alonzo Mourning had Patrick Ewing's picture plastered all over his bedroom walls at his home in Chesapeake, Virginia. And when he got to Georgetown, he played just like him.

He kept John Thompson's legacy of producing big men alive. Mourning was one of the best shot blockers in the history of the game. He was a human eraser who led the country in rejections as a freshman with 5.8 blocks a game. He was a consensus first-team All-American in 1992 when he averaged 21.3 points, 10.7 rebounds and five blocked shots, becoming the first Big East player ever to win the regular-season MVP, the Defensive Player of the Year and the MVP of the conference tournament.

He and Patrick stayed close after he graduated. They would work out together in the summer, and Patrick is the godfather of Alonzo's daughter. In 2000, after he helped lead the U.S. to a gold medal in Sydney, Mourning developed a serious kidney ailment and Patrick offered to donate one of his kidneys to him if he needed it. Fortunately, that wasn't necessary. Mourning is still playing and signed a free agent contract with the New Jersey Nets before the start of the 2003-04 season.

Johnny Dawkins was Mike Krzyzewski's first big recruit and the star of his first Final Four team in 1986. Coach K got him out of Washington, D.C.—you think Lefty was mad? Dawkins scored 2,556 points and averaged 19.2 points during his career.

He was a first-team All-American in 1985 and 1986 and the winner of the Naismith Award his senior year. He played in the NBA, and now he's back on the Duke staff as an assistant coach. It shouldn't be long before he has a head coaching job of his own if he wants it.

Maybe I'm prejudiced toward Jersey guys, but I love gym rats. And **Bobby Hurley Jr.** was the ultimate gym rat. His father, Bob Hurley Sr., is one of the great high school coaches in the country at St. Anthony's of Jersey City. And his son was the perfect student.

Bobby was the epitome of a point guard, a four-year starter who set the NCAA career assists record and was the catalyst for Duke's championship runs. He was the Most Outstanding Player in the 1992 Final Four and a consensus first-team All-American his senior year.

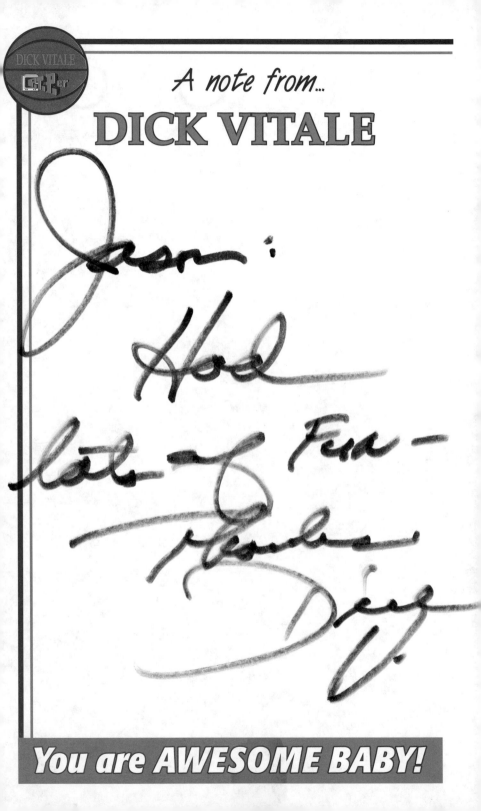

I went to a Duke practice his senior year, and he was still diving for loose balls. I said, "Yo, Bobby. It's not like you have to make the team."

But that's the way he played.

I know Mike Krzyzewski cried after Bobby played his last college game—a loss to Cal and Jason Kidd in the NCAA Tournament.

Ray Allen was the best player in UConn history, a first-team All-American in an era when the Big East also had Kerry Kittles and Allen Iverson.

I was speaking at a banquet in Columbia, South Carolina, when Allen was honored as high school Player of the Year in that state. They were raving about him at the time, and I was saying to myself, "Could he be that good? Is he as good as all those people are saying? He wasn't recruited by that many people."

Well, he made an impact right away. He stayed only three seasons, but he averaged 23.4 points, 6.5 rebounds and 3.3 assists as a junior and shot 46.6 percent from the three. He made every All-America team.

He also became a star in the entertainment world, playing the role of Jesus Shuttleworth in Spike Lee's movie *He Got Game*. I had a bit role in that movie, where I had to evaluate the character from an announcer's standpoint.

Shane Battier could be a future Bill Bradley, a brilliant student who was a complete player and led Duke to the 2001 national title.

Battier played four years at Duke and finished among Duke's all-time top 10 in scoring, three-point field goal percentage, rebounding, blocked shots and steals. He was the NABC Defensive Player for three consecutive years and the Verizon Academic All-American his senior year. He also won the Wooden Award and was voted one of the ACC's 50 greatest players.

I will never forget that the night they beat Arizona for the championship, Elton Brand—who came to Duke in the same class—was sitting right in front of me. Elton plays for the L.A. Clippers. I know he has a lot of cash in his pockets. He had on the Armani suit and he looked like a million bucks. But you just knew that, deep down, there was a little emptiness. I wish I'd had a camera to take a picture of him to let kids see how he was missing out, not being on the floor with his buddies when Duke cut down the nets.

No one—except Gary Williams—felt that **Juan Dixon** could make it big because of his background. But he had one of the two best six-game NCAA Tournament runs, along with Glen Rice of Michigan, who led the Wolverines to the 1989 national title.

When Dixon was growing up in Baltimore, he lost both parents to the drug scene. He was raised by his brother and was just 145 pounds when he came to Maryland. During his freshman year, when he sat out to improve academically and to develop physically, he had the opportunity to practice every day against Stevie "Franchise" Francis. Believe me, that was a major help in becoming the superstar that he became. Gary Williams once told me, "Dick, we got a special kid. He didn't get a whole lot of notice, but watching him work out with us his freshman year, I know he's going to be a heckuva player."

It just took a little time.

He played behind All-American Steve Francis for a season, but he kept working. He was in the gym at 11, 12 at night, working on his game. Then he just exploded. He became All-ACC for three consecutive seasons and a consensus first-team All-America selection in 2002 and the Terps' career scoring leader with 2,269 points. He led Maryland to its first national championship and was named Most Outstanding Player of the Final Four. He averaged 25.8 in March Madness, the most points by a player since 1989.

Sean Elliott was the best player ever to play for Lute Olson and the best player I covered in the Pac-10.

He was a local kid from Tucson who stayed home and played on Lute's first Arizona Final Four team in 1988. He was the consensus National Player of the Year the next year and was the only player in school history to lead the team in scoring for four consecutive seasons.

His pro career with San Antonio was cut short after he was diagnosed in 1994 with focal glomerulosclerosis, a disease that prevents the kidneys from properly filtering waste from the blood. He received a kidney from his brother, Noel, and on March 14, 2000, seven months after the operation, he made a brief return to basketball in front of 46 family members and close friends. He now works for ESPN.

Dwayne "Pearl" Washington had more charisma than any player I've watched in the history of the Big East. They still tell the story about him scoring on eight straight possessions in high school and then running by the opposing coach and saying, "Don't you think it's about time to call a TO?" Or the time he drained a halfcourt shot against BC at the buzzer and ran off the floor before it dropped, just waiting to hear the roar of the crowd, and then called his mom.

He came to Syracuse with a big ballyhoo out of Boys and Girls High in Brooklyn, and he lived up to it. He picked up his nickname in Brooklyn because of the luster of his game. It was magical to go up to the Carrier Dome: 30,000, rocking and rolling. He was a three-time All-American who had great body strength, who could get to the basket on anybody. He had super ball-handling skills—the ball was like an extension of his hand.

He left for the pros after his junior year, but didn't have the quickness to stick. He ran youth programs in Houston and Boston and is currently the supervisor of recreation at Syracuse. In December

1995, while residing in Boston, he suffered a seizure in his bed and was taken to a hospital. The next day, he underwent four hours of surgery to remove a large tumor from the front of his brain. Fortunately, it was benign.

Antawn Jamison was the first star of the post-Dean Smith era and helped Bill Guthridge bridge the gap by combining with Vince Carter to take the Tar Heels to the 1998 Final Four.

He was the unanimous national Player of the Year as a junior in 1998, when he scored 822 points, the second highest total in UNC history, and grabbed a single-season school-record 389 rebounds.

And even though he was at Carolina the same time as Vince Carter, on the college level, I've got to give the edge to Jamison. He had the quickest release on his shot of any player I've seen. I can still remember Jay Bilas, who works at ESPN, putting a timer on him to determine how quickly he could get it off.

I know you're saying, "Dickie V, how can you have so many Duke kids on your teams?" But how can I leave out Danny Ferry?

Danny Ferry was a complete player whose ability to put the ball on the floor and shoot from outside made him the best player in the ACC. There's just something about these guys who are coaches' sons.

He was the ACC Player of the Year for two seasons and national Player of the Year as a senior. He played on three Final Four teams and was the first player in conference history with 2,000 points, 1,000 rebounds and 500 assists.

Along the way, I've left out some tremendous players. These are the guys who have dazzled me, so we've got to have some Honorable Mentions. Mine would include Jim Jackson, Ohio State; Mark Price, Georgia Tech; Marcus Camby, UMass; Jacque Vaughn, Kansas; Nick Collison, Kansas; Shaquille O'Neal, LSU; Ed O'Bannon, UCLA; Rumeal Robinson, Michigan; Mark Macon, Temple; Calbert Cheaney,

Indiana; Derrick Coleman, Syracuse; and Waymon Tisdale, Oklahoma.

I can hear people screaming now, "Wait a minute. What about Shaq? Take it to the Rack. How can Shaquille O'Neal only be an Honorable Mention?" Hey, Shaq was a terrific player with great potential when he played for LSU, no question. He averaged 21 points and 13.5 rebounds a game and led the nation in rebounding one year. But I'm going to tell you this, LSU did not cut the nets down, did not make a run to the Final Four.

I'm not saying the guys I picked are better players than Shaquille O'Neal is now. I'm just saying they had better college careers. But I'll tell you this, he could go down as the best post player in the history of the NBA.

It all depends on Shaq and how dedicated and committed he will be to becoming the best of all time. That means he'll need to work at the free throw line during the off season; that means he'll have to get into the greatest shape possible and really have that hungry energy it takes to be number one.

Speaking about that drive to be the best, I will never forget one day many years ago when I was assigned to do the Foot Locker Slamfest, which involved athletes who did not play professional basketball. Talk about stars, man, we're talking prime time—Deion Sanders, Ken Griffey Jr., Cris Carter, Barry Sanders, Olympic track and field star Mike Powell—every major athlete. And the judges were former hoop greats such as Wilt "the Stilt" Chamberlain and Calvin Murphy, who might be pound for pound, inch for inch, the best ever to play the game—remember, he was only 5'9", and that, my friends, is stretching it. John Havlicek was also on the roster to evaluate the dunks of these wannabe basketball players.

But what made this day truly interesting was that as soon as I arrived at the Phoenician Hotel in Phoenix, I was summoned by our producer, Kim Belton, who is one of the greatest to have ever played at Stanford and is a member of their Hall of Fame—and they'd be proud to know that he's outstanding as a producer, as well, when dealing with the game he loves. Well, Kim told me excitedly, "Hey, you have to get to Wilt Chamberlain's room immediately. He wants to see you as soon as you arrive."

"Wilt Chamberlain?" I asked him. "What is this about?"

"I don't know, man. But he seems upset."

First I found my buddy John Saunders, who's ESPN's and ABC's Mr. Versatility. He's sensational whether he's hosting shows involving the NHL, college football, college basketball—you name it, he can do it. And I love him dearly for his humanitarian efforts on behalf of one of our closest friends, Jim Valvano.

I said, "John, you must come with me, man."

When we walked into Chamberlain's room, he was spread out on this huge bed with his head up on a pillow. As soon as he saw me, he began to scream at me with a sense of pride you could just feel, "What are you talking about on the air, Dickie V? I heard you the other day when you said Kareem Abdul-Jabbar was the best all-around center of all time. You said that Bill Russell was the biggest winner and the greatest shot blocker. Are you serious? Do you know what my numbers are against Russell? And do you know what I would do to Kareem?"

I said, "Wilt, you forgot to mention that I said you were the best *athlete* of all those guys. But I'm glad you were listening, at least."

"I can't believe you felt that guy Jabbar was better than me."

After John and I had said so long to Mr. Chamberlain and left his room, we looked at each other and began to laugh. Chamberlain was just a guy who was filled with pride in himself and his abilities. That's what made him so special.

Yes, my friends, that's what it takes. You must believe you're the best in order to be the best. If you think you're mediocre, you'll never be anything more than mediocre. Do you get the message, Shaq?

He certainly has a chance to overtake Wilt the Stilt, Kareem and Bill Russell if he keeps improving and continues playing for several more years.

And, hey, what good's a list if you can't talk about it, baby?

5

BRUSHES WITH FAME

D id you know I once did the Letterman show? It happened back in 1996 when the NCAA Final Four was at the Meadowlands in East Rutherford, N.J.

Actually, the writers for *Late Night with David Letterman* on CBS came up with a bit for me to do from our set, which was located at the New York Coliseum. They called it "Ten Reasons Why Dick Vitale Is Nuts" and had me read it on the air.

Here's a quick rundown.

10. I like to run through the locker room wearing nothing but a referee's whistle and yelling, "Baby."

9. I keep repainting the roof of my house to match Dennis Rodman's hair.

8. Five seconds after my first child was born, I dumped Gatorade on my wife.

7. I'm on a strict diet of shoelaces and floor wax.

6. I've invited David Letterman to host the next ESPY Awards.

5. For a cheap rush, I take hits of stale air from an old basketball.

4. My pet project, ESPN 3, is a new channel devoted to coverage of my Rogaine treatment.

3. When I make love to my wife, I always go for the three-pointer, baby.

2. I've referred to everything as "baby," except for an actual baby.

And the No. 1 reason why Dick Vitale is nuts: Right now, I think I'm whispering.

Ha ha. Very funny.

Actually, I had a pretty good time with it. Did you know David Letterman is a basketball fan? He grew up in Indiana and he roots for Ball State, his alma mater.

Man, I love the Big Apple. New York, New York, my kinda town—just as my favorite, Francis Albert Sinatra, would say.

This one time, my wife and I went there for the U.S. Open tennis tournament. One night, we were coming back to our hotel from a Broadway play. We took a cab to the Grand Hyatt in Manhattan. Man, we had a difficult time getting to our hotel because there were all kinds of limousines and police officers lined up all over the street. There were barricades set up everywhere.

Finally, I said to a couple of guys, "What's going on?"

They said, "You kidding me? MTV awards tonight, man. It's the event of the year. And throwing the biggest party of them all, over at Cipriani's, is Sean 'Puffy' Combs." By then the superstar had stopped going by the name Puff Daddy and was calling himself P. Diddy.

One of the guys recognized me. "Dickie V, I can't believe you're not at his party."

People were going into the place in tuxes. You should have seen the way they were dressed—my wife and I were just wearing casual clothes.

You had to have a special pass just to get in, but this security guy came up to me and said, "Dickie V, you've got to come to the party. P. Diddy's a big hoops fan."

"Jeez, I've got no invitation."

So he stepped inside for just a second, came back out and said, "Hey, man, they want you in there."

So Lorraine and I went in. They were having a bash. Women swinging on trapezes from the ceiling. Beautiful girls dancing. And who comes walking in? I thought it had to be the hero of all time because the music stopped and people started clapping.

And it's announced, "P. Diddy has arrived."

Well, we made eye contact. He called me over, put his arm around me. We started talking, taking pictures. And I just had to call my daughters to let them know who their dear ol' dad was hanging out with.

Those are just a couple of the bonuses I've gained in my life from the exposure I've had on ESPN and ABC.

Hey man, my job has opened doors. It's allowed me to meet some of the biggest celebrities of Hollywood as well as those of the sports scene. Man, I've got pictures of me with the best of the best. I've hung them all on a wall in my memorabilia room that I call my Wall of Fame.

You've got to be unique and special to make that wall, man. I have the best of the best. The crème de la crème. Man, are you kidding me? I'm up there posing with the likes of Tiger Woods, Michael Jordan, Wayne Gretzky, Mark McGwire, Sammy Sosa, Alex Rodriguez, Ken Griffey Jr., Shaquille O'Neal, George Foreman, Kevin Costner, and Bill Cosby.

It's my personal Who's Who, baby.

Why do I have that wall? Because I'm like everybody else. People get enamored with celebrity; they get excited about seeing people who've been in the limelight. And I'm no different—except that I've been lucky enough to meet many of those who have made it to the top.

Let me tell you about the time I met Roseanne Barr.

One of the things I'd always wanted to do in my life was to go to a heavyweight championship fight. Well, I got to go to the Tyson-Holyfield fight in Las Vegas with my wife, Lorraine. Charley Steiner—who was ESPN's voice of boxing at the time and has gone uptown to do the New York Yankees games—helped get us tickets. Great seats—and I paid for them, baby. Paid big time.

We also got invited to the big party put on by Showtime before the fight. And what a party it was. I walked in there and I couldn't believe all the big names walking around—Madonna, Sylvester Stallone, Wesley Snipes, Shaquille O'Neal, Michael Keaton, Jack Nicholson, Donald Trump, Kelsey Grammer. The room was filled with one superstar after another. I was the least known in the bunch. I was like a groupie, man, walking around with my eyes wide open, and I couldn't believe all the stars gathered there.

Then, out of nowhere, Roseanne approached me and said, "I don't like you."

I was completely stunned, "Oh, my God."

For all of you out there who ever want me to be quiet, that's the way to go. I had no idea why she felt that way. I had never met her before.

She proceeded to tell me, "What you did was a shame."

I was like, "Man, what is this?"

"You know what I'm talking about, Shapiro."

Shapiro? Shapiro? I couldn't believe it. She thought I was Robert Shapiro, who had represented O.J. Simpson in his murder trial and who was also present at that party.

Well, after a moment, when she found out who I was, she was so embarrassed. All of a sudden she was my buddy, taking pictures with me, introducing me to different people. She even took me over to say hello to Madonna.

Also in the room was the talented Rick Reilly of *Sports Illustrated,* who was there to do a story about the party and the big title fight.

He said, "Dick, what's going on?"

Well, I told him about being mistaken for Shapiro, and sure enough it popped up soon afterward in the pages of *SI.*

By the way, if you're like me, man, you never miss the last page of *Sports Illustrated.* I mean, when you talk about geniuses who bang on a typewriter for a living, they don't come much better than Reilly.

The party was just awesome, baby.

I was like a little kid. Again, I had to call my daughters to tell them, "You're not going to believe who your mom and dad are at a party with."

But talk about a case of mistaken identity.

And here's another one. I was the grand marshal at the Apple Blossom Festival in Virginia a couple of years ago. They had a lot of celebrities there like Jim Palmer of Baltimore Orioles fame and NBA Hall of Famer Moses Malone.

Moses had always been one of my favorites.

In fact, we tried to recruit him when I was at Detroit. Smokey Gaines, my assistant coach, had us in the ballpark—Moses visited us in Detroit.

Moses lived in a little house with boarded-up windows. He slept on the couch. You had to knock on the door and give a special code just to get in, because so many people were driving him nuts.

Moses wound up signing with Maryland. Then he broke Lefty Driesell's heart when he changed his mind to sign with the Utah Stars in the old ABA.

So, anyway, I saw him in Virginia.

Moses told me he'd built his mom a new house. Moses is a guy with a heart of gold. Man, he really held a special place in his heart for his mom. Moses never forgot where he came from, which unfortunately is what many players do when they get the big cash.

So a week after the festival in Virginia, my wife and I were in L.A. and went to dinner at Spago's. I've gotten to know the waiters there, so the first thing I asked the waiter when we got there was, "Anybody big tonight?"

"Yeah," he said, "I'm putting you next to Moses."

And my wife went, "Moses. That's great. We were just with him a week ago. We'll get a chance to shoot the breeze."

"Hon," I said, "you've got the wrong Moses. He's not talking about Moses Malone."

"No," the waiter said, "I'm talking about Charlton Heston."

My wife was so embarrassed.

So we sat next to Charlton Heston. He was such a nice guy. But he probably didn't even know who I was. It didn't matter to me, though.

I've met a lot of other movie stars, too, including one of my favorites, John Travolta.

I love him as an actor, John Travolta. *Saturday Night Fever,* baby.

I like to tell people that before I got into coaching, I had a big crop of hair like Travolta. But that was before I had my first team meeting with the varsity squad at East Rutherford High School back in the mid-60s. I had gotten fired up to meet my team, but when I saw them as they walked in, I said to them, "This is the varsity meeting, not the JV one."

They replied, "We *are* the varsity team."

Immediately, my hair began to fall out. And along with it, I lost any chance I might have had at being compared to Travolta.

Anyway, I got a chance to meet the real deal one time when my wife and I were in L.A., and I had arranged to play golf at the Riviera Country Club, even though I'm not much of a golfer. In fact, I'm a hacker.

So Lorraine, my daughters and I drove up to the club. The guard at the gate came out and said, "Oh, my God, I can't believe it. Dickie V. Come over here and take a picture with me. I'm a big basketball fan."

Then he said, "What a day it's been. I just met John Travolta and now Dickie V."

"John Travolta?" I screamed. "How'd you meet John Travolta?"

"He's over in that house right now."

"In that house?"

"Yeah, they're shooting a movie with him and Sean Penn."

"Well, I'll tell you what I'll do," I said. "You're going to get a picture with me. But you've got to arrange for me to meet John Travolta."

"That's no problem," he says, "I'll get ahold of him."

The movie was *She's So Lovely*. The director, Nick Cassavetes, had gone to Syracuse. His father, John, was a famous director and had written the screenplay 10 years earlier. It turned out that Nick had tried out as a walk-on for the Syracuse basketball team. He knew me right away.

Small world, baby.

Nick said, "Sure, come on in. I'll arrange for you to meet John."

So he arranged for all of us to come over to the set by his trailer.

And I'm telling you, John Travolta couldn't have been nicer. He's from Englewood, New Jersey. We started talking about Bergen County, about his aunts and uncles. I thought I was talking to the most regular guy in the world. In fact, it was while listening to him speak that I was reminded of all my aunts and uncles—my mom and dad each had had nine brothers and sisters. I'm not sure, but my gut feeling is that he's not a big sports fan, but, man, was he absolutely beautiful to me and my family.

His brother was there, too, and before Travolta headed off to work, he asked his brother to show us his sports cars, which mean a great deal to him.

John Travolta was so genuine.

And then there's the one who got away. I'm still mad at myself for just missing this one.

Danny DeVito is one of my favorite actors of all time. I just laugh when I see his face. I don't know why, but I immediately think of Rollie Massimino. I mean, Danny DeVito—I can just imagine that when he walks into a room, it's got to be absolutely hilarious.

Lorraine and I were having breakfast in Beverly Hills, at a place called Al's Deli, the home of Larry King, who starts his day off there whenever he's in town. Anyway, when we came out of the restaurant to get our car, this guy came over to me. He's a basketball fan, so he started talking to me.

We were chit-chatting, and I said, "You must see a lot of stars here."

"Yeah, like the guy who just left. See that guy pulling out? That's Danny DeVito."

"Where?"

I jumped into my car, man. I wanted to catch him.

But DeVito peeled off at the light. I thought about following after him. That would have been a funny scene. Can you imagine Dickie V chasing down Danny DeVito on the streets of Beverly Hills? It sounds like a movie, man. It's something out of an Eddie Murphy flick.

Thanks to ESPN, I even got involved in politics—in a way. And it's all due to Digger Phelps.

Digger is connected to the White House because he and George H.W. Bush are very tight. He also knows George W. Bush.

True story: We interviewed President Bill Clinton at the 1995 Final Four.

This was Arkansas playing against UCLA, in Seattle, for the national championship. We were sitting in the studio, and Digger said, "We've got to get Clinton on the line; he's a big Arkansas fan."

I said, "You can't get the president."

But Digger started making calls. He was calling FBI guys. He was calling Secret Service guys he knows. And before long, we got the word: Clinton is going to come on with us. And we're going to do the interview while he's in a restaurant in Arkansas getting ready to watch the game.

Off the air, Clinton asked me, "Dickie V, who do you like?"

I said, "Hey, man, Ty Edney's not going to play. You Razorback fans are home free."

So Clinton said to the crowd, "We're in great shape. Dickie V says they've got no shot."

Little did I know, though, that Cameron Dollar would step up big time and Jimmy Harrick's Bruins would beat Arkansas, 89-78.

Politics just isn't my thing.

But thanks to Digger, I got a chance to meet another president.

I love going to big games on Saturday across America. I love the atmosphere of college football. I always wanted to go to a game at Texas A&M. So I went down there for the Texas A&M-Notre Dame game a couple of years ago.

I got there early in the morning. The cadet corps was marching. It was a beautiful day in College Station.

Well, then I noticed this entourage following some vans. Not limousines, just vans. I also noticed that everybody else was getting stopped. I wondered what was going on.

All of a sudden, a van stopped, and out steps George H.W. Bush, the former president.

And who got out with him? Digger Phelps.

As they began walking, I started yelling, "Digger, Digger."

Digger stopped. He looked at me. I think it took him a minute, but he finally recognized me.

He knew I couldn't get by that barricade because the Secret Service was there, so he went back and asked them to let me in.

So there I was, talking with the former president, having my picture taken. And all of a sudden, the Secret Service said, "We've got to go now."

So Digger turned to me and said, "I've got to go to lunch now."

I just stood there, pleading, "Digger, I'm your buddy. Can't I come?"

I mean, my buddy Digger really big-timed me—I'm only kidding, Mr. Phelps. But I've reminded him about it a hundred thousand times.

Not that he's needed me to.

After Digger left coaching, he joined George H.W. Bush's cabinet. He actually had an office in Washington, D.C., where he served as special assistant to the director of the Office of National Drug Control Policy.

When Bill Clinton won the presidency, Digger lost that position. I think that's why he started saying that he was going to run for president in 2000—he liked the address.

And if he won, he was going to make me ambassador to Italy. Thanks, bambino.

I also got a chance to meet Wayne Gretzky.

When you think about great superstars, you think of Magic in basketball, Alex Rodriguez in baseball, and Gretzky in hockey. They're just synonymous with their sports.

I was at a Notre Dame-Southern Cal game. Digger and I were having dinner over at Parisi's, a popular off-campus Italian restaurant in South Bend, and guess who joined us for dinner? Wayne Gretzky.

What a scene. I mean, people were flocking over for autographs. Not mine. Not Digger's. They wanted "The Great One."

I finally said, "Hey, man, we're trying to eat here. Let the guy eat."

Wayne said, "Oh no, no, no. If I'm going out in public, I've got to expect this."

He is the most down-to-earth guy. I mean, Gretzky is as regular a guy as you'll ever find for someone who is such a superstar.

He'd made out a list. He told me one of the things he wanted to do was to be at a Notre Dame-Southern Cal football game because he'd heard so much about it. So when he finally came to South Bend, he spoke at the pep rally and told the crowd there—14,000 strong at the Convocation Center—"The one thing I regret about my resume is that it doesn't say that I played hockey at Notre Dame."

And the place went nuts, screaming, "Gretzky . . . Irish . . . Gretzky . . . Irish."

He gets it.

That's why I love Magic Johnson and Michael Jordan. They understood what it was all about, too. They understood, with a smile, that the cash register went ring-a-ding ding.

Whereas a lot of guys don't get it. They've got chips on their shoulders. They're angry, and they wonder, "Why doesn't anybody ever call me for anything? Why don't I ever get any endorsements?"

Why? Who wants to be around people who are constantly moaning and groaning?

Not me.

I've been in the limelight a little, and I'll tell you it has its good and bad sides—just like everything in life does.

I remember when my girls were going to Notre Dame, I told them, "With fame comes responsibility. You have to be careful. If you go to a party and see something going on at that party that you know is illegal, you've got to get out of there. If something ever happened—

if there was a raid—whose names do you think are going to be in big headlines? Two hundred kids might be there, but your name and your father's will be in the headlines. 'Dick Vitale's Daughters Arrested.'"

I was lucky. They listened.

Jim Simpson, my original partner at ESPN, gave me some good advice a long time ago. He told me, "You want to make certain that whenever you go out into public, you're shaved and dressed neatly, because people are going to form opinions on every little thing about you."

Now, some guys don't care about that. But I do. I give a damn about all that. I feel I have an accountability, a responsibility to the public, and I try to uphold that. I find that as my visibility has in-creased—thanks to the growth of ESPN—I've had to be more alert and watchful of my actions.

People know who I am. They know what I'm about. So I have to go the extra step. All that comes with the territory, but it's a small price to pay for the life I've had.

And for all the people I've met.

I think my body language lets people know that they can ap-proach me, wherever I meet them. Al McGuire always teased me about being All-Airport, All-Lobby, "You're always in the lobby with people." Man, I flat-out love people. I like being around people. I like going to restaurants. I like going out and just being with the fans.

My wife and I were down at the River Walk at the 1998 Final Four in San Antonio, which is one of the great cities, along with Indianapolis and New Orleans, to host the best sporting event of them all. We decided to go for a ride on the river in one of those barges, and John Stote, who runs Anaconda Sports, which produces my basketball, "The Rock," gave me a bunch of basketballs. I started flipping 'em all over the place, and the crowd went bananas as guys started diving for the balls.

It was thrilling to hear the fans chanting my name.

But then I threw one and almost hit Dan Issel, the former Kentucky star, who was eating lunch outside. There could have been guacamole everywhere, baby.

Finally, Lorraine stopped me, saying, "Somebody's going to get hurt. You've got to be careful."

When you're easily recognized and you go out, you've got to expect that some people will come over to you. That's obviously going to happen. Now some people don't like that, and I can respect that. If you don't want to be bothered, you shouldn't go out. But as for me, I enjoy it.

People ask me, "Well, jeez, don't you get annoyed when you're eating, and people are bugging you for autographs and all that?"

No, not at all. Man, are you kidding me? If they didn't ask, I'd put a sign on, saying "Please ask. My name is Dickie V."

And that would be just for the adults. The kids are another story. Being a fan myself, I get what they're about. And I try to give them what they want.

The first time I went to Maryland's brand new fieldhouse to see them play Duke, the Terrapin fans were teasing me and having loads of fun, calling me "Dukie Vitale"—by the way, Chris Fowler started that. He was busting my chops one day on TV. Instead of calling me "Dickie," he called me "Dukie." Thanks a lot, Chris. Man, I owe you big time because I don't know how many times since then I've been asked why I love Duke so much. And I just laugh when I hear that, because I'll never apologize for speaking about a program as successful as Duke's. They've earned every line of every compliment I've ever given them.

I'm such a hot dog before a game, I'll even play a one-on-one with a little kid. I remember once down at LSU, I went onto the floor and started playing one-on-one with the sons of an assistant coach there, Butch Pierre. He has twins, the little guys were about seven years old then, but they could really handle the rock.

So I went out on the floor and started playing against the twins. And got so into it that I blocked one of the little guys' shots, and the crowd got all over me. Here I was, six feet tall and one of the kids was maybe four feet—maybe.

Another time, I was on the court with Brad Daugherty at Georgia Tech. Brad had been a superstar at North Carolina, the No. 1 pick in the NBA draft, and a star of the Cleveland Cavaliers in the NBA. Now he's one of us at ESPN.

So we were playing one-on-one, shooting around. "Come on, Daugherty," I said. I've got my back to the basket, and he was checking me. I threw in a sweet underhand, like a reverse layup, and the sucker went in.

The crowd went out of its mind.

I'd been as lucky as could be—seven-foot first-round draft pick, he was.

And he said, "Come on; try that again."

"Uh-uh, I'm not giving you a second shot, Brad. You had your chance."

I just try to lighten up the moment. I try to get involved as much as I can. I love it. I just feel like a little kid when I'm out there.

One time, dancing with the cheerleaders, I got the crowd going crazy in Illinois, doing a dance—my "Disco Dick" routine. I can't dance a lick, but I was out there giving it my all, baby. They got the band playing and the place went berserk.

This past year, I did the Oklahoma-Texas game, a big game down there in Norman, Oklahoma. I was up in the crowd with the fans before the game, taking all kinds of pictures and just mingling with the kids, having a blast, taking photos with all the cheerleaders—and telling everybody in America to eat their hearts out because I'm surrounded by pretty young girls who all want to hug this bald-headed old guy. And where were they when I was 21 years old? None of them were there for me then. None of them.

At Kentucky, it's the same thing—getting serenaded with the "Dickie V" chants.

Generation after generation of fans have passed me down the stands now, it seems. I meet so many people today who say, "Gee whiz, I was in the crowd when you came up in the stands 10-15 years ago." Young people have always been fantastic to me. I think that's why, at age 64, I act like I'm about 12. College students are really able to enjoy life to its fullest—they're my kind of people.

It's amazing, the reactions that I receive from student sections all around America, whether I'm at Stanford, Michigan State, Illinois, Pittsburgh, Missouri or any place else. Sometimes I'll ask my partners, "Man, what have I created?"

They've got the Izzone up there at the Breslin Center at Michigan State. It just blew my mind last year when they made me an honorary member. They've only got two of those so far—me and Steve Mariucci, Tom Izzo's best buddy and the coach of the Detroit Lions. They lowered this giant banner from the top of the ceiling before the game. It was a picture of a guy with a great body—and my head—wearing a jersey that read, "Dickie V, Isn't the Izzone Awesome, Baby?"

Student enthusiasm like that can give a team an edge. Basketball is all about that kind of emotion, passion and excitement. The bottom line is that the home-court advantage is much more of a factor in basketball than it is in football. It is just so unique.

In basketball, shooters have a lot of idiosyncrasies. They can be very superstitious about being in a comfort zone. The vision and sight lines have to be just right. They normally are at home.

But when the players go away and don't have that same feeling of comfort, it affects them. And the most dreaded college basketball fans are Duke's Cameron Crazies. They're bright, creative, funny. No surprise there, with a student body whose average SAT score is over 1400. They know how to get under the skin of their opponents.

I remember when Herman Veal of Maryland had trouble with a sexual assault charge, they threw condoms onto the floor. When Chris Washburn of NC State was accused of stealing a stereo, they threw records out onto the floor. When Olden Polynice was accused of plagiarism at Virginia, they threw out term papers. When Lorenzo Charles of NC State was arrested for supposedly stealing a pizza, they had a guy dressed up as a delivery man hand him a pizza before the game.

It got a little out of hand, and obviously, you couldn't blame the administration for stepping in to make certain the group would control their actions.

You see some places where they allow beer into the arenas. That's just looking for trouble on the college level. I mean, you're just looking for problems when kids are stumbling in, half-blitzed, before the game starts.

I'm also bothered by some of the behavior that takes place after big victories, after the national championships. It's happened at Michigan State and Maryland, where there were riots on campus.

In many cases, it's not even the students. It's people in the city looking for an excuse to come out and celebrate. They're sick. That's not celebrating; that's hooliganism, plain and simple. They get a five-star rating for being a hoodlum.

Fans throughout the sporting world seem to have gotten nastier these days. They're not afraid. Remember what happened in Chicago at the White Sox game in the summer of 2002? Fans jumping onto the field, attacking the Royals' first base coach? Fans attacking players, throwing batteries at them—that's a no-no. What happens in international soccer just blows my mind. I don't ever want to see that happening in this country.

The game of basketball is so emotional that I worry sometimes about the antics of the fans because you can see and feel every move made by the coach. It's not like football, where the coach is jammed in with all the big guys on the sideline and you can't find him; or baseball, where the manager is tucked away in the dugout and you can't get to him. In basketball, the coach is standing out there in the open. Man, he is exposed.

Everybody can see his pain as he walks down the sideline. Sometimes the crowd is in such a frenzy you worry about some wild scenes that might break out.

Today's fans feel they have a right to vent at a coach. And they do have a right—to a certain degree. They have a right to yell and scream about his coaching choices, but if they start attacking his family, then they've gotten too carried away with emotion. Sometimes they take out their frustrations on the players. In Boston, for example, Antoine Walker of the Celtics actually went into the stands after a fan who had been on him for *seven* years.

On the whole, though, I've found most fans to be very supportive. I've seen fans really get after their teams, and that's okay. I just object to the people who take it too far.

The Cameron Crazies are better behaved these days, but they're just as vocal. And they wouldn't be quite so boisterous if not for the success that their team has had. Everything is related to success, man— the packed house, the coach, the players. Why is it crazy at Duke? Well, they're 29-2 every year. So there's a genuine love affair between the fans and the team.

Sort of like the one between me and the game.

I'm lucky to be in a sport that mirrors my personality. Can you imagine me doing golf or tennis? Wow, I want to sit next to Johnny Mac. Johnny McEnroe and Dickie V going one-on-one. What a combination that would be.

Fan reaction has just been thrilling. It gives me goose bumps sometimes. I've said to myself, "Wow, it's a great feeling that I've reached so many people and I get to feel like a little part of the fabric of the game."

I don't know. Some people may say that takes away from the game. The game, obviously, is the No. 1 thing.

But it's who I am.

During March Madness, I don't know how many times I hear this: "Who's going to be in the Final Four? Who's going to be in the Final Four?"

Like I know so much.

Even my daughters want to know. One year, Terri called me and said, "Dad, Dad, we're going to have an office pool at work. Can I get some advice? I don't know anything about these teams."

So I gave her my advice, and after the Tournament was over, she called me back to say, "Thanks a lot, Dad. I finished last."

During the off season, the one question I hear everywhere I go is, "Who's going to be No. 1?" It happens 20-30 times a weekend.

Another question I hear frequently is, "What is Bobby Knight really like?"

Fans are always seeking the inside story about the "General," Robert Montgomery Knight. There's no doubt that the fans are sharper than ever today, and they're more vociferous, too. They're at a higher level, man, running on a higher octane. And I'm sure it's gotten that way because of all the television analysis. You just turn on the TV and every major event is dissected. A fan can watch ESPN, ABC, all the networks, read all the local papers. Every major game gets broken down into the strengths and weaknesses of each team.

Sometimes it can be a bit too much.

At times, even the Final Four seems like it gets beaten to a pulp, like everyone can't wait until the event itself is over so they can go back and argue over the particulars. Let's just play, man. Let's play.

I'm still wondering what I must sound like to these fans on the air. For over a decade, we've had sound-a-like contests at the Final Four. Brad Nessler, one of my favorite partners, shocked me in Atlanta one year. He was in the audience with his beautiful bride, Nancy.

When he finally got up on stage, he was way better at being me than me. He was incredible.

I'll tell you, some of these guys who imitate me, it blows my mind how they've got it down. But others? I say, "If I sound like that, please, I beg you, don't let my boss, Mark Shapiro, know because, man, I am flat-out stealing money."

I guess I sound okay to some people, though, because I get some interesting mail, I'll tell you that—real exciting letters from fans.

I also get some really touching letters. One particular letter stands out in my mind.

I had given a speech on ESPN about the game of life. I spoke about drugs, alcohol, making good decisions, and looking in the mirror. You can't play the con game. The mirror knows everything that you're doing with your life.

This former drug addict sent me a letter. He wrote about how he heard me speak on ESPN. In his letter, he said that when he went and looked at his little boy sleeping in bed—his little son was about one year old—he started crying because he felt that he was playing the con game, that all his life he had been conning and conning people. And he couldn't con any more. Now he knew he was cheating his little son as much as he was cheating himself, and he thanked me for helping him to realize this.

I don't know what ever happened to him, but I do know how meaningful his letter was to me.

I got another letter from a couple of guys who were in prison. They told me they wished they would have listened to more adults when they were younger. They also wished they'd had people who could have directed them in a positive way.

The response I got from so many people after that "Game of Life" speech was just incredible. I had parents writing to me, saying that we need more people to talk with kids about life, to share their theories and experiences with today's youth.

A lot of coaches try to do just that. They really try to discipline their players. Yet today it seems that if you jump on someone or you discipline him or her, you're immediately criticized, you're ripped, reprimanded. I know years ago, man, when our coaches got on us, it was because they cared about us. That's all it is. And I try to remind kids about that. I've had the good fortune of speaking to a lot of groups.

I would say 99 percent of the mail I receive is positive. But there are some wacky people out there.

I remember one particular Kentucky-Florida game. After Kentucky beat Florida, I said, "Kentucky is now the college basketball capital of the world after they defeated Florida last season. They are on cloud nine."

You tell me, what's wrong with that?

Well, this guy writes me that he's got a trademark on "Kentucky is the basketball capital of the world" and he wants me to send him $1,000.

That's just crazy, man.

Most of my mail goes to ESPN; the station sends me a bag of it at a time. One of the responsibilities that my daughter Sherri has each morning is to sort all my mail—requests for autographs, requests for auction items. I get a lot of these types of requests. Also each day, Sherri pulls articles from the websites of newspapers from all over the country so that I'm able to keep up on what's happening in the basketball world. Man, I'd be lost without her help.

I just take the letters as they come in—I have them all stacked on my desk in different piles for different requests—and I answer every piece of mail that I get. It's important to me—I feel that if people go out of their way to write me, then I owe them a reply. I'm honored and flattered that somebody has taken a moment to drop me a note. I even answer back those who criticize. Heck, they're entitled to a reply.

Someone once contacted me about a boy who had lost his eye; he had been hit with a golf club in the back yard at a party. Someone swung a golf club and accidentally shattered his eye. The family was devastated. They'd read something about me and how I had lost my eye at a young age—so young, in fact, that I don't remember much of the accident—so they asked me if I could contact him.

So I did. I stayed in touch. I got to meet the youngster. I invited him to be my guest at the preseason NIT games in New York. He comes from a great family in upper New York, and he's doing well right now.

To be a part of someone's life is rewarding. It can be a lot of fun, too.

We were in Indianapolis for the 2000 Final Four; and I had a schedule that was so intense, you wouldn't believe it. I went to my room at the Canterbury Hotel, where my wife and I were staying, and there was a stack of all these drawings and invitations sent to me by Lynn Wide, this fifth-grade teacher at P.S. 79. They were from all her kids. "Dickie V, please come to our school. You're in Indianapolis. We know you're here. Please stop by." This fifth-grade teacher had found out where we were staying and had the kids write to me.

Lorraine looked at me and said, "Look at this—the whole class. You've got to go down there." So I did. I had myself a great hour at the blackboard teaching math—breaking down fractions with the least common denominator, baby—and I mean, I was having a blast with the class.

I reminisced about my days as a sixth-grade teacher. Then I gave a little talk to the youngsters about how they should never, ever believe in the word—*can't*. "Don't allow that to be part of your vocabulary," I told them. It was fun city, man. I couldn't wait to pass out basketballs and books to the kids. They were so nice, they came to visit us at our set and I got a chance to introduce Chris Fowler and Digger and the whole gang to them.

Several years previously when I was in Indianapolis, I'd gone to the Riley Children's Hospital. I was never more touched. They do a phenomenal job there. The medical staff at Riley does a sensational job with all the people they treat. I know Bobby Knight's been there a number of times. People don't know that side of him—spending time with youngsters, bringing gifts to them. Anyway, I went over to the pediatric oncology ward, where many of the youngsters were battling cancer. To see these children with smiles on their faces was very touching. And I tried to say a cheerful word or two.

I remember a little girl, who had a beautiful smile, asking me, "Did you know Damon Bailey?" I remember that—"Did you know Damon Bailey?"

"Yeah, I knew Damon Bailey."

The nurses told me she was going in for major surgery the next day. Major surgery, on an eight-year-old girl who was battling cancer. I left her room and had tears streaming down my face because I couldn't believe that this kid was facing such a crisis, yet she was smiling and talking about her heroes, the Indiana basketball players.

So when I returned to Indianapolis for the 2000 Final Four, I visited Riley Hospital again. There is one scene I will never, ever forget to the day I die. This other little girl must have been no older than 18 months. She was sitting in her hospital bed; her mom and dad were sitting by her side. She had a bandana wrapped around her head. She was just the cutest little thing going—with big blue eyes. She was playing in the bed and the mother and father were smiling and hugging her, trying to make her feel comfortable.

I had no idea what was wrong with her. I usually find out before I get to the room, but I hadn't had a chance. I knew it was something serious, though. As I was telling the mother to have faith, that everything was going to be fine, the father just kept looking at that door. He was so focused, man. You could see it in his eyes. I found out later, when I asked the nurses why he'd seemed so intent on the door, that he'd been waiting for a doctor to come in to announce the results of a test that would reveal whether or not a tumor found in his little girl's brain was malignant.

I thought to myself, "We in the world of basketball worry about all these little things like winning games. This father is dealing with the big game—the game of life. He's waiting for a report that will reveal whether his little girl's tumor is malignant or benign." My friends, that just puts what is truly important into perspective.

To the nurse I said, "You've got to do me a favor. Here's my number at the Canterbury. Call me up. I want to know the status of that little girl."

I had to know that. It would bother me all afternoon.

As my wife and I were going to the car, the nurse came running out after us: "The test came out inconclusive. We just got the report. Inconclusive."

"Oh, my God," I said to myself. "What that father's got to go through now, waiting for another test?"

So I asked the nurse to please call me when they knew.

Finally, she called me at the hotel and left a message. It was good news. No malignancy, no cancer. I jumped with joy when I heard that.

You never know when you're going to need other people's help.

If an off-duty St. Petersburg fireman by the name of John King hadn't been in the Tropicana Room at Tropicana Field in Tampa, I wouldn't be writing this book today. It was one of the scariest moments of my life. I was there, having dinner with my wife and a friend, Rocky Ross, a die-hard Michigan booster, prior to getting ready to see the Tampa Bay Devil Rays play. I'm a season ticket holder and go to about 40 games a year.

All of a sudden, a lump of melon stuck in my throat. I started choking. I was turning blue. I finally looked at my wife and she started pounding me, hitting me.

It was scary. I thought I was a goner. I couldn't breathe.

I was going, "Ungh, ungh."

Suddenly, this big guy jumped up in the back of the room. He came running over and he performed the Heimlich maneuver on me. And, to my great relief, that melon popped right out of my throat.

I can tell you, I had tears rolling down my face. It was scary, man. I am so indebted to John King. We talk about heroes in the sports world—and I certainly respect the talent of a Barry Bonds and the ability of a Michael Jordan—but the real heroes are the firefighters and police officers who are willing to give up their lives to save others. Police officers, firefighters, and teachers are the most underpaid professionals for the kinds of responsibilities they have.

Many people don't know how valuable the Heimlich maneuver is, so I decided to tell them whenever I got the chance. Then I was contacted by Dr. Heimlich himself. He came to a Cincinnati home basketball game. We met, had our pictures taken together, and he thanked me for all the positive publicity.

But I should be thanking him. And John King. Again.

Lou Holtz, the former football coach of Notre Dame, had this wish list of 100 things he wanted to accomplish in his life. He wanted to skydive, wanted to be on the Johnny Carson show. I know he made Johnny's show; I'm not sure about the skydiving.

But the one thing I would love to do in my lifetime—and so far I haven't gotten it done—is to meet the Pope. I envy Rick Pitino because he had an audience with the Pope when Kentucky went on a summer tour of Italy.

I would give anything, but so far I haven't been able to make that happen in my life.

I've been to Rome. Maybe if I go back . . .

That would just blow my mind.

6

THE FOUNTAIN OF YOUTH

Several years ago, I was invited to play Syracuse coach Jim Boeheim, one on one, up in Rochester to raise lots of money for charity. So I go up there, thinking it's going to be a fun situation.

And you can't believe how serious this guy was.

He's all dressed up in his uniform, comes out in front of hundreds and hundreds of people, and he makes like Magic, man. His buddy and former teammate in college, Dave Bing, would have been proud. Oh, man, I would have given anything to have coached Bing when I took over as head coach of the Pistons, but he'd left only a few years earlier. You talk about class—this guy was not only a Hall of Famer as a hoopster, today he's become one of the giants in the metropolitan Detroit area steel business. Bing has set a great example for today's athletes to follow.

Getting back to Boeheim—oh, man, he really pounded on me one on one. I couldn't do a thing to stop him. He stole the ball. He rebounded. He drove, hit jumpers. Incredible. I'm surprised he didn't take me out to the golf course afterward. He has a two handicap. Mine is something like 30.

He grabbed the microphone and said, "Hey, Dickie V, you always talk about us playing some cupcakes in the pre-conference schedule. But today, you were the biggest cupcake of them all."

That's where he made a mistake.

I took the microphone from him and said, "Hey, Jimmy B, you may beat me with the J. But you're not going to beat me on the microphone.

"Now that you've embarrassed me, I get the last word. I want you to know that, if your kids would ever play as hard as you played today, there'd be some banners flying out there at the Carrier Dome."

And now I can just hear him saying to me, "Hey, Dickie V, remember telling me about the banners? Well, there's one flying here now. It's flying high. And that's more than you've ever won."

And he's right.

Syracuse finally won a national championship in the spring of 2003, beating Kansas, 81-78, in the big Louisiana Superdome in New Orleans. And Jim Boeheim was finally recognized as a genius, an Albert Einstein of hoops. Suddenly everybody wanted to know about his 2-3 zone.

Jimmy's been playing that zone for years, man. The zone has a way of camouflaging a team's liabilities, and it was very effective for Syracuse because of the agility, the movement and the length of their players. Just look at Hakim Warrick, Kueth Duany, Jeremy McNeil and Carmelo Anthony—those guys are all 6'8" or bigger; they have long, 747 wingspans, and they play the passing lanes really well. If you're struggling with the jumper from the perimeter, they're going to allow you to take that shot; and if you're not knocking it down, it's lights out.

That was their great asset.

They played with the minds of opposing teams. And we in the media made a monster out of it and created this huge psychological weapon for them.

The Syracuse zone had an effect similar to the 1979 Michigan State matchup zone. Jud Heathcote, who won the national championship that year behind the brilliant play of Magic Johnson, had people buzzing about how to attack that zone. Boeheim did the same, psychologically, in 2003 with his 2-3 zone. To me, half of the battle occurs before the game ever begins.

I remember Jud going to clinic after clinic, talking about that 2-3 matchup. And guys were scribbling down all these notes.

I finally asked him, "Jud, do you think it's pretty good because you have two guys by the name of Greg Kelser and Magic Johnson?" I really believe Michigan State could have played any defense they wanted—man-to-man, matchup, 3-2, 1-2-2—and that as long as those two were in the lineup, the team was going to win.

One of the assets of coaching is the ability to understand the strengths and weaknesses of your team and adjust your style to fit your personnel. If you've got a team that can't press and run, you can't go 90 feet and start trapping people. And at the college level, you can recruit to your style.

Still, the biggest problem for teams playing Syracuse during the 2003 season was a youngster named Carmelo Anthony, a 6'7" freshman from Oak Hill Academy in Virginia.

I thought we'd never see another diaper dandy like center Pervis "Never Nervous" Ellison of Louisville. Pervis was the best freshman I'd ever watched in terms of dominating in the Final Four. He got 25 on Duke in the 1986 championship game. But his performance takes a back seat to what Carmelo did. And Carmelo did it with style, did it with grace, did it in a special way.

He went off for 33 points and 14 rebounds during a 95-84 victory over Texas in the semis. Then he scored 20 points, grabbed 10 rebounds and had seven assists against Kansas.

I remember speaking to him before he ever played his first college game—against Memphis in the Coaches vs. Cancer games in

November 2002 at the Garden. We were both on ESPN radio with Dan Patrick. I remember grabbing Carmelo and telling him, "Coach has told me so many great things about you. Just go out and play, enjoy the year. Don't worry about playing to the camera."

So many young kids have a tendency to try to live up to the billing they have coming out of high school and go out and try to please everybody.

You could see it that night against Memphis. John Calipari was doing everything to stop him, doubling him, and Anthony still went off for 27 in a loss—but he was a disaster at the free throw line. And he worked hard to improve that aspect of his game.

I remember saying, "They've had some great ones at Syracuse. I remember Derrick Coleman, Billy Owens, Pearl Washington, Sherman Douglas. But take it to the bank—this will be the greatest frosh ever to wear the Syracuse uniform." You could have been blind and still seen this kid was on another level.

Carmelo is from a tough, drug-infested, war-zone neighborhood in Baltimore notoriously dubbed "The Pharmacy." "I lived right in the middle of it," he admitted. "I could have gone left, could have gone right. I could have made a messed-up decision."

Instead, Carmelo, who grew five inches—from 6' to 6'5"—in the ninth grade, found an escape route through basketball. He was the second best player in his class—behind Amare Stoudemire of the NBA Phoenix Suns—and could have been an NBA lottery pick last spring when he was a senior. But he chose to enroll at Syracuse instead because his mother, Mary, a custodial worker at the University of Baltimore, urged him to go.

Carmelo Anthony and guard Gerry McNamara, who scored 18 points and made six three-pointers against Kansas, were two freshmen who played critical roles for the Orange. That young team also had another freshman—guard Billy Edelin—and three sophomores—guard Josh Pace, forward Hakim Warrick and center Craig Forth—in its top eight rotation.

McNamara moved into the starting lineup the first game of the year after the NCAA suspended freshman guard Billy Edelin a ridiculous 12 games for playing in an adult winter league the previous year, when he was working through a year-long suspension from classes.

Over 2,000 fans from McNamara's hometown of Scranton, Pennsylvania, made the pilgrimage up I-81 to the Dome when Syracuse played Notre Dame. They went wild when McNamara beat the Irish with a three at the buzzer. McNamara became a cult hero in his hometown after he led Bishop Hannon, with a graduating class of 105, to a PIAA small schools state championship, scoring 54 in the finals against powerful Trinity Catholic of Harrisburg.

Coleman's Pub in the Tipperary Hill section of Syracuse wanted to make him the grand marshal of the Green Beer Delivery Parade on St. Patrick's Day. McNamara said he had to take a pass on that for obvious reasons.

McNamara's a classic gym rat who spent hours shooting jumpers after CYO practice with his father, Gerry Sr., a former high school star and ex-marine. By the time he was 12, McNamara was already a local legend, having won a state free throw shooting contest by making 25 straight foul shots and then leading his Holy Rosary team to the state title. That was only the beginning. McNamara was recruited by Duke, but settled on Syracuse because he wanted to stay closer to home. "Syracuse has been a great place for me," he said. "Coach Boeheim has been here forever. He's not going to go anywhere."

The previous three NCAA championship teams—Michigan State with Mateen Cleaves and Morris Peterson, Duke with Shane Battier, and Maryland with Juan Dixon and Lonny Baxter—had been powered by seniors. And the two biggest stars on the Kansas team were both seniors—forward Nick Collison and guard Kirk Hinrich.

But the talent gap between upperclassmen in the marquee programs and the top 30 freshmen is not nearly as wide as it has been in the past. There was a time when most freshmen—even Michael Jordan of North Carolina—had to be satisfied with being members of the supporting cast. Players like Georgetown center Patrick Ewing and Pervis Ellison were once the exceptions rather than the rule.

But Roy Williams, who coached Kansas in the 2003 championship game before leaving for North Carolina, can see that trend is starting to change. "When I started at North Carolina 25 years ago," he admitted, "we'd tell kids, 'During your four years here, we're going to go to the West Coast, we're going to New York, we're going to take you to Hawaii.' Now, half the dadgum kids in the country, top 50 kids, have already been to Hawaii. You tell them that now and they say, 'Yeah, long plane ride.' That's the way they look at it.

"The kids nowadays are more worldly. They've had more experiences, been more places. Nick Collison has been around the world with USA Basketball. He's made five different tours during his college career and he also went in high school. The day I saw Kirk Hinrich play for the first time, he had just returned from Moscow—not the one in Idaho—I mean Moscow. I haven't even been there, man.

"Freshmen are no longer freshmen, even when we start the year, much less at this time of the season. It started to change about 12 to 15 years ago when summer basketball just exploded. When I first started, you went to Five Star Camp, BC camp. That was it. There was nothing else going on. Then I saw Nick Collison play like 12 games the summer before his senior year in Vegas. That's a long way from Iowa Falls, Iowa."

We're getting more and more instantly dominant performances from kids stepping in right out of high school because a lot of them have played 60, 70, 80 games in the summer.

Carmelo is a classic product of the system. He steps in, and right from day one, he's a major impact player. Ask him if he didn't learn and get a lot of competition from the AAU circuit. He played for Baltimore Select, a high-powered, Adidas-sponsored travel team. Then he transferred from Towson Catholic to Oak Hill Academy in Virginia, a nationally ranked private school that plays a national schedule. He flourished in that atmosphere.

Guard Bracey Wright of Indiana comes out of The Colony High School in Texas, plays AAU competition, and right out of the gate, he wins the MVP Trophy at the Maui Invitational in Hawaii. At New York, the Garden, the Preseason NIT—the MVP? Rashad McCants from North Carolina, who had been a big star in the Bob Gibbons Memorial Day tournament the spring of his junior year.

It's happening all over the country.

Boeheim says he feels the best freshmen have a chance to shine earlier because so many underclassmen are leaving early for the pros. "The kids are just better. They're more suited, more ready to play," he said. "They're probably not as ready as they think they are—that's life—but they're more ready these days, and there are not as many great seniors. You don't have a Kobe Bryant who's played four years and is waiting for you there. It's a lot easier for a younger player to have a chance to make a big impact and compete against more experienced players."

Jimmy wound up running his offense through Anthony and McNamara. "They're unusual freshmen," he said. "Gerry had 54 points in the Pennsylvania state championship game. He's a big-time player who wants to take big shots. He has no fear. The other guy—I think he's shown what he is all about."

Carmelo was out the door before you knew it. Gone. He went third in the draft to Denver and signed a $3.7 million deal with Nike. It wasn't LeBron money, but it should help him buy a new house for his mom. During the NBA draft, it was such a touching moment when our Stuart Scott tried to interview Carmelo's mom, who could not speak and had tears flowing down her cheeks because she was pouring out all the emotion she felt at her son being drafted so high. It's beautiful to see young athletes give back to the people who helped make it happen for them.

Now LeBron and Carmelo have hooked up together to do a Nike commercial. And they can't wait to go head to head with each other on the court and have some fun.

In fact, there now are some NBA scouts who are starting to wonder if Carmelo won't make a greater impact his first year in the league than LeBron. The LeBron-Carmelo debate is like asking who you like better, Willie Mays or Mickey Mantle? The bottom line is you can't go wrong. It's like Michael Jordan and Magic Johnson—they're both superstars.

As Oklahoma coach Kelvin Sampson puts it, "What can't he do that LeBron does?" He feels that, while Anthony may not have James's chiseled 6'8", 240-pound body yet, and while he may not be able to sell as many tickets as high school's resident superstar, he is quicker, a better shooter, has an equally excellent feel for the game and has had the benefit of playing against a higher level of competition for a year.

Boeheim wished him well. He said he would recruit Anthony all over again—even knowing he was going to have him only for one season. "I don't think there's a coach in the country who wouldn't take that guy," Jimmy said. "Duke takes three or four guys a year who could go after one year. That's college basketball right now. Until the NBA establishes an age limit, you just have to adjust to it. What we've tried to do for the last seven, eight years is get pretty good players. Until this past season, we haven't had enough to make a real good run—although we did in 2000 when we lost to Michigan State in the Sweet 16.

"We'll try to recruit a guy we think will be in college a couple of years. A lot of those guys end up staying three, four years. You never know when you recruit a Nick Collison. And he stayed four years at Kansas."

Great players come and go so fast these days.

Players with superstar talent today are thinking NBA right from the start. I think the era of seeing two kids the caliber of Nick Collison and Kirk Hinrich of Kansas on the same team and staying four years, going the route won't happen any more. It'll be the exception rather than the rule. Everybody's chasing the dollar, racing to get to the top of the mountain. Guys are filling up players' heads with delusions of grandeur. We don't have kids out there like David Robinson and Tim Duncan who realize that the money is going to be there anyway and that there's no greater time than strutting your stuff at school, being the big man on campus.

I ran into Grant Hill, the former Duke star who now plays for the Orlando Magic, at an airport. He grabbed me and he said, "Dickie V, keep telling those kids to stay in school. Man, it's the best time of your life. I'm telling you. It's all business once you leave. It's a completely different world."

But how do you tell a kid like LeBron or a kid like Carmelo to stay in school? You just can't when they're in such demand. The system is so wacky. NBA commissioner David Stern is right to argue that there should be a 20-year-old minimum age limit. So many veteran players are losing job opportunities. They get cut for a bunch of young kids who're taking their spots on the roster. But the youngsters have to learn that it takes time for them to develop.

It amazes me how the Players' Association doesn't fight on behalf of a veteran player who ends up losing his job for some young kid who will have to sit on the pine for several years before he's ready to play. It just drives me wild how everyone gets hurt in this equation— the college team gets hurt through the loss of some quality players, the players miss out on a chance to hone their game and thereby develop greater marketability for themselves, and the NBA certainly suffers because the quality of play gets watered down because too many players are entering before they're fundamentally ready to compete. To me, that's a no-no.

All of these defections to the pros have made the NCAA Tournament more unpredictable than ever.

Had the NCAA Tournament been a best-of-seven format instead of one and out, I really believe Kentucky would have won the 2003 national title. But Marquette caught lightning in the Mideast regional finals and was able to pound the Wildcats behind Dwayne Wade's triple double—29 points, 11 rebounds and 11 assists. It was one of the greatest individual performances I've ever witnessed in tournament play.

It was Jordanesque.

As it is, one bad night and the party's over. That's the beauty and the essence of the NCAA Tournament. It's generated plenty of other dream-shattering performances—where the hopes of the student body, the coaches, and the players were all taken away.

The one people probably talk about the most is Princeton's 43-41 upset of UCLA in the first round of the 1996 Tournament in Indianapolis, the year after the Bruins cut down the nets in Seattle. Princeton had come close before. But this time, the Tigers—who were a 13th seed—were able to get the job done.

It was an especially sweet victory because it was Pete Carril's final season as a college coach, and because Princeton—a methodical, highly disciplined Ivy League team with no scholarship players—won it at the end with a trademark play. With just four seconds to play, Gabe Lewullis beat Charles O'Bannon and took a pass from Steve Goodrich for a back-door layup—a move that left Jim Harrick and his team shocked.

Carril was voted into the Basketball Hall of Fame, and he was even invited onto *The Tonight Show With Jay Leno*. Eventually, he was hired by one of his ex-players, Geoff Petrie, the GM of Sacramento, to come out to the West Coast and install his offense there.

My favorite first-round upset? It's a tie. It's between Coppin State—who came out of nowhere as a 15th seed from the MEAC in 1997 to beat South Carolina, when everybody was going gaga for Eddie Fogler's club—and Richmond, a 15th seed from the Colonial Athletic Association, beating Syracuse 73-69 in 1991. I put the latter in there because of my admiration for Dick Tarrant, the coach of Richmond. Tarrant was a sensational high school coach at Passaic, New Jersey, when I was about to begin coaching at East Rutherford. I always knew that if he had a chance to coach quality big-time players, he would be a major success. His Spiders also upset Charles Barkley, the "Round Mound of Rebound," in 1984.

Hey, speaking of Barkley, I remember going to a practice at Auburn, and Sonny Smith, who was coaching there at the time, asked me to say a few words that might inspire Mr. Barkley. Let me tell you, I couldn't believe as I was watching him practice that he was just going through the motions and not really using his exceptional talent. I remember telling him so and saying, "Charles, you have a chance to be really special, but it's gonna be up to you to develop a sense of pride and the work ethic to get yourself to the next level."

Charles always kids me about that talk. Let me tell you, this guy is one big, lovable character. Every time I see him—get this—he drops to his knees, bows and says, "Dickie V, working in TV is like stealing money. I've watched you doing it over the years and told myself, 'If he can do it, man, I can do it.'"

Charles is certainly doing it big-time on TNT.

But there have been plenty of other great upsets apart from the Richmond and Coppin State ones. Santa Clara shocked Arizona in 1993, the second of four straight first-round defeats for Lute Olson. Cleveland State, a 14th seed, stunned Indiana in 1986. Weber State, a 14th seed, bounced North Carolina out in 1999. And Hampton, a 15th seed, upset Iowa State in 2001.

March has become one huge celebration at ESPN, man, starting with Championship Week. Last year, after IUPUI won the Mid-Continent tournament, their coach, Ron Hunter, went crazy. He was pounding the floor with joy. Afterwards, while we were in the studio, Chris Fowler started asking Digger and me how we celebrated after big victories.

They ran a clip of Digger doing a high step and a little jig after Notre Dame beat Syracuse one year.

I said I'd also danced after Detroit beat Marquette in 1977 to clinch an NCAA berth.

"We don't have any video," Chris said. "Would you show us?"

So I got up and went crazy, doing some disco steps. Imagine— a guy in his mid-60s with dance fever. I mean, John Travolta would have been proud of me, baby. He would've been proud.

Another good thing about March Madness at ESPN is that I get to stand up on my soapbox. This past year, I screamed and yelled about how the Big East got a raw deal when Boston College and Seton Hall didn't get bids. Now, I was talking about how the teams were selected, not whether the teams could win if they got invited. Teams like Auburn—I know, they beat St. Joseph's and Wake Forest and marched on to the NCAA Sweet 16—but I didn't think they should have gotten in because they had a horrendous strength of schedule and some bad pre-SEC losses.

A lot of their fans were mad. I got letters from some of them, complaining I was anti-Tigers, anti-Auburn. That's not true. I was just talking the facts. I didn't mean Auburn couldn't win two games in the postseason. There are a lot of teams in the NIT that could have won two games at the big dance.

And you know what's funny? I got a call on my birthday from Cliff Ellis of Auburn—wishing me a happy birthday.

Some teams seem destined to reach their goals. The Indiana team in 1976 was the best I ever watched. I know some people will get all over me about not picking Lew Alcindor's group at UCLA. But Indiana that year represented everything I believe in as far as a team concept. Bobby Knight's team finished 32-0 and had that great starting five of Quinn Buckner, Bobby Wilkerson, Scott May, Tom Abernathy and Kent Benson.

I would love to have done a game where that team and one of Bill Walton's UCLA teams went head to head. I would love to have seen that, baby—the perfect team against the Big Redhead. Or how about Lew Alcindor? Either one of them—they were the two best centers ever to play college basketball. I would love—*love*—to have seen if Bobby Knight could have come up with a game plan to offset the dominance of either Walton or Alcindor.

But that's never to be.

The amazing thing about Alcindor is that the NCAA did everything humanly possible to try to make the game tough for him. The Rules Committee even took away the dunk. They did all kinds of things to try to hurt him, but they couldn't stop him.

Now, who's the best team since I've been involved with ESPN? I really loved those Georgetown teams with Patrick Ewing, man. I loved the way they played. They took you out of everything you did with defense.

I've always liked athletes who are multidimensional and can play a variety of positions. I liked full-court pressure when I was at Detroit, and the kids I had at that time—Terry Tyler, John Long, and Terry Duerod—were perfect for that system. We were 25-3 my last year there. All three of my stars got a chance to play at the highest level—the NBA. We were pretty good at Detroit, but we weren't on Georgetown's level.

Patrick Ewing, Reggie Williams, Michael Graham, Michael Jackson, Billy Martin, Gene Smith. They had all kinds of bodies. They played my kind of basketball. They came after you. They beat you on the offensive boards. They pressured. They really just played aggressive basketball.

Check out the destruction they laid on Kentucky in the 1984 Final Four. The Hoyas almost blanked them completely in the second half of a 53-40 victory. Kentucky shot just three for 33. After the game, their coach, Joe B. Hall, said that it must have been some kind of extraterrestrial phenomenon. Georgetown had that effect on everybody. In the finals against Houston, they went off on a 26-8 run to start the game and then cruised to an 84-75 victory. Ewing, who was a junior at the time, was named MVP after holding Hakeem Olajuwon to just 15 points, well below his average.

Today, the NCAA Tournament has become more of a grab bag than I can ever remember. There are so many good teams out there. TV has opened up the world of recruiting to a lot more schools. A coach can say, "Hey, man, watch us. You might like it here in the Mid-American Conference. You might like it here at an Atlantic 10 school." Years ago, you didn't know what existed unless you visited, man, but now you can see some of those teams on TV.

And there are more good players in the talent pool than ever before. With all the summer play, basketball has become a game of specialization. Coaches have a very difficult time evaluating players off the summer. There are so many scouting services like Bob Gibbons's *All-Star Report*, Clark Francis's *Hoop Scoop*, and Tom Konchalski's *HSBI* out there. There are so many recruiting shows on the radio. And, of course, coaches are always trying to impress by getting guys who are rated the best of the best.

But there are guys out there who can really play, sleepers like Tim Duncan and David Robinson who don't get the national publicity but turn into stars once they get to college.

The key is to be able to spot those players. A basketball team is only five players, man. If you come up with a superstar and find four others who know their roles, you can go out and shock a lot of people. You don't need the numbers the way you do in football.

Today's parity and balance have occurred for several reasons— firstly, scholarship reduction to a maximum of 13 has leveled off the playing field; secondly, players leaving early have allowed the mid-major and high major schools to be able to compete with the big-time programs, since their players often stay all four years; thirdly, the development of late bloomers has gotten recruiters to start keeping an eye out for kids with potential and who will really work hard to develop their game. Basketball is a game of rhythm, a game of timing and chemistry. It's not always about having the best talent. It's about having a coach who understands the strengths and weaknesses of each of his players. And the coach who can maximize the strengths and minimize the liabilities usually comes out on top.

It's created a chance for the middle-of-the-road guy—the mid-majors, I call them—to play against the big guys and to compete with them.

That's a compliment, not a knock.

Coaches of teams like these don't want to hear the term *mid-major*. I know Mark Few of Gonzaga goes bananas. "Hey," he says, "we're not a mid-major." But I'm not saying their coaching or their talent level is mid-major. I'm talking about visibility, about conference affiliation, budgets. They don't have the dollars that the big-time conferences have.

All I'm saying is, with brilliant coaching and talent, you can not only go out and compete, you can win.

We've seen that happen over the last few years. Check out Gonzaga or Kent State.

The big question I have is whether we'll ever have another situation when a mid-major team will make it to the Final Four. The last time that happened was 1979 when a kid from French Lick, Indiana named Larry Bird led Indiana State to the national championship game against Michigan State and a kid by the name of Tony Price did a phenomenal job leading the University of Pennsylvania out of the Ivy League to the Final Four.

Teams have come close a few times.

Two years ago, Kent State went to the Elite Eight, beating Pittsburgh before they were knocked to the sidelines by Indiana. Gonzaga went to the Elite Eight in 1999, beating Florida in the second round before being knocked out by Connecticut, the year the Huskies won it all.

Just recently, in 2003, it was Butler's turn.

Two seasons before, they won 25 games, beat Indiana and Purdue and were denied an NCAA bid. It was a total injustice.

This time Butler got in as an at-large pick and proved they could play, making a great run to the Sweet 16. They beat Mississippi State—whom some people had already penciled into the Final Four—in the first round. Then they came back and shot the lights out to send Louisville to the sidelines. Rick Pitino told me that Butler executed the three-point offense as well as any team he'd faced since coming back to the college game in 2001.

So, yes, David can play with Goliath.

Teams like that definitely deserve an opportunity, but they don't get the same chances as the big guys. The big guys have three chances: They can either have a great record and qualify based on that, they can win their conference tournament and qualify, or they can get in if they finish .500 in their conference.

Unless they win their conference championship, though, the little guys are usually knocked out.

I've always hated the fact that a lot of big-time programs dodge these teams—avoid the mid-majors like the plague—and don't give them a shot. I know what that's like. I was at Detroit and I was always begging and pleading with my counterpart Digger Phelps when he was at Notre Dame. I wrote him and called him. I desperately wanted to play the Irish.

You know what, though? If I were in his shoes, I might think the same way—but he could have been a nice guy and given me a shot.

Just before the start of the 2003 NCAA Tournament, I was doing our ESPN Selection Show and I went chalk city. I had all four No. 1 seeds—Arizona, Kentucky, Texas and Oklahoma—in the Final Four. Rudy Martzke of *USA Today* and other critics really teased me for going for all the favorites.

But I wasn't the only one—a lot of people thought that the heavyweights would make it.

As it turned out, only one No. 1 seed, Texas, got to the Final Four, and they had gotten to play their regional final in San Antonio, where there were 30,000 fans wearing orange for their game against Michigan State. You would have thought it was a football game, the way those fans down there were going wild watching T.J. Ford.

I've always had trouble with the NCAA allowing teams to play so close to their campuses in March. I'm not trying to take anything away from Syracuse's achievement. They took advantage of the opportunity they had, playing the regionals in Albany—just a couple of hours from campus. But it's hard beating a team when you have to go up against a fan following like they have and the adrenaline rush those fans can supply.

It's totally unfair.

Syracuse blew away top-seed Oklahoma, 63-47, at the sold-out 15,000-seat Pepsi Arena.

There's no reason whatsoever for the NCAA Selection Committee to place teams in their own back yards. Fairness, man, fairness. Everybody should have the same shot. Don't tell me it's a level playing field when you've got a team playing Texas in San Antonio or

Syracuse in Albany. Syracuse might have been a No. 3 seed in the brackets, but they became a 1-A seed by playing up in Albany.

Basketball is a game of emotions, of adrenaline, of feeding off the energy provided by your fans and teammates.

So how are there upsets? If you were to rate the players on a scale of one to five, with five being the best, as Howard Garfinkel—the Garf—would say, the upset occurs when the three-star player plays like a five for a night and the five-star player decides to slide and glide. And a lot of that is driven by the spark the players get from the fans.

I remember Jim Boeheim teasing me the day before they played Kansas. He came by our ESPN tent where Chris Fowler, Digger and I were doing some shows and said, "Dickie V, you haven't picked us yet, so don't start now." He knew I had been saying all year that they were underrated.

Hey, speaking about things that are underrated—are you serious? Jim Boeheim has now become a hero to many men—ever since the national TV cameras flashed shots of his beautiful wife, Juli, during the championship game. I mean, if a guy as regular as him can get someone that beautiful, there's hope for many. (Jimmy, relax, I'm only teasing.) In fact, if I had to rate the three biggest "upsets" in marriage, they would have to be:

1. When Julia Roberts said yes to Lyle Lovett. That was like Duke getting beaten by, let's say, Occidental—a total mismatch.

2. Jimmy Boeheim with his wife would be like Syracuse getting beaten by Cortland State.

3. My guy, Sonny Vacarro, and his beautiful wife, Pam. Man, I don't know where these basketball guys get such a magical touch.

I guess I shouldn't be talking, though, because many have teased me for overachieving with my lady, Lorraine.

Anyway, I felt that the Big East was underrated all year, and I felt they got a raw deal when the NCAA gave them only four bids, wiping out Seton Hall and Boston College—even though both teams had won 10 games in the conference.

Jim Boeheim always had faith, though, just like Jim Valvano had.

Syracuse's game against Kansas came right down to the end. Kansas had a wide-open look for a three that could have spelled disaster for the 'Cuse. But Hakim Warrick—whom I thought was the most improved player of the year—came out of nowhere for the block of the year, the rejection of the year.

For me, that's a great game—when it goes to the buzzer. I call it a Maalox Masher. When you have that kind of game, it's always special—certainly when it's for the national championship.

The game I've always treasured was 1983 North Carolina State-Houston, Jimmy V cutting down the nets. His team was a heavy underdog—I didn't think they'd get out of the ACC Tournament. But beating Jordan and company in the final to earn a bid, then moving past Ralph Sampson in the West Regional final and going on to win the national title—it was just incredible. And the way they did it—so dramatically, an air ball at the end by Dereck Whittenburg, the catch by Lorenzo Charles and then the dunk at the buzzer. The passion, the emotion displayed by Jimmy V—it was just unbelievable.

When I think of great Academy Award-winning performances by a coach to win the national championship during my 25 years at ESPN, I also think of:

• Larry Brown directing Kansas after a 12-8 start to the national title in 1988 with a win over Oklahoma.

•Rollie Massimino of Villanova pitching a perfect game to beat Georgetown, 66-64, in 1985. The Cats shot the lights out that night— shooting 90 percent in the second half and 78 percent for the game against one of the great defensive teams of all time.

• Lute Olson, Arizona, 1997, beating three No. 1 seeds—Kansas, North Carolina and Kentucky—to win it all.

• Gary Williams leading Maryland to the school's first title in 2002 behind Juan Dixon, a guard from Baltimore who had not been a heavily recruited superstar.

Move over, James Cameron, these guys each deserve an Oscar.

I felt so good for Jim Boeheim for a couple of reasons. First, he had gone through a tough time a couple of years ago, going through surgery for prostate cancer. Secondly, he had been maligned by his own people since 1987 when Syracuse lost in the finals to Indiana.

Derrick Coleman missed the first half of a one-and-one in the final seconds of that game and Keith Smart made that jump shot from the baseline to lift the Hoosiers to a 74-73 victory in the same Superdome.

Well, Jim had just bolted onto the court to celebrate after the 'Cuse came out victorious this time—he had just put on his national championship T-shirt—when his cell phone rang.

And who was on the other end of the line?

Derrick Coleman.

"I told him he was finally off the hook," Boeheim said.

Boeheim couldn't help mixing the present with the past when he spoke about his program. Just before the end of the regular season, Sherman Douglas, a guard on that '87 team, returned to campus to have his number retired in the Carrier Dome and spoke with members of the current team. "He told them he thought they had the ingredients to get to New Orleans," Boeheim said. "He said he thought they could win it all."

I've gone on some incredible emotional outbursts over the years, saying Jim has done so much for the program that they should name the court at the Carrier Dome after him. I mean, the guy bleeds Orange. He's just as excited about the Syracuse team as my guy Tommy Lasorda, who bleeds Dodger Blue, is about his. I was overjoyed when I learned that the school had announced they would give Boeheim his day and name the floor after him. He's a guy who is putting together Hall of Fame numbers. Every year, he's posting 20-25 wins. Boeheim has won 653 games and coached the Orange to the NCAA Tournament finals three times in 27 years. He coached a 1996 no-name team to the NCAA finals against Kentucky, and now he's coached this young team to the top of the mountain.

Jim's been a Syracuse guy all his life, first as a player, then as an assistant coach, and now as a head coach. He's never even thought about leaving. Rick Bay, the AD at Ohio State, once called him about an opening there. Jim thought about it for about 10 minutes, then said, "Thanks, but no thanks."

One time, Jim was sitting around with Rick Pitino and Rick's wife, Joanne, in Hawaii. They were talking about the perfect place to live.

Rick said, "San Francisco."

Joanne said, "New York."

Then Jimmy pipes up, "Syracuse."

Their Chamber of Commerce will be happy to know he's a big fan of 100 inches of snow.

Besides, he has other things on his mind these days. Times have changed for Boeheim. He's not only the Syracuse coach, he is also the father of three young children—four-year-old Jimmy and a pair of three-year-old twins, Jack and Jamie.

Talk about a 48-hour day.

The 56-year-old Boeheim took his wife, Juli, and the two boys with him to Albany, New York, for the NCAA East Regionals. Jamie stayed home. "She's in her own little world," Boeheim said. "The two boys play basketball all the time. She sees the ball and goes, 'Phew.' Then she throws it behind her. She'll probably turn out to be the best player in the family; but right now, she has no interest."

In between looking at tapes to prepare for the game, Boeheim found himself trying to keep his kids entertained. Fortunately, there was an arcade just outside his hotel room at the hotel. "I gave them $5 to play the games, ride the rides," he said. "That kept them occupied."

He even found time to change Jack's diaper 15 minutes before he was scheduled to leave for the East Regional final against top-seeded Oklahoma at the Pepsi Arena. "I guess it's good," he said. "You have to focus or you're going to get dirty, so it takes your mind off of the game."

Father knows best.

Jim must have gotten his second wind later that spring. Every year, he helps run "Basket Ball," a charity event to raise money for Coaches vs. Cancer. Last spring, they brought in The Temptations. I heard Jim got up on stage to sing "My Girl" with the group and did all kinds of dance steps.

I wonder if he threw in a little Disco Dick.

7

ABSENT FRIENDS

I t's hard to believe it's been 20 years since my late buddy, Jim Valvano, cut down the nets and won the national championship at Albuquerque, New Mexico, in 1983 as head coach at North Carolina State.

During that title game, the Cougars actually had a 52-46 lead and looked like they were about to break open the game. But then Jimmy V's team committed a series of fouls and Houston coach Guy V. Lewis's Cougars came up empty at the free throw line. Eventually, State pulled ahead to win the game when Dereck Whittenburg— with five seconds left—put up a 30-footer that was rebounded by Lorenzo Charles, who scored the game-winning dunk shot at the buzzer for a 54-52 victory.

Jimmy V spent the next minute running around the court, looking to give somebody some love, looking for somebody to hug. It was all over *SportsCenter*.

It's even harder to believe it's been 10 years since Jimmy died of cancer.

The memories linger on.

Jimmy V always had to be the life of the party. I thought he had really missed his calling. He was a natural for TV, man. He could have been Seinfeld before Seinfeld came along. He was such a funny guy, he would have been phenomenal on sitcoms. When he walked into a room, he just lit it up.

He was the king of the one-liners.

Ron Morris, who wrote the book *The Illustrated History of the ACC,* listed some of Valvano's best quips:

• "My mother said I was vaccinated with Victrola. I haven't shut up since."

• "In America, I am an Italian. Down South, I'm an Eye-talian. I had to go to Italy to become an American."

• "People down here want me to hunt and fish. I tell them I'm from New York. What are you going to do in New York—fly cast at a fire hydrant?"

• "I asked a referee if he could give me a technical for thinking bad things about him and he said, 'Of course not.'

"I said, 'Well, I think you stink.' And he gave me a technical. You can't trust them."

• "I got a call from a fan after we blew a lead in a big game against North Carolina and lost at the buzzer. He said, 'If you ever do that again, I'm going to come over and shoot your dog.'

"I got his address to write him back.

"I also said, 'P.S., I don't have a dog.'

"He said, 'I'm going to send you one—just don't get too attached to it.'"

I'll tell you about a great night. I've always made myself available for people to poke fun at me if it's to help a worthy cause. Well, when the University of Detroit wanted to roast me in order to raise money for their school a few years back, I just couldn't say no. I mean, I'll always be indebted to the people in Titan territory for giving me my first opportunity to be a major college coach.

The place was sold out. And sitting up on the dais with me were Jimmy V, Abe Lemons, Dale Brown, Chuck Daly, and local Detroit columnist Joe Falls, who was inducted into the baseball Hall of Fame in 2003. Man, they made their cracks and really had a lot of fun at my expense.

Then Jimmy gets up for the boffo finish.

He pulled out a letter, dated 1980, and said, "I'd like to read this letter to you beautiful Titan fans and all you Pistons fans."

It was from Willis Casey, who had been the NC State AD at the time. It read, "Dear Dick: We are sorry to inform you that we have hired Jim Valvano of Iona as our new head coach. Thank you so much for your interest in the position at North Carolina State."

Nobody else had known about it before that night. I couldn't even get an interview, and Jimmy had gotten hold of my job application.

"I beat you again, buddy," he said.

But I loved Jimmy for his enthusiasm and spirit.

He fought for his reputation on the court, too, man.

One time when NC State was playing North Carolina, I was doing the game. State had the lead, but, over the airwaves, I said, "Don't leave this telecast. Dean Smith is Michelangelo, the best in the business in the last four minutes. He's a miracle man."

Jimmy called me the next day and said, "Hey, man, we're winning the game. You're supposed to be a buddy, and yet here you are talking about the miracle worker, talking about what a great guy Dean Smith is. You never said anything about us—and we won the game."

"You're right," I admitted, "but Dean Smith truly is the Michelangelo of coaching, man. Jimmy V, you've got to admit it, he's an artist at work. Plus, he's a Hall of Famer."

Valvano looked like he might be headed in that direction, too, after the Wolfpack shocked America.

Elvis, eat your heart out, baby. This is my flying Elvis impersonation at the 2000 ESPY Awards show at the MGM Grand in Las Vegas. Man, I'll do anything for ESPN.

It all started back in September, 1979, when I joined ESPN—not long after the fledgling network had hired Bob Ley. Here we are on the sets of *SportsCenter Plus* (top) and ESPN's *College Basketball Report* (bottom).

Hey, here I am in the middle of the Illinois student section, the Orange Krush. Sharing time with the students and fans is something I love doing when I visit campuses throughout America.

I had the good fortune to be the featured speaker at the 1984 Naismith Awards ceremony when Michael "the Magnificent" was honored as the collegiate Player of the Year. He went on to become the greatest ever to play the game.

I feel blessed to have worked with so many wonderful partners during my career. Among them are Robin Roberts (left), who's become a star now on *Good Morning America*, and Keith Jackson (right), who with his "Whoa Nellie!" has become Mr. Football.

Here I'm talking hoops with two very special people—the late Jimmy V, who meant a great deal to me, and Hall of Famer Mike Krzyzewski.

© ESPN

How lucky I've been to work with broadcasting standouts like Mike Patrick (left) and Brad Nessler (right). These guys have put me in a comfort zone that allows me to be myself.

My buddy John Saunders and I hang out with Olympic track star Mike Powell before the Foot Locker Slam Fest. Powell was one of the athletic stars who participated in the contest.

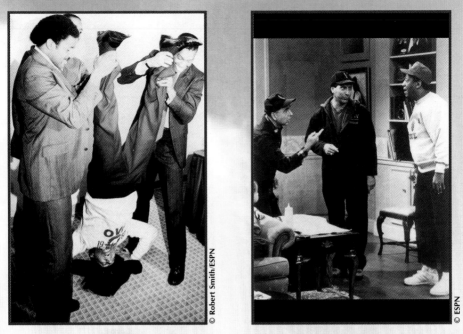

"**Austin Peay vs. Illinois in the 1987 NCAA Tournament? (left)** Are you kidding me? Austin Peay has no shot. If they win, I'll stand on my head." As you can see, Austin Peay won—and their players helped me keep my word.

Here I am with two of the funniest guys I've ever met (right)—my late friend Jimmy Valvano and Bill Cosby. Valvano and I were playing V&V Movers on *The Cosby Show*. Let me tell you, Valvano had Cosby in stitches.

Dickie V with his own sitcom? Not quite. *Hoops Malone* was actually a series of commercials ESPN put together to promote college basketball. Here I am with my TV family.

Bob Ley and I shoot the breeze with the late Al McGuire and Billy Packer about the game we all love—college basketball. McGuire was one of the warm, genuine characters in the game, and Packer is a hoops guru with CBS.

Here I share a laugh with one of the greatest minds ever to grace the basketball hardwood, the Michelangelo of coaching, Dean Smith of North Carolina.

David Robinson, "the Admiral" as I liked to call him, was a first-class student athlete who became a prime time player on the NBA level. He'll now be a success in the real world.

© Norvelle Kennedy

© Jeff Camarati/ESPN

Say what you want about "the General," Bob Knight (left), but he's a guy with integrity and has always praised genuine student athletes, such as Robinson or **Mike Krzyzewski (right, teasing me about my bald dome)**. Krzyzewski played for Knight at West Point and has since become a Rolls Royce Hall of Fame coach.

Jimmy Boeheim, a guy with a heart of gold, took time immediately after winning the 2003 NCAA championship to take a photo with my daughter, Terri, her husband, Chris Sforzo, and my granddaughter, Sydney.

© Einstein Photo

© Einstein Photo

At Sonny Vaccaro's Roundball Classic (left), Lorraine and I were able to shoot the breeze with Magic about his Showtime days with the Lakers.

Grant Hill (right) learned from his mom and dad that being a good person is as important as being a good player. His father, Calvin (at left), was a star running back with the Dallas Cowboys.

© ESPN

Let me tell you, being around the students has kept me feeling young. I have a blast no matter what campus I go to or what I do, whether it's leading the Michigan band in "Hail to the Victors" (top) or being passed up through the stands by Duke's Cameron Crazies (bottom).

I love picking up the microphone and speaking to youngsters all over America, especially about making good decisions in the game of life.

Here I am at the age of 64 (left), acting like I'm 12, shooting the J against a 10-year-old.

Hey, did you know I could play a horn? (right) And if you believe that, I've got some real estate to sell you, baby.

P. Diddy (top), Burt Reynolds (bottom left), Jack Nicholson (bottom right), and my guys Tommy Lasorda and Herman Boone (center)— Boone's life was portrayed by Denzel Washington in the movie *Remember the Titans*. You'd better believe these guys are up on my Wall of Fame.

While he was trying out for the Chicago White Sox during spring training, MJ lived in the same subdivision as my family in Sarasota, Florida.

Man, do I love horses. And what a thrill it was to be in the paddock area with the champ, Muhammad Ali, at the Kentucky Derby.

Hey, Rick Pitino knew of my love for horses and asked me to join him and two of his buddies in buying a two-year-old horse that we named It's Awesome, Baby. It was amazing to watch the horse win for the first time at the Maiden Special on July 4, 2003.

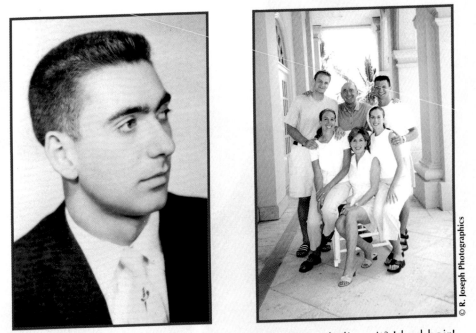

© R. Joseph Photographics

My high school graduation picture (left)—can you believe it? I had hair!

My wonderful family (right)—my daughter, Sherri, and her husband, Thomas Krug (left); my daughter, Terri, and her husband, Chris Sforzo (right); and my wife, Lorraine (center). As Bobby Knight once teased me, any woman who can live with me for over 30 years deserves sainthood.

The three newest joys of my life—I've already taken my granddaughter, Sydney (top), to a Notre Dame-Florida State game. I can't wait to dress my twin grandsons, Connor and Jake (bottom), in their Notre Dame uniforms and take them to their first game in South Bend.

Are you serious? I've been inducted into seven Halls of Fame—not bad for a guy who can't run, shoot or jump and has a body built on linguine. Here I am with my wife, Lorraine, at my induction into the Florida Sports Hall of Fame. You'd better believe I feel like I'm *Living a Dream*.

Dick Vitale

The irony was that they almost hadn't gotten into the NCAA Tournament. State was just 17-10 heading into the ACC Tournament and was looking at an NIT bid if they didn't win the title. But they swept by Wake Forest and North Carolina, then shocked Virginia and Ralph Sampson, 81-78, in the finals.

That was just the start of the electrical storm to come. The Pack erased a six-point deficit with 24 seconds left, then went ahead to defeat Jimmy Harrick's Pepperdine team in double OT in the first round and ended with that dramatic victory over the heavily favored Cougars.

Houston was 27-2 entering the tournament and had all kinds of shining stars like 7' center Hakeem Olajuwon, who was by then known as "Akeem the Dream," Clyde "The Glide" Drexler, Michael Young and Larry Micheaux. Olajuwon came to Houston from Nigeria, where he had been a soccer goalie. But he had turned into a big star and eventually became the No. 1 pick in the draft.

The team was so famous, it even had its own fraternity—the Phi Slamma Jammas.

And the Cougars lived up to their hype during a 94-81 victory over Louisville in The Pit, going on a spectacular dunk-a-thon that wiped out an eight-point deficit and completely turned the game around. It was a preview of what people thought basketball would be like in the 21st century.

NC State, on the other hand, just managed to squeeze by Georgia, 67-60, to get to the finals. Watching that game was like watching two JV teams scrimmage compared to the fireworks displayed in the Houston-Louisville game.

Nobody gave Jim Valvano much of a chance.

But he had a couple of tricks left in that magic wand of his. The day before the game, he told the media, "If we get the opening tap, we won't take a shot till Tuesday morning."

State lulled Houston to sleep by slowing the tempo down long enough to pull into a 52-52 tie. State had the ball with a minute left when Jimmy yelled, "One shot!" We all know what happened next.

It was shock city, an incredible David-versus-Goliath upset. Shock city. And Jimmy had the perfect line to celebrate.

"How do I like Albuquerque?" he asked. "Albuquerque is the greatest city the Lord ever made. My wife is pregnant and—she doesn't know this yet—I'm going to name the kid Al B. Querque."

Jim Valvano was on a roll after that. He won 20 or more games in each of his first eight years in the job, won two ACC titles and reached the Final Eight three times.

And he also knew how to make that cash register ring-a-ling-ding, baby.

There was a big article in *USA Today* that reported he was making something like $600,000-700,000 with all the extras, which included his speaking engagements and various endorsements in addition to his coaching and administrative responsibilities. Our producer at ESPN wanted me to interview him, and they were going to show with graphics what the paper had reported.

He'd said he didn't mind coming on *SportsCenter*, so when we had him on, I hit him up with the numbers.

"Jimmy, you've got a lot of professors screaming and yelling and calling each other over how much you're making," I said. "They say you're pulling in $600,000-700,000 a year."

And, as only Jimmy V could do with his sense of humor, he replied, "No. Hey, that was like two years ago. If they're going to report it, they should at least get it right. I'm making a lot more than that right now."

He knew what he was worth.

Obviously, Jimmy made some mistakes along the way, too.

Jimmy thought he could change every kid for the better, even Chris Washburn. Remember, Washburn was a 6'11" center from Hickory, North Carolina, who was America's guest. There were about a hundred guys recruiting him. If he had picked up the phone and called any of them, they'd have sent the limo or had the private jet fired up in a heartbeat. Jimmy was guilty of just one thing—he was a better recruiter in the hunt for Washburn than his competitors. He and his buddy, Tommy Abatemarco, recruited the kid when he was one of the top five prospects in the country. They thought that the kid would take them to the promised land.

They almost made it happen, too.

The good times ended for Valvano in 1990, a season after Peter Golenbock, who, with help from a former student manager, wrote a book entitled *Personal Fouls,* in which he alleged that Valvano and NC State officials had repeatedly covered up for failing students. The book claimed that Washburn—who played for the Pack in 1984 and '85 before he left for the pros—had scored just 470 out of a possible 1600 on his SAT. It further claimed that Washburn had been allowed back on the team after he'd pled guilty to stealing a stereo from an undergraduate, for which he received a suspended sentence and was ordered to perform community service.

Washburn, a first-round pick of Golden State in 1986, was banned for life from the NBA in 1989 after testing positive for substance abuse three separate times. Man, that '86 draft has to rank as one of the sorriest of all time in terms of the players taken who were involved in the drug scene. That was the year Lenny Bias was taken at No. 2 by the Boston Celtics. William Bedford of Memphis and Roy Tarpley of Michigan were also part of that draft. It's sad when you think how good these guys could have been if they'd only listened to the right people.

Golenbock's book also charged that players had traded shoes for cash at a local store and suggested that Jimmy had too many outside business interests. Bruce Poulton, the chancellor, resigned. Jimmy also resigned as AD but stayed on as coach for another year. When State visited Duke that season, the Cameron Crazies littered the floor with sneakers.

What bothered me about the book was the fact that it never presented the side of Jimmy that was positive, how he influenced so many kids. It offered only the views of those who were disgruntled and had a chip on their shoulders, as opposed to sharing the opinions of those who loved him, too—kids like Chris Corchiani, Tom Guglilotta, Dereck Whittenburg, Sidney Lowe, Rodney Monroe, Thurl Bailey, and a host of others.

The one thing I want to make very clear is that Jimmy V received a letter from the NCAA enforcement office stating that he was not guilty of any involvement in recruiting violations. But trust me, his heart was broken big time when all of this started to appear in the papers.

Jimmy eventually left NC State under a cloud of controversy and negative publicity. He had felt a lot of pain when the book hit the stores. It became a nightmare for him because he felt that the book was so one-sided. I certainly agreed with him.

Jimmy always had a way to find humor in even the most dismal situations. In fact, I've always loved one of Jimmy's lines—he said once, "Everybody gives me heat. They get on my case, man, about players not graduating and point to my graduation rates at NC State. How come they don't factor in my graduation rates at Johns Hopkins and Bucknell? Throw them in there, man, and I've got a hell of a graduation rate."

Jimmy found out the hard way that you can take on one or two kids who are borderline academically; but when you start to take on more than that, it can end in disaster. But it all comes down to the pressure to win. When you're living in the same neighborhood as North Carolina and Duke, it's tough to compete.

And Jimmy was about competition. I know that from experience.

Jimmy had played for Rutgers before he got into coaching. He was part of some outstanding Rutgers teams that were coached by Bill Foster. Dick Lloyd was able to obtain a wealth of information when he had served as an assistant under Foster. And believe me, I gained much of that same knowledge when I was Dick Lloyd's assistant. Foster, who went on to Utah, Duke, and South Carolina, was one of the most innovative minds I've ever met in the game. Through him and Lloyd, I was able to meet Jimmy Valvano.

Then when I was at Rutgers, we played against him when he was the coach at Bucknell—I would tease him how it was cupcake city, baby, cupcake city. Then we really got to know each other in the recruiting wars.

Once I started to cover his games on TV, we really got to know each other, and man, our relationship just blossomed when Jimmy came over to ESPN after he got out of coaching. His last season at NC State was '89-90—he coached his team to an 18-12 record—and then he joined us at ESPN for the 1990-91 season.

He had a way with so many people.

Bill Cosby called ESPN once to talk about which Atlantic 10 team would join the conference champion in the NCAA Tournament.

Bill was a big Temple fan, and he defended his alma mater. Jimmy was a Rutgers graduate, and he supported his team. Those two ended up making a bet. If Rutgers made the field, Jimmy said he and I would be guests on *The Cosby Show*. If Temple made it, the Cos would appear on our ESPN Tournament Selection Show. Both teams made it, and we got to appear on Cosby's show.

We played the part of V and V Movers on the show. I showed up on Monday in New York, figuring the shoot would last an hour or so, that I would do my thing and then leave. But I was greeted by Jimmy V with, "Where have you been? You've got to be here for at least four days."

You've got to spend much of that time in the studio. There are all kinds of meetings with writers, dress rehearsals, and after all that, then you do the actual show in front of a live audience.

It was a blast. I was there from Monday to Thursday, having an awesome time, baby.

Cosby asked us to dinner, so we went to a nice Italian restaurant in the Village, and it was a riot. I was humbled—so was Jimmy—big time. People kept coming up to the table with cameras, wanting to take pictures, asking us, "Excuse me, can you take my picture with Mr. Cosby?"

"Hey, what about us?" we replied. "Can't we be in the picture?"

"We don't want your picture. We want Mr. Cosby."

You want to know what a star really is? Go out with a guy like Bill Cosby and you'll find out. Jimmy V and I certainly found out that we were little players on the big scene compared to Mr. Cosby.

Then I watched Jimmy V do his magic. He had an unbelievable sense of humor, and soon he had the funniest man in the world on the floor, laughing hysterically. Remember, at that time, Cosby's sitcom was the toast of the nation and was No. 1 in every poll.

Jimmy told me that Tommy Lasorda asked him once to be a celebrity batboy for the Dodgers. He got all dressed up in his Dodger Blue. Now, I'd have gone for something like that, but Tommy never asked me.

Another guy whom Lasorda did ask, though, was the NBA's Mike Fratello. One thing about Lasorda is that he's consistent—all Paesano, baby. Can you imagine? Lasorda, Valvano, Fratello—all he'd have to do is ask Vitale, and we'd have what sounds like an Italian construction company.

Jimmy told me that one of the thrills he had in being around Tommy Lasorda and the Dodgers was that he got to meet Francis Albert Sinatra. "Yes," Jimmy V said, "it was just golden having the chance to share words with the Chairman of the Board."

I would have given my right arm to have been there. I thought the world of Frank Sinatra, and I did get my own chance to meet him at the Pine Knob Center in the suburbs of Detroit when I went back to present him with a basketball.

I felt so bad for my wife, though. She had gotten all geared up to meet him, but security would only allow the presenter to go in. I didn't know what to say.

"Well, you go in," she said.

So I went in and gave him the basketball. He probably had no idea who I was, but I got a chance to have my picture taken with Ol' Blue Eyes. You know *he's* on my Wall of Fame—front and center, baby.

So, anyway, when Jimmy joined ABC and ESPN after his tenure at NC State, he took to it like he was a natural. And then, a year later, Jimmy began to complain vociferously about back pain.

We were doing special shows from the 1992 Final Four in Minneapolis. Jimmy would stand up when we weren't on the air and complain about his back pain. The red light would come on the camera, though, and he'd sit right back down and be as funny as ever. And then, when the lights would go off, he'd turn and groan, "Oh, my back is killing me. Oh, the pain in my back."

"Jimmy, man, get an aspirin," I told him. "You'll be fine. Stop complaining. You'll be fine."

Little did any of us know this would end up being a much more serious problem. Two months later, he went to the doctor, thinking he had a disc problem. Then he found out the tragic news—he had acute and aggressive bone cancer.

When he told me, over the phone, there were a lot of tears shed between us. I can remember our conversations almost word for word, and we would share stories about our children and our lives. And Jimmy would break down, saying he couldn't believe that this was happening to him at such a young age. Man, it crushed me to hear him crying like a baby.

The disease got progressively worse.

I'll never forget him telling me, very emphatically, one time, "You find out about true love and what it really means when you're faced with a life-threatening situation like I am. Man, I found out about love. Let me tell you, Dick. Love is when you're throwing up all over after chemotherapy and your family is at your side, trying to comfort you. Love is when you're in such pain that you can't even pull up your underwear and your wife is there to help. That's love, man; that's love."

Also, I can't forget this one night when I was at ESPN for the weekend and Jimmy was there as well. We were each staying at the hotel across the street from ESPN's main campus in Bristol.

I was having dinner when I received a call to join Jimmy up in his room to watch *The Frank Sinatra Story* on TV. When I arrived in his room, he was pounding the walls and screaming as loud as could be about the pain that was running through his body. He ran to the bathroom and started popping aspirin after aspirin, and then he told me, "Just think of your worst toothache, and that's the kind of pain I feel—except that I feel that throughout my entire body and it just doesn't want to go away."

We hugged and hugged. I get so emotional when I think of that moment to think that he had to go through such a painful period. My friends, that's why I get so worked up many a time on TV when I'm giving out the 1-800-4-JIMMYV number to raise money for cancer—because there are so many beautiful, innocent people whom we all know who have to battle through that disease. Believe me, it's not a fun time for anyone involved, especially the family.

Jimmy wasn't afraid to share his feelings. I'll always remember how touched I was to receive a handwritten note from Jimmy V about a week after we had spoken on the phone about his battle with cancer. He wrote to me, "Dickie, slow down, man. Slow down. You're going at too fast a pace." I guess that's always been my way, but just the fact that he'd told me that let me know he cared about me.

I know I cared about him, too.

Jimmy was in New York City on March 4, 1993 for the ESPY Awards at Radio City Music Hall, where he was scheduled to receive the Arthur Ashe Award for Courage.

Duke coach Mike Krzyzewski and his wife, Micki, had been on the same flight with Jimmy and said he'd been ill on the plane. Now, let me tell you why I love Mike Krzyzewski so much—he and his wife are special people. I mean, Mike is such a humanitarian. I could go on and on, story after story about the love he showed for Jimmy during his tough battle. Mike and John Saunders were so close to Jimmy at a time when he needed them most. That's why I have such great respect for both.

When I saw Jimmy at the hotel, he was throwing up and just feeling miserable.

I remember talking to Jimmy's wife, Pam, the night before, after having been to the rehearsal. I called to let Jimmy know that it was going to be a special night. They were going to announce the V Foundation, and Jimmy was going to be the first recipient of the Arthur Ashe Award for Courage.

Jimmy was so determined to beat this disease that he was doing everything possible. And his doctor had suggested that he might be able to join the lucky few who have had success in the battle with the cancer that he was faced with. I knew he had just gone for his regular checkup and was anxious to hear the report from the doctor. That was when he found out really bad news.

I asked Pam to get Jimmy to come to the phone and she said, "He's in his room, crying. He just learned from the doctor on his regular checkup that the cancer has spread throughout his body."

I begged her to get him on the phone, and Jimmy finally came on. I can still hear his words: "Dick, you think I'm thinking about awards, man? I'm thinking about my wife. I'm thinking about my kids—Nicole, LeAnne and Jamie." We were both in tears. He said how much he loved them and how he would miss them. Jimmy was not thinking about going to the ESPYs.

I told him, "Please, make sure you come to the event."

Well, he did. And Mike Krzyzewski was a big help in making certain that Jimmy was there for this special night, when the formation of the V Foundation would be announced.

Shortly before the show, I asked the crew to bring a boom mike to where Jimmy was sitting. That way, after receiving his award, he could say a quick thank you and not have to struggle toward the stage. But when Jimmy found out about that, he got angry.

"I didn't come here for a simple thank you," he told me. "I've got something to say. You get me to the podium."

One of the great actors of our time, an All-Rolls Roycer, Dustin Hoffman, introduced the Arthur Ashe Award and spoke about what it epitomizes. Dustin then introduced me to present Jimmy V with the award.

Mike Krzyzewski, Joe Theismann and yours truly had to carry Jimmy to the stage and then walk him back to his seat as he received a thunderous standing ovation from all the stars present.

Man, I thought Jimmy would just say a quick "thank you" and sit down after I presented him with the award. But he electrified the audience with one of the greatest speeches that I've ever heard. Jimmy rocked the house. The crowd at that place and the TV audience heard something they will never forget. Jimmy V was at his best.

I was stunned watching him. He had the crowd in the palm of his hand as he poured out his heart about battling cancer. I still get goose bumps when I think of what he said.

He talked about cancer, about life—about how one day, you're on top of the world, and the next day, you're fighting for your life. And that's what Jimmy was fighting for.

Then Jimmy said, "There are three things we all should do every day: We should laugh every day. We should spend time in thought. We should have our emotions moved to tears—it could be from happiness or joy. If we laugh, we think, and we cry, that's a full day. That's a heckuva day."

He told the audience always to dream big dreams. Then Jimmy, with his voice breaking, offered this advice on life: "Don't give up. Don't ever give up."

If you didn't get moved by those words, something was wrong with you.

The next day, he received calls from President Clinton, Johnny Carson and Bill Cosby. Sometimes when I want to get motivated, I turn on the tape of that speech. It's still used by many whenever they need motivation.

Jimmy died on April 28,1993. He was 47.

Let me tell you. Nothing breaks your heart more than going to the cancer wards in hospitals. I've met lots of people—young kids—battling that disease. I walk out and think that sometimes we can all—including yours truly—be so selfish, when we complain about the little things like travel and schedules and so on. Sometimes I leave with tears in my eyes, because it hurts so much to see people suffer.

But Jimmy V decided to do something more about cancer than just cry.

When Jimmy was 17, he'd written his life goals on an index card. He wanted to become a coach, to win a game in Madison Square Garden, and to cut down the nets after winning a national championship. Shortly before his death, Pam Valvano found another index card in the pocket of one of Jimmy's sports coats. He'd made a new list: he wanted to learn to play the piano, to learn to paint, and to find a cure for cancer.

In February 1993, with the help of ESPN, Jimmy formed the V Foundation to raise money for cancer research.

He told all of his buddies, "I want to beat cancer. I might not be able to beat it by myself, but I'm going to beat it by you guys not forgetting about me and raising millions of dollars to help find a cure." He had a game plan on how to put this foundation together.

Bob Lloyd, Jimmy's teammate who retired at age 50 after a successful run in the corporate world and now lives in Maui, has devoted his life to his buddy and heads the board of directors. He puts on a wine festival in the Napa Valley that raises approximately $1 million annually. Mike Krzyzewski, John Saunders and yours truly are co-chairs of the Jimmy V Golf Classic, our golf outing every summer that raises a million-plus for the V Foundation for cancer research. The head of the golf classic is one of Jimmy's closest buddies, Frank McCann, who gave up a job in the corporate world to head up the golf classic for his late friend, whom he loved dearly. Jimmy's brother, Nick, is the CEO of the V Foundation, and with the help of Jimmy's wife, Pam, and his children, the V Foundation has flourished.

Pam was so excited when she called me in the spring of 2003 to tell me that Bill Cosby was going to do a special show that summer in honor of Jimmy and in celebration of the 10th anniversary of the Jimmy V Golf Classic. Man, it'll be like old times when they re-air the "V and V Movers" segment that Jimmy and I did with Bill on his sitcom.

I'm so proud to say that with the efforts of people like Bob Lloyd, the Valvano family, and all the others involved with the V Foundation, over $30 million has been raised and utilized in research grants across this nation to battle a disease that we all despise.

Which brings me to Mark Kelly.

I got a call from the Make-a-Wish Foundation in 1992. This youngster from Long Island wanted to spend a weekend with me at the Final Four.

"Well, certainly," I said. The caller from Make-a-Wish told me that Mark had gone through seven major operations to battle the cancer that had spread in his body. So he came out to Minneapolis with his mother, and we hit it off. While he was there, Jimmy V and I entertained him and introduced him to the coaches and all the people on our set.

Well, it just shows you how things sometimes do work out in the end.

When the Make-a-Wish Foundation sends kids to Disneyland— or wherever they want to go—it means the youngsters are really struggling. It's a tough time in their lives. Anyway, the beautiful part of this story is, 11 years later, Mark Kelly is cancer-free.

He goes for tests regularly, but he is living proof that the research being done by doctors today can get your life back on track and moving in a positive direction.

Mark now works for ESPN and does a wonderful job in the research department. At the Jimmy V Basketball Classic in 2002, I had the chance to speak to the crowd at the Meadowlands in New Jersey about the V Foundation. I invited Mark to be there as an example to show that our efforts can work, that all those dollars raised and put toward research have helped people like Mark Kelly to go on with their lives in a positive way. I will never forget the wonderful response of the crowd when I told them about Mark's story.

You know, it's ironic that 20 years after Jimmy V had that magical night in Albuquerque, Syracuse coach Jim Boeheim won his national title. Jimmy B is a cancer survivor. He beat prostate cancer because of early detection.

And when I think of Jimmy V, I can't help but think about Al McGuire, the great Marquette coach, who passed away at the age of 72 on January 26, 2000, at a hospice in Milwaukee after developing a blood disorder that was reportedly acute leukemia. The school band played "Danny Boy" and "You Can Call Me Al" at his memorial service that weekend when Marquette played Tulane.

Jimmy V and Al McGuire were both American originals.

Al coached Marquette to a 295-80 record in 13 years from 1964 through 1977. The Eagles made 11 straight postseason appearances. McGuire, who sent 26 of his players to the NBA, was inducted into the Basketball Hall of Fame in 1992.

His greatest asset was his ability to understand people. And he never forgot his roots, either. The son of Irish immigrants, Al grew up in the Rockaways around the family bar. As a kid, he spent a lot of his time on a playground overlooking the beach. Al overachieved athletically.

I was a big fan of basketball years ago when Marty Glickman called the games on radio and the McGuire brothers—Dick and Al—played for Frank McGuire (no relation) at St. John's along with backcourt star Jack McMahon when the Johnnies went to the NCAA Final Four in 1953.

Al was a street fighter out of New York. He was a guy who always gave you the impression: "Aw, I never coach. I just sit back, throw out the balls and watch the game." Bull. Forget about it. This guy was a master psychologist, man. He could have received a doctorate in psychology from Harvard, he was so sharp. He knew people—he knew how to orchestrate a team, he knew how to size up the officials, he knew which official he couldn't jump on, he knew what player he could get on.

Al was one of the first white coaches to recruit inner-city players. He wasn't afraid to take the subway to Harlem, and he assembled a team filled with kids from inner-city New York and Chicago that won an NIT and got to two Final Fours.

McGuire did not discourage players from declaring early for the pros if he thought it was in their best interest—as in the case of Jim Chones in 1972. "I looked in my refrigerator and it was full," McGuire said. "I looked in Jimmy's refrigerator and it was empty."

Al was a Damon Runyon type of character and the first $50,000 coach in college basketball history. His teams constantly played before sellout crowds in the MECCA. His 1977 team with Butch Lee was good enough to beat North Carolina and win a national championship in Atlanta.

That night, at age 48, Al McGuire walked away from coaching.

Why?

My take is that Al had reached the pinnacle—that unbelievable moment at the top that all coaches dream about—and thought, "I've got it all now. So why not just jump on my motorcycle, man, and head on down the highway?" I think he'd had enough. He was tired of coaching and ADing, tired of the Xs and Os, tired of going to the gym every day.

He also felt it was time to move on with public speaking and TV. It turned out to be a great decision. The next year, NBC offered him the chance to become a college basketball analyst, joining play-by-play man Dick Enberg and Billy Packer, even though Al had no network experience.

He was "Showtime" before the Lakers earned that nickname, man.

McGuire's teams always walked with a swagger, which sometimes upset opposing coaches. Once, before their game, Notre Dame coach Johnny Dee had his players hand out mustard packs to the Marquette starters during introductions.

McGuire gave his players complete freedom of expression. He let them wear those bumble-bee uniforms with flapping shirt tails that were designed by the players.

Al drove a motorcycle, collected toy soldiers and had his own unconventional wisdom. Among other things, he said:

• "The best players come from neighborhoods where there are cracked sidewalks."

• "If a waitress's ankles are dirty, it means the chili is good."

• "You can always tell a Catholic school by the length of the cheerleaders' skirts."

He even developed his own language, which found its way into the *Milwaukee Sentinal.*

There were *prime time players,* and then there were *dance hall players*—like himself—who didn't have a lot of talent but had a lot of resolve. *Uptown* meant a postseason invitation. There was *Park Avenue,* where everything is first class, and *Tenth Avenue,* where everything isn't. There were *aircraft carriers*—big centers; *blue chippers*— great players; and, for close games, *white knucklers.* An agent was a *backroom lawyer.* Shooters who got fancy received *diving points.* And officials were *zebras.*

When he was at NBC, Al showed up at Duke one time decked out in safari gear with a hunting hat, chair and whip. He was cracking that whip and throwing peanuts to the Cameron Crazies. Sometimes he didn't know the names of players, but that didn't stop him. Once, Packer got the guy who was holding Al's cue cards to drop them. Al had no idea who the player was, so he just called him "Treetop."

As Billy Reed wrote in *Basketball Times,* we are losing some of the great characters we've had in college hoops—guys like Jimmy and

Al, Rollie Massimino of Villanova, Lefty Driesell of Maryland, Dale Brown of LSU, Louie Carnesecca of St. John's, Abe Lemons of Oklahoma City, and Digger Phelps—guys who made the game so much fun.

They were showmen. They were as big as the game itself.

We have a new breed of sophisticated coaches these days. Television has created them. Everybody is trying to be this classy guy. They're all so reserved at press conferences, so guarded with every comment. People aren't as loose and as free today as some of these guys once were.

I miss that.

So, as a tribute to Al, here's my All-Al McGuire team. These are coaches who've been electrifying at the microphones and at press conferences, guys who've been unique on the sidelines, guys who've had such personality and flair that they generated their own excitement.

We've got to start with my guy, Jimmy Valvano. I'd get a kick out of it every time when he would say, "My name is Jim Valvano, Iona College." He told me one time, "People would ask, 'What? You own a college?'" He always had those great one-liners.

Then we go to Lou Carnesecca. Luigi. He's in the Hall of Fame. I loved doing his games. He'd put on that lucky sweater of his on the sidelines. And he'd dance—man, he was Mikhail Baryshnikov after a big play on the sidelines.

And what about Lefty Driesell of Maryland? I know he didn't win the national championship. But what about the excitement the Ol' Left Hander brought to the campus of College Park when he said, "We will be the UCLA of the East!" He finally won an ACC Tournament in 1984, and I can still remember him talking about how he was going to put that gold trophy on the hood of his car and drive it all over the state of North Carolina.

My buddy Mike Patrick—whom I personally feel is Mr. ACC and who has such great love, understanding, and knowledge of the game—and I have shared many a laugh when trying to picture Lefty on his victory drive after that '84 championship game.

Rollie Massimino of Villanova would always pour out his heart and soul on the sidelines. He'd start out in his nice suit and wind up looking like Columbo by the end of the game. Talk about emotion, talk about linguini, talk about a guy who enjoyed every moment—he had the rumpled-up clothes and all those wonderful expressions.

When Billy Tubbs, who just took over at Lamar, was at Oklahoma, he could be a funny guy—except when you were playing him. He'd press all over and he'd say, "If I can get 200, I'll get 200." I still think about the time he grabbed the microphone to try to calm down the crowd at Lloyd Noble Arena after a bad call. "I know the referees have done a poor job, but don't throw anything on the floor."

Digger Phelps coached Notre Dame to a Final Four in 1978. But he always likes to let you know about his accomplishments—even 10 years after he left. I've heard five million times in the studio about that win over UCLA when they knocked off the Bruins in 1974 after they had won 88 in a row. We're on the set and we're talking about somebody winning a big game, and he's in my eardrum, "Dickie V, Dickie V, you'd better remind them—UCLA. Who put an end to it? Who put an end to it?"

No list would be complete without Dale Brown, the preacher man. Dale loves to travel. He once tried to recruit Arvydas Sabonis from Lithuania. And he loves to talk about recruiting Shaquille O'Neal. He was in Europe when he ran into this kid on an army base in Germany. The kid was so big, he thought he was a college kid. Dale went over to say hello.

Dale asked him, "What school do you play at?"

And the kid said, "I'm only 12 years old."

I can just see Dale's eyes light up—"I'm going to stay in touch."

And he did. He eventually got Shaquille to sign with LSU.

I received a call from Dale in May 2003, after I'd read in the paper that he'd had a stroke. I was shocked. My God, I couldn't believe it. Dale is 67. He doesn't smoke or drink. He's in great shape physically. But he suffered a major stroke in April at his home in Baton Rouge and had to be taken to Our Lady of the Lake Hospital. When he arrived, he heard his wife talking to the doctor, who told her he didn't know if Dale was going to make it. His carotid arteries were 95 percent blocked, and doctors weren't sure they could even do the surgery.

Then, before the decision had been made, Brown claimed, there was a miracle. The arteries were suddenly clear and the blood clot had disappeared.

"I always thought I'd die falling from the Matterhorn or being eaten by Big Foot," said Brown, who has climbed the mountain and searched for the legendary creature.

Brown is back in his office, running two miles a day.

There are only so many miracles to go around, though. Some people die before their time. I can still remember Hank Gathers—a first-team All-American from Loyola-Marymount who led the country in scoring and rebounding in 1989—collapsing on Gersten Pavilion, his home court, the next season during the semifinals of the West Coast Conference Tournament.

I was lying in bed watching the highlights on *SportsCenter* when I saw him collapse. It was so scary. In the Catholic religion, St. Jude is the patron saint of miracles. My mother had given me a St. Jude card years ago, when I lost my eye as a kid—before I'd reached the age of five—and I still keep one in my left pocket all the time. I took that card off my nightstand that night and started praying, "Please, don't let this be."

Unfortunately, it was.

Gathers died later that night of a heart ailment.

The conference tournament was suspended, but Loyola still went to the NCAA Tournament because they were the regular-season champions. When they got to the West Regional finals, Bo Kimble, Gathers's high school teammate in Philadelphia, went off for big numbers. Kimble paid tribute to his friend by shooting a left-handed free throw at the start of each of the Lions' three victories, as Gathers had done.

He made them all.

"They could have gone over the backboard, but America wanted them to go in," Kimble said 10 years later when the school retired both his and Gathers's number.

Can it really have been that long ago? Time flies.

The one sad part of my life now is that I'm at an age where so many friends and people I've come to admire and respect are either ill or have passed away. It hurts because you know it's winding down to the last chapter.

It seems like only yesterday when Dave DeBusschere, the most famous player ever to wear a University of Detroit uniform, was a key player on those world championship teams with the Knicks in the '70s. He died May 14, 2003, but he had affected my life big time. He always denied it when I saw him, but I firmly believe he played a role in my getting the University of Detroit job.

I'll tell you how.

One day, I was in the Knicks' locker room. I was very close friends with Willis Reed because he and I ran a charity game for a youngster, Sammie Davis—no relation to the entertainer—who had lost both his legs and one of his arms in a train accident. Through Willis's name and contacts, I was able to get many NBA stars to play every summer in Clifton, New Jersey, to raise money for this youngster.

I told Willis I'd like to meet Dave DeBusschere because he represents all the things I love about basketball—toughness, defense, setting the screen, making the open shot. Dave DeBusschere had it all. He was the consummate team player.

DeBusschere came over and we started talking. He made you feel like he was your best friend. Now, I'm looking for a job because Dick Lloyd had resigned at Rutgers and it didn't look like I was going to get the head coaching job. DeBusschere was heading into the shower, but he stepped back out and said, "Hey, why don't you apply at my alma mater? They're looking for a coach."

Willis turned around and said, "Hey, Dave, that's a great idea. Why don't you call for him? He'd be great with young kids."

And that was the end of it for that day.

All I know is that, two weeks later, the phone rang at my house. It was Bob Calihan, the AD at Detroit, the guy who had coached Dave DeBusschere. He said, "We'd like to fly you in." I thought it was a joke because he said, "Hey, you pay your way out and we'll reimburse you when you get here."

When I got off the phone, I said to my wife, "Reimburse me?" I didn't have a lot of money then. I was making about $11,000 as an assistant coach.

I said to myself, "Suppose this is not true. Suppose my friends are playing a joke on me."

So I called him back: "Mr. Calihan, this is Dick Vitale."

He said, "Yeah, I just called you a little while ago."

"Oh, I just wanted to make sure."

I went there and I was fortunate enough to get the job. I guess since it was a Catholic school, when they asked me what it would take for me to be their coach, I said, "Well, I'm making $11,000 as an assistant at Rutgers. Give me $15,000."

They looked at me in shock and said, "Okay, let's hire this guy."

Man, I could have used some financial advice. Where were all my buddies—guys like Valvano, McGuire, and company who knew a little about negotiating for cash—when I needed them?

I guess they figured they got me cheap, giving me $15,000 instead of having to pay some established head coach $20,000-plus. Maybe I got the job because of economics instead of ability.

Afterward, every time I'd run into Dave DeBusschere at different functions, I'd say to him, "Man, Dave, I really appreciate it."

He'd say, "Dick, I didn't do anything. You got it on your own merit."

I still believe, to this day, that he wanted to remain in the background, but that he'd called his former coach and said, "There's a young guy out of the East. You ought to at least take a look at him."

Another guy who affected my life was the late Larry Donald, the editor and publisher of *Basketball Times*. He received the Curt Gowdy Award from the Hall of Fame in 1998, the same year I received that award for broadcasting. My buddy Dick Weiss, who worked with me on this book, also received the award that year for his superb journalistic ability.

But Donald was there for me when I needed a friend. I had just been let go by the Pistons, and he would meet with me regularly at this Denny's over in West Bloomfield. I was wondering where I was going with my career, and he got me involved with his magazine. He constantly offered me encouragement, telling me, "Someday, Dick, you're going to find a niche." It would make me feel so good, even though I was down because I'd just been fired, and he would say, "With your enthusiasm and passion, you will be a success in some endeavor."

Man, I've always felt indebted to Larry for those words of encouragement. To this day, I still write for *Basketball Times* because of my feelings for Larry.

Just a week before Larry died, we were talking at the 2000 Coaches vs. Cancer Classic at Madison Square Garden. I was running onto the court to get ready to do my opening for the show and he stopped me to say, "Wait until you see my publication, Dickie V. I have Seton Hall at No. 1."

I told him he was out of his mind. "There is no way," I said. "I know it's my alma mater and all, but Seton Hall is too young. They're all diaper dandies."

He said, "Yeah, the recruiting class that Tommy Amaker has put together—featuring Eddie Griffin—is going to be sensational."

That was our last conversation.

Then I got the call that Larry had died of a heart attack while he was taking his daily walk around Pinehurst, North Carolina, where he lived and had his office.

The memories live on, though.

I still remember Larry walking into the Detroit locker room back in 1977 after we had won 20 in a row. He came over and said, "Hey, you're doing great, huh, Dick? But you'd better win Wednesday."

"What do you mean?" I asked.

"You'd better beat Marquette or you're not going to get to the big dance."

I said, "Wait a minute. We're like 23-2, and you're telling me I have to beat Marquette to get to the NCAAs?"

"Dick," he said, "I'm telling you. They're only going to take two independents from the Midwest. And they're going to take Marquette and Notre Dame. The only way they're going to take Detroit is if you shock and stun them by beating Marquette in Milwaukee."

Well, we went over there the year Al won the national title and beat Marquette at the buzzer. We got into the tournament, and Larry said, "I know you don't believe me, but that was the clincher. They had no other choice."

You know what? Now that I think about it, Larry was right. But then, he was always two steps ahead of the curve.

So were Jimmy, Al, and Dave.

Rest in peace, friends.

8

THE PRESSURE COOKER

Sometimes coaches push the envelope.

Last fall, Cincinnati coach Bobby Huggins was in the Pittsburgh airport at the end of a four-day road trip. He was rushing from the rental car return lot to catch a flight to Milwaukee, where he was scheduled to do a Nike coaches' clinic. Then he became nauseous. He started having chest pains and began having problems breathing.

Huggins phoned longtime friend J.O. Straight—a Pittsburgh businessman who had been involved in an age-group traveling team and was the legal guardian of former Cincinnati All-American center Danny Fortson—on his cell phone and told him he felt like he had an elephant sitting on his chest. Huggins asked Straight to call 911. A woman who asked if he was in distress also called emergency services. "I was sweating. My pants were soaked all the way down," Huggins recalled later at Conference USA media day in Chicago.

Huggins almost died that day.

When the paramedics arrived, they gave Huggins a nitroglycerin tablet, but it didn't work. They put Huggins in the ambulance and had to use a defibrillator—not once, but twice—to restart his heart. Huggins had a 90 percent blockage in one artery and at least some degree of blockage in others. A metal stint had to be inserted during surgery.

The next day, John Calipari of Memphis visited him at Beaver Medical Center. When Coach Cal showed up, he said to Huggins, "Yo, it's not time to die. I haven't beaten you yet."

"But, seriously," John said later, "we can laugh about this stuff now; but it wasn't funny then. When I showed up, I could see the burn marks from the paddles they had to use."

Six weeks later, Huggins was back coaching, putting in 12-hour days as he prepared for his team's season opener against Tennessee Tech.

Huggins is a working man's hero in this blue-collar factory town. He was heavily romanced by West Virginia last March when that Big East job opened, but turned down a $1 million-plus offer. He also turned down an offer from the NBA's L.A. Clippers two years ago.

The bottom line is that he just can't pull himself away from Cincinnati.

These are his people, and this is his program. It's a special connection that is beautiful to see. It's a side of Huggins that many fans may not know or appreciate.

Huggins never gave any thought to taking off this season. He never considered lowering his voice a few decibels in practice.

"Same ol' Hugs," UC sophomore forward Jason Maxiell admitted.

Well, almost.

Huggins approached his comeback with the same unbelievable intensity he had used to become one of the best coaches in college basketball. He's started exercising again for the first time since college, working out on a treadmill, a stationary bike and a rowing machine. He's walking three times a day, something he'd never done before. His heart is being monitored regularly. He is trying to control his schedule, and he is getting more rest.

Huggins is the driving force behind Cincinnati basketball. He has a 517-184 record over his career heading into the 2003-04 season. He has the second highest winning percentage of any active coach in Division I—behind Roy Williams of Kansas.

Huggins has always been an intense competitor.

"The doctors did not tell me to tone down my personality on the floor," he insisted. "The first couple of weeks, yeah. But I think they're smart enough to know they can't control what I am going to do. I'm not going to just sit there and get beaten."

"He's competitive about everything he does," Dallas Mavericks guard Nick Van Exel told an AP reporter—Van Exel played for Huggins in the mid-90s. "There's always a competition. When he thought we were playing too soft, he would come out at practice and take the first charge. He'd tell guys to run him over. He would lead off a drill by challenging the whole team to run him over. Whoever hated him the most would go first and try to run him over, and he'd stand in there and take it."

Huggins will be the first to admit he hasn't taken any charges since his return.

One step at a time.

Huggins discovered he has a lot more friends than he thought, though. His wife, June, and his girls, his parents, and his three brothers and four sisters were all at the hospital the first day. And Huggins received flowers that night from Van Exel.

Leonard Stokes, one of his players, actually drove to Pittsburgh two days later and sneaked onto Huggins's floor in the cardiac wing. The rest of the team visited Huggins at Christ Hospital after he was transferred back home. They just wanted to see with their own eyes that their coach was okay.

It was equally touching when Huggins took part in "Breakfast with Bob," a continental breakfast and 20-minute scrimmage for the fans the first day of practice. When Huggins walked onto the floor at Shoemaker Center with his wife, he received a standing ovation from the 3,200 in attendance.

Through it all, Huggins has maintained his sense of humor. While he was on the way to the emergency room, Mark Block, an ambulance worker, tried to comfort him.

"Don't worry, Coach. I won't let you die. I'm John Calipari's cousin," Block said.

"Oh, no," Huggins replied. "I may as well close my eyes. I've got no chance."

I called him up to ask, "Hey, Bobby, why not a year off? Get yourself healthy, get yourself trimmed down. Just concentrate on that and let one of your assistants take over on an interim basis for a year."

Man, he stopped me in my tracks. He didn't want to hear any of that. He was all over me like I couldn't believe on the phone.

"What, are you crazy, man?" he said. "I'm feeling okay. I'm ready. I'm doing my workouts. I'm getting myself ready."

And he did. He's still coaching, God bless him. And I hope he coaches 20 more years at the very least.

Huggins couldn't wait to get back to the pressure cooker.

Coaches get so into it, they begin to feel they're invincible.

Jim Calhoun is an important figure in the Big East and a historic figure in New England basketball, having won a national championship in 1999. He is also the heartbeat of Connecticut's program, the leader of a young team that rallied to make the NCAA Tournament and then reached the Sweet 16 in 2003.

But the 60-year-old Calhoun missed five games this past season following surgery to remove a cancerous prostate gland. When Calhoun came out of the operation on February 6, his urologist suggested he wait four weeks before returning to coaching. But the doctor knew that Calhoun wouldn't listen, so he advised him just to ease his way back in so he wouldn't become a victim of his own fatigue.

Calhoun waited all of 13 days before he tested his stamina under game conditions. He showed up for UConn's game with St. John's on February 19.

It was just too hard for him to stay away.

"I learned how much I really liked this team, learned how much I missed it," he said. "One of the toughest days for me was when the kids were leaving for Virginia Tech the day before my surgery. They left and I was sitting alone at my desk and looking around, thinking, 'Where is everybody?' I felt an incredible sense of loss. I wasn't frightened about the surgery. I felt only anticipation—let's get this thing over and done; let's get rid of it and march on."

The day after his surgery, Calhoun walked around his hospital room 45 times. After he got home from the hospital, he proceeded to drive his wife, Pat, crazy. "Pat has decided one thing after having had me home for two weeks—she's not ready to have me retire," he said.

I'll bet Jim agrees with her.

Calhoun was in constant contact with his staff, making at least 10 phone calls a day. He came back to practice Thursday afternoon and made up his mind to coach the game Friday night. "I decided that, 'Yeah, I'm okay and, anyway, I'm just going to sit there,' but then all of a sudden—I guess it's like riding a horse or a bike—I just got back on and official Jim Burr and I started exchanging ideas about our philosophies on life," he said. "I had asked George Blaney to help me as much as he could. I think one time he got a bruised shoulder as I knocked him out of the way when I jumped up on the sideline and he said, 'Well, I guess we're back to normal.'"

I'd been in Chapel Hill getting ready for an ACC game when Calhoun called me the day before his surgery. I remember that he felt very touched by all the messages of hope and support that he'd received from so many people in the basketball community. Jim was very upbeat and had a positive attitude, and I believe all those words of encouragement helped him immensely.

The Connecticut students brought signs and posters with them to Calhoun's Corner, located on the baseline at Gampel Pavilion, the day he came back. Several enthusiastic undergrads even spelled out his name in blue paint on their bare chests.

As he walked onto the floor before the St. John's game, bathed in the spotlight of a CBS camera, he could sense the noise level start to rise in the sold-out campus building. The standing ovation lasted a good 90 seconds. When he reached the bench, two St. John's players—Marcus Hatten and Elijah Ingram—came over to shake his hand. It was one of the more poignant moments of this past college basketball season.

"I told George Blaney I wish I could just be on the bench and not have to walk out there," Calhoun recalled. "I may not be the most humble person in the world, but I'm not someone who seeks the spotlight. I wanted to get on with the game. I didn't want this to be a distraction.

"But I guess when you've been at a place 17 years and every place you go, people are saying, 'Come on, Coach, come back' and you hear about a billboard sign saying the same thing and you receive hundreds of thousands of letters and Mike Krzyzewski of Duke, who is on the way to Wake Forest, is calling the house—it all just gives you pause."

I can relate to Jim Calhoun's and Bobby Huggins's health problems, though, because I went through some tough physical times myself when I was coaching.

I know I brought them all on myself. I could never relax when I was coaching. Every day, I'd be thinking, "Oh, my God, I'm sitting here eating dinner. What are my competitors doing? They're out recruiting. They're out talking to kids. I've got to get on the phone. I've got to write letters." Every day I felt the challenge of having to do it.

I had no balance. I was working the phone lines, recruiting 24 hours a day, seven days a week. I was either calling kids or seeing kids, constantly. I was a workaholic. I always felt that if I wasn't doing it, my competitors would be. I always felt that because I wasn't on the same footing with Michigan or Michigan State, I needed the winner's edge, that little extra. I pushed myself beyond the norm.

Remember, I never had the luxury of coaching in a marquee college program. And that's the one thing I missed in my coaching career. Sometimes I wish I had listened to Jim Valvano. When I left for the NBA, he warned me, "Don't do it, Dickie. You're a college coach. With what you're achieving at Detroit, you'll have an opportunity to get a major job."

I'll tell you what else I did—I took everything personally. If a kid got into trouble, if something happened academically with a player, I felt it was a reflection on me. I think we in the media are all guilty of judging coaches many times by what happens with players off the court. We also constantly criticize coaches over their graduation rates. But let me tell you, as former Alabama coach Wimp Sanderson once said, "If a player really wants to graduate, with the guidance available today, it is simply up to that kid." I say amen to that.

A kid's sense of discipline, of responsibility, begins to develop from birth. It starts at the beginning when they're in the crib, with hugs and squeezes and loads of love. It doesn't start at 19 or 20 when they get to college as a recruit. All of us like to think that we can change every kid going, that we're going to be miracle workers, that we'll make sure that nothing bad happens to them.

Al McGuire said it best when he told his players, "Hey, I'm not trying to be Father Flanagan, man. I'm here to coach. I'm not here to handle all your problems and all your headaches. I'm certainly here for you, but I'm not here for all the nonsense."

Father Flanagan—I labeled Jerry Tarkanian that when he was at Vegas. "If a kid had a problem," I said, "he'd go down to Tark, and Tark would just try to be Father Flanagan. 'Come on down. I'll try to help you.'"

I tried to be Father Flanagan, too, and I paid the price.

I was coaching at East Rutherford High School in New Jersey. We were getting ready to play a state semifinal game—and all of a sudden, I'm bleeding like crazy. I had blood coming out of my mouth, blood coming out of my nose, blood just everywhere. They rushed me to the hospital and gave me six pints of blood.

Fortunately, my team was ready to play, and my assistant Bob Stolarz did a great job in guiding them to the big win, which meant they'd be going to the championship game in Atlantic City.

Man, I told my doctor, Joseph Latona, "I am getting out of here."

He said that if I wanted to leave, I'd have to sign out on my own. The hospital didn't want to release me, but I had to be at courtside, man. So I went there at my own risk.

Can you imagine that? Here I was, an ulcer patient in need of rest, putting myself into the state championship game—and, of all things, it was a Maalox Masher. I mean, I had a quart of milk next to me, and I was downing it. We finally won that game by one, which was the best medicine. Better yet, my star, Leslie Cason, had 45 points—he really put on a one-man show. And fortunately, I was okay. After the game, I was put on medication. I probably needed the men in the white coats to come get me—that's what my wife seemed to think anyway.

While I was at the hospital, I remember the doctor saying that the normal person has a hemoglobin count of 12. Mine had been about six. I'd lost six pints of blood. I was a basket case.

But the problem didn't stop there.

When I was coaching at the University of Detroit, I couldn't go to sleep at night. I'd be tossing and turning, worrying about recruits. "Where are they going? This kid might go here. That kid might change his mind."

And right after I was fired from the Pistons, I started bleeding internally again. I was at home. I was feeling very dizzy and weak. I figured that I must be bleeding again, and then I passed out. Luckily for me, Lorraine was home and able to drive me to the hospital. If she hadn't been there, I don't know what would have happened. I might not have survived.

Man, I say this all the time—had I not gotten into television, I don't think I would have made it to the age of 50—let alone 60—because of the pace I put myself on, the pressure I put myself under, when I was coaching.

I recently discussed this intense pressure with Mike Greenberg and Mike Golic on their radio program, *Mike and Mike in the Morning*. Now they are a couple of great guys, and Golic is a former Notre Dame All-American. We talked about the pressures of coaching and why they keep coming back for more and more when the heat is so extreme. Let me tell you, you just get addicted to it. There is no more special feeling than that big-time victory—but those losses can just tear your guts out.

Yes, I'm lucky I do all my coaching now on TV, where I haven't lost a game in 24-plus years. That's why I say I have the best job in basketball now.

Today, the pressure on coaches keeps getting more intense as the interest in the game keeps getting bigger.

Some people say that TV ratings for college basketball are down. But are they really? Brent Musburger—talk about your diehard sports fanatic—and I were sitting in a hotel one Saturday morning, having breakfast. We looked at the TV schedule in the paper, and without exaggeration, there were 12 games listed for that day. So a lot of people *are* watching college basketball—it's just that they're watching so many different games, it's incredible. It's not like it was years ago, when all televised games appeared on just one network. That increased visibility puts more pressure on coaches to perform and to get their players to behave.

I've never seen anything like the hype that's out there today. When I was coaching in college, I dealt with the beat writers and that was it. Now, if you're a coach at a major university, whatever happens in your program is going to be news. If a player misses practice, gets into a shouting match with a coach, take it to the bank—it's going to be on the Internet and all over TV. The media scrutiny and evaluation today have created a pressure cooker for the coaches that's a monster. It's just unreal.

If you're a coach, that game you're coaching tonight is the only game that means anything. All those other games are so many fond memories, great history, and wonderful conversation topics. But a coach today is conditioned to feel that his worth is determined by the success he has on any given night.

And if he doesn't have it, he feels like a total failure.

I recently had a conversation with Bobby Knight. I was in the locker room with him when Texas Tech was getting ready to play a big game against Kansas. Bobby was completely frustrated with the way his team was playing.

I was trying to tell him, "Bobby, your team doesn't have the personnel you had at Indiana."

"What do you mean?"

Coaches all believe they can get it done with their work ethic alone. I've watched Knight putting together a game plan in practice sessions. He feels that if his players follow his game plan, they're going to win, no matter who they play or who they are.

I said to him, "Here you are, you're a Hall of Famer, you've won national titles. I can see it's tearing you apart."

"The minute I lose that drive," he told me, "that's when I know it's over."

That's just the way coaches are made.

Yet I still feel that we in the media are responsible for some of the pressures that coaches face. We have a tendency to rave about certain coaches, to the exclusion of others. That's unfair. Very unfair.

And I'm as guilty as the next guy.

I pick my All-Rolls Roycers. It doesn't make life any easier for the coaches who are getting held back by the bottom line, even on the mid-major level.

A coach from a non-marquee program approached me once and said: "Hey, man, you're from the University of Detroit. You are supposed to be like all of us. Did you forget where you started coaching?"

Man, it hit home.

"You were there when you operated with the small budgets," he continued. "Yet you competed with Michigan and Marquette and all the biggies. Well, that's where I'm at. And it hurts me to hear you always talking about Mike Krzyzewski and Bobby Knight as being the best. Heck, it's not an even playing field that we're on."

Hey, I know that. I've always known that. Things are not equal. It's not the same for every coach. The key to success in college basketball starts with one factor—recruiting. And it helps if you have an All-Rolls Royce program.

Just ask John Wooden—that 2-2-1 zone was sensational, and the way they trapped, pressed, and played as a team was terrific. But it also helped to have guys on the team named Lew Alcindor, Bill Walton, Gail Goodrich, Marques Johnson—and all the other greats who wore the UCLA uniform. And Coach Wooden would be the first to tell you that.

But he'd also say his job was to blend the talent that he had. That's where he excelled as a teacher. That's where he was a wizard. He was able to get superstars to understand their roles.

There's a story that I've heard that really shows the coaching ability of John Wooden. According to the story, when Sidney Wicks started taking some bad shots, Wooden pulled him out of practice and said, "Sidney, Sidney, I'm going to tell you simply. You aren't gonna play if you take shots like that, my friend, or you will be sitting on the bench.

"If you want to take some good shots, do you see the big guy over there?" He pointed to Lew Alcindor, now known as Kareem Abdul-Jabbar, "Well, Mr. Alcindor makes 70 out of 100 shots. You get right up on that glass to get the other 30 he misses and convert them into baskets, you can keep playing."

And the rest of the story, as Paul Harvey would say, is that Sidney must've gotten the message, because he became an All-American Windex man.

But let's get back to my mid-major coach. Referring to coaches like Wooden and Coach K, he said to me, "We're going in with Volkswagens and they're going in with Rolls Royces. They can say, 'Oh, wow, we're on TV 30 times a year. We have a program that's going to be in the top 15 in the nation every year.' Try to deal with that. Let's reverse roles; let's take some of the stars you're talking about and put them on the campuses where we have to operate."

When I think about it, that's a legitimate argument.

Obviously, there are coaches who are making big bucks these days. There are several that belong to the millionaire's club. Can you imagine what professors out there are thinking when they see the dollars being paid to the superstars of the coaching fraternity? They go bananas when they hear somebody's making millions. In many cases, they're making more than anybody in the state, including the governor. But there are a lot of coaches who don't make that kind of money.

You might wonder why the big guys make the enormous amount of money that they do, but think about this—at that level, the pressure to keep winning so that the revenue keeps flowing into the university is intense. They are corporate superstars.

And keep this in mind—if they are given the ziggy, many of them are never able to reach that same level again. They're viewed almost as damaged goods. A lot of brilliant guys have had their reputations tarnished simply because they weren't in the right situation. If a coach loses a job, how many times does he get a chance to get back? I'm telling you, it's not very often.

That's why some coaches have been pushing the idea of tenure.

Al McGuire sang its praises. "Hey, the professor in the classroom, he gets tenure. He gets that, he has a lifetime job." Tenure would not be a bad thing for a coach, but I don't think we'll ever see it.

Sometimes the pressure is ultimately too much.

Take the case of Dick Fick.

In his heyday, Fick had coached at Morehead for six rollicking years, from 1991-1997. His first team finished 14-15 and produced the nation's leading scorer in Brett Roberts. In 1994-95, the Eagles finished second in the Ohio Valley Conference, and Fick shared Coach of the Year honors.

Fick always knew how to put on a show. One time, when Morehead played Kentucky at Rupp Arena, Fick, upset at some calls, pretended to hang himself by his tie and even fell flat on his back at courtside. His antics led ESPN to create a weekly Dick Fick Award for Demonstrative Coaching, which actually was started by our own late Jimmy V.

That was the high-water mark of his career.

In 1997, he was fired. He finished with a 64-101 record. Fick moved to Cincinnati to coach youth and high school basketball and to try to find someone to give him another chance. He was also in and out of alcohol rehab. Eventually, he wound up back in his hometown of Joliet, Illinois. Pat Sullivan, head coach at St. Francis of Illinois—an NAIA school—who had known Fick when he was a high school star, gave him that chance a couple of years ago when he hired Fick as an assistant.

I will never forget a segment on *SportsCenter* that revealed how much Sullivan truly cared for Fick. That piece would bring tears to anyone's eyes. I was so blown away by it, I immediately wrote a letter to Sullivan to tell him how special he was. He wrote back to say he was doing all he could for Fick from the bottom of his heart.

It was in February 2003 when Sullivan gathered his team around Fick. Sullivan had asked Fick's mother and a psychologist to attend as well. It was an intervention. Fick had been abusing alcohol.

One by one, the players went around the room and told Fick how much they loved him and asked him to try one more time to get help for his problem.

So Fick went through detox and then went to rehab, but it just didn't work out. He was already on the road to self-destruction. He got divorced from his high school sweetheart in April. And even though Keith Inzler, a former Morehead player and assistant at Joliet JC, was driving him to AA meetings, it was already too late.

Fick was found dead on April 28 in the Joliet apartment where he lived by himself. He was 50 years old. Police had gone to Fick's apartment after a friend found his body and telephoned for help. Sullivan said the cause of death was internal bleeding resulting from ulcers.

What a sad end to a promising career. A story like that just breaks my heart.

These sad incidents speak for themselves and show that in the world of coaching today, it's not all fun and games. I often say, "It's fun and games, man; it's Christmas—a holiday—the day you're named coach at a big-time job. You've got the press conference and all. You're ecstatic." But it changes—for the worst—quickly. Coaches get so knotted up during the course of the season when they begin to feel that heat, especially if the ball doesn't bounce their way. Sometimes there's such a thin line between being a superstar and being an average coach.

Nowhere is that pressure greater than it is at Kentucky.

Tubby Smith is one of my favorites. He won a national championship in 1998, the first year he had the job.

But at Kentucky, it's always "What have you done for us lately?"

I did the Louisville-Kentucky game in December 2002. Talk about pressure—not only is this matchup one of the great rivalries in basketball, like Duke-North Carolina or Purdue-Indiana, but the pressure of Louisville-Kentucky has increased incredibly now that Rick Pitino has joined the mix. The game was at Freedom Hall, and Kentucky got blown out, blitzed.

I remember talking to Rick Bozich, a basketball lover and columnist at *The Louisville Courier Journal,* the next day; and he told me, "Man, you should hear the talk shows. Tubby's getting whacked. People are saying that if Rick were here, things would be different."

During that game, I said—and I know it's on tape—"Kentucky will win, will have a big-time year and they are Final Four material—and this guy will get them there." What I respect about Tubby is that he didn't go back to the locker room, pout and sulk. He took all the heat; guys were jumping on him about style of play, bringing up that out-of-control, soap opera scene from the previous year. *As the World of the Wildcats Turns*—players had gotten into fights with one another and others had wanted to transfer. It had been chaos.

What I loved about Tubby is that he went to work immediately. He sold his team on the importance of defense, and it all came together for them in a game against Vanderbilt. They were getting beat early, but played a brilliant second half defensively. From that moment on, that team started to believe. They believed in the system, they believed in what he was trying to get across, and they went on a roll.

They certainly rolled Florida last January in Rupp.

Florida had just been named No. 1 in the country that day. Here they were, the toast of the country for the first time in the history of the school—and they just got pummeled. I remember talking to Billy Donovan after that game, and I said, "Billy, I feel so bad for your kids and you, but tonight your kids didn't compete. They didn't fight. They got embarrassed, humiliated."

He said, "You're right; we went from No. 1 a few hours earlier to where we are now. We don't even believe in ourselves."

Kentucky went on to win 24 straight games, finishing 16-0 in the SEC regular season. They looked like they were headed for the Final Four. But then, in the Sweet 16, Keith Bogans—their best player—injured his ankle, and Marquette ended up spanking them in the Elite Eight.

Tubby knew he'd hear about it—again.

But he signed on for more, inking an eight-year, $20.25-million contract extension on April 18. That number is guaranteed if Smith stays at Kentucky for the length of the contract.

I think Tubby Smith expects the pressure. Coaches like Krzyzewski, Gary Williams, and Roy Williams do, too. It comes with the territory.

You wouldn't believe it, but a guy came up to me recently and started teasing me about Duke. He said what a bust they were. They couldn't do this, couldn't do that. I thought, "How many teams wish they could have had the kind of year Duke had?" But they've set the bar so high, people expect them to be in the Final Four every year and then can't deal with it when that doesn't happen.

What was Duke this year? They were 26-7. Those types of years get you into the Hall of Fame. Then the fans come up to you and it's, "What's happened to Duke?"

Come on.

Back in 1997, Kansas was 35-2 and lost a heartbreaker to Arizona in the NCAA Sweet 16, and people said that Roy Williams couldn't win the big one.

That's the mentality that exists in college basketball today.

Unfortunately, some coaches just lose it.

Mike Davis of Indiana stormed onto the court at the end of a loss to Kentucky while the ball was in play. He got into official Bert Smith's face for close to 30 seconds to protest a no-call.

In a postgame conference, Davis quickly apologized to the Indiana fans, the officials and players after he was assessed two technicals and tossed with 2.6 seconds left, costing his team—which trailed 65-64 at the time—any chance they might have had to win the game.

Davis faced a possible six-game suspension by the Big Ten, but Indiana AD Terry Clapacs appealed. He admitted there had been interaction, but claimed Davis had not intentionally incited the crowd. Davis issued a letter of apology to the officials and received a public reprimand from the school. Jim Delany, commissioner of the Big Ten, handed down a suspension of one game. That was certainly fair, because Davis had realized soon after the game how wrong he was.

Even that one-game suspension, though, stood in stark contrast to the Big Ten's treatment of Penn State's football coach Joe Paterno—an icon in his sport. They had let Paterno off without so much as a slap on the wrist just two months earlier. Paterno had repeatedly criticized Big Ten officials both during and following three heartbreaking conference losses, including one to Iowa. When Delany, a man of integrity, was asked about those incidents, he admitted that he'd looked the other way with Paterno because of his reputation, who he was and what he had contributed to the sport.

But to be fair, this was the third time Davis had been at odds with the conference. He was fined $10,000 for postgame comments criticizing officials after losing to Butler in the 2002 season. Then following a loss at Illinois that same year, when his assistant Ben McDonald got a bench technical, he received a letter of reprimand from the Big Ten and paid a $10,000 fine out of his own pocket.

Of course, it's not just coaches who have to deal with the pressure of trying to live up to everyone's expectations.

I read recently in *The Washington Post* that Nic Wise, a 5'9" point guard from Hightower High in Katy, Texas, committed to Lute Olson at the University of Arizona.

He's only in ninth grade.

That's right. Forget about teenyboppers going to the NBA—at least LeBron James is old enough to drive.

Wise is another Texas blue chipper who had been courted by both Arizona and Texas. He figured he may as well just get it over with so he'd no longer be besieged by scouting services who were constantly calling the house and bugging him.

He claims he's wanted to go to Arizona since he was in the sixth grade, playing for Josh Pastner in AAU age-group ball. Pastner is now a full-time assistant at the university and is one of the rising stars in the profession. Wise, who is coached by his father, told *The Post* he was impressed by Olson and the fact that Arizona was turning out so many quality guards like Michael Bibby and Jason Gardner. He's constantly watching the Cats play on TV.

It will be interesting to see if he actually winds up there.

This is starting to happen elsewhere, too. Just last year, Robert Vaden and Desmond Gaddis—a pair of ninth graders from Indianapolis—committed to Purdue. Vaden has already changed his mind and has now committed to Indiana.

Coaches think all these prodigies will take them to the promised land when—or is it *if?*—they finally show up on campus.

Every year, I hear about dazzling future college stars. I can't wait for November, because for me, one of the great things about my job at ESPN has been the anticipation of seeing the new diaper dandies.

Who can forget this past season when freshman guard Bracey Wright of Indiana went out to Maui and walked away with the MVP trophy? Who can forget when North Carolina won the preseason NIT in New York—due to the performance of another freshman, Rashad McCants?

But there have been a lot of guys who haven't lived up to their billing. They were scholastic superstars. Once they arrived on that college campus, though, they turned into major disappointments.

Some of them have even made my All-Broken Heart team.

My second team lines up with forward Curtis Hunter, guards Anthony Perry and Sherron Wilkerson, center Duane Spencer, and forward Lester Earl.

Hunter was a McDonald's All-American in 1982 who was described as having "a Michael Jordan jumper" when he signed with North Carolina. But he averaged just 4.2 points and 1.5 rebounds for his career.

I love Bob Hurley, the coach at St. Anthony's of Jersey City, who has a reputation of producing great guards. Perry, a 1997 McDonald's All-American, was supposed to follow in the footsteps of David Rivers and Bobby Hurley Jr. when he signed at Georgetown. He was supposed to be a great shooter. I don't know what happened.

He averaged only 8.7 points as a junior and scored just 6.7 points and shot 42 percent and played only 17 minutes a game as a senior.

When you think of the John Thompson teams at Georgetown, you think of Patrick Ewing, Dikembe Mutombo and Alonzo Mourning. You don't think of Duane Spencer, a 1992 McDonald's All-American. This is one 6'10" aircraft carrier that didn't float. He averaged 8.7 points and six rebounds before transferring to LSU.

And speaking of LSU, what about Lester Earl? He was one of the big names in the country in 1996 when he signed to play for Dale Brown. He was a Mr. Basketball from Glen Oaks Academy in Baton Rouge who had 25 points and seven rebounds in his debut versus Troy State. But it was downhill from there—he eventually turned state's evidence against Brown in an NCAA probe, claiming he received $30,000 from a booster to go to LSU. Then he resurfaced—with no penalty—at Kansas, but was just a role player there.

All I heard one summer was, "Wait until you see this kid, man. This is going to be a future Super Hoosier, one of those big guards who'll be a dominator." Wilkerson averaged 7.5 points for Bob Knight before being bounced off the team due to a domestic battery charge having been filed against him his sophomore year. He did average 25 points his last two years at Rio Grande, an NAIA school, but he was off anyone's radar screen by then.

My first team—center Ajou Deng, forwards Winford Walton, Barry Spencer and Joey Beard, and guard Kevin Walls—were even bigger busts.

Walls, a 1984 McDonald's All-American, was a great scorer in high school. He signed with Louisville, following Milt Wagner and Billy Thompson, the original members of the Camden Connection who helped lead the Cardinals to the national title in 1986. Walls was a sub on that team, and he averaged just 3.8 points and 1.6 assists in his second season before quitting following an incident when he re-fused to enter a game against South Carolina his junior year because of a knee injury.

I remember the 6'10" Deng getting rave reviews. He sat out his freshman year at UConn, but in practice, he dominated a team that had great stars like Rip Hamilton. There were fans in the Husky Na-tion who thought he'd be a lock first-round NBA choice—he never panned out. Deng transferred to Fairfield, where he averaged 4.8 points per game and four rebounds per game in his final year as a grad stu-dent—not exactly NBA dominance.

When Walton signed with Syracuse in 1996, the folks there had visions of him becoming the next Derrick Coleman because he was from Detroit. But he was never eligible to play for the Orange and ended up transferring to Fresno State, where he posted decent numbers—11.1 points, 6.1 rebounds and 39.1 field goal percent-age—in 1997-98 before deciding he could make it in the NBA. He didn't.

Joey Beard was a 1993 McDonald's All-American from the same high school as Grant Hill in Reston, Virginia. He also signed at Duke. But that's where the similarities ended. Beard averaged 1.3 points and 2.4 rebounds for the Blue Devils his freshman year before transfer-ring to Boston University, where he became a decent player in the America East Conference.

Finally, there's Barry Spencer, a 1980 McDonald's All-Ameri-can from Detroit Central Catholic. 1980 was the year after I got into TV, so I was reading about him on a regular basis in the Detroit papers. Everyone wanted him—Michigan and Notre Dame, to name a couple. Eventually, he signed with the Fighting Irish but averaged just 5.8 points a game as a freshman and never really became the superstar he was projected to be.

They're all in my missing persons file.

9

BIG BROTHER
IS STILL WATCHING

March Madness is my time of the year. There's nothing like the spirit generated by all those NCAA teams chasing the gold trophy. Yes, March is my favorite month for sports, usually.

But 2003 was a different story, man. There were so many scandals rocking the sport at places like Georgia, Iowa State, Fresno State and St. Bonaventure, I felt as though I could be a reporter for *The National Enquirer.*

I found myself in the middle of a doozy. Sadly, it involved a close friend.

Jim Harrick, who was coaching at the University of Georgia, should have been excited about seeing me. I was in town to do his team's big, sold-out SEC game with third-ranked Florida for ESPN at the end of February.

But he had other, bigger problems on his mind.

He was under siege, living in a bunker in the wake of a widening NCAA investigation into allegations of academic fraud and financial improprieties from a former player, Tony Cole.

In an interview last fall, Cole told ESPN that Harrick and his son, Jim Jr., who was an assistant at the school, had covered a number of his expenses before he was enrolled—including wiring $300 to cover the cost of a phone bill while he was staying with a friend of his mother in Baton Rouge in August of 2001 and paying $1,200 at two hotels—and doing work for him in two correspondence courses at Lincoln Trail Junior College in Illinois. Cole also claimed Harrick Jr. gave him an A in a summer school course called "Principles and Strategy of Basketball," even though Cole never attended class.

Cole had a troubled past. He'd spent time in three junior colleges before he was accepted at Georgia. And he'd spent more than his share of time in the courtroom. Cole was dismissed from the Community College of Rhode Island in March, 2000, after having been accused of groping two female students who worked in the athletic department. On January 14, 2001, during Cole's freshman year at Georgia, an incident occurred in Cole's dorm room involving Cole, two other Georgia athletes and a woman, who says she was raped. Two days later, Georgia suspended Cole, teammate Steve Thomas and football player Bernard Williams pending the outcome of an investigation.

Cole never played another game for Georgia. In April of that year, he was indicted on a charge of aggravated assault with intent to rape. Thomas and Williams were also indicted on multiple charges, including rape. Later that summer, Williams was acquitted, and charges were dropped against Thomas and Cole. But Georgia AD Vince Dooley sent Cole a letter telling him he would not be reinstated. The letter accused him of starting a fight in practice, acting abusively toward Harrick Jr. and other staffers, and abusing telephone privileges on road trips.

Cole was kept on scholarship, but he dropped out of school in January, 2003, after having been arrested for criminal trespass in the athletic weight room. He was banned from campus.

The kid had such a shaky track record that I had to wonder whether there might be something to the allegations.

But I started hoping and praying that Jim would have an answer for all the accusations. I mean, when somebody is my friend, I will be loyal to them until the end. I was actually rooting for my buddy to come through this mess in a positive way. He went to my daughters' weddings. My family is close to Jim and his wife, Sally. I was hoping maybe it was just the kid making up the allegations; maybe he was just bitter and was looking for some revenge.

Cole had painted a bleak picture of what was going on down there. Among other things, Cole claimed that he received $900 from a booster and that Harrick let him use his credit card to buy a TV at Circuit City.

ESPN tried to get a response. Jeremy Schaap tried. He called, he wanted to set up an interview with Harrick to get his side of the story, but Georgia refused to call back. So he went down there and caught up with Jim on the way to his car in the parking lot. He got some heat about that, but all he was trying to do was get a one-on-one interview.

Anyway, I went there at the beginning of March and made a call to Jim's office. They said he wasn't in, but they gave me his number at home. I called, got his wife, Sally, and she put Jim on the phone. I asked, "Jim, are you coming down to the office?" He told me, "I'll be there in 30 minutes."

Dan Shulman, a rising star with a magical voice from out of Canada (hey, what's this about Canada producing stars for ESPN? My buddy John Saunders is also Canadian), was doing the play-by-play. Dan and I sat with Jim in his office at Stegman Coliseum, and I asked him about the allegations. He was able to completely rebut each one. He talked about his graduation rates and claimed Tony Cole and the rest of the players went to the summer school class taught by his son. He told me, "It will all come out."

"Why don't you tell that to the national TV audience?" I asked. "We'll get a camera."

At first, Jim said, "No, I'm not doing any interviews. My lawyers advised me not to do any. The school doesn't want me to do any, and I'm not going to do any."

He started getting worked up.

Then I brought up Rhode Island, his previous employer, and that touched a nerve. Earlier that week, a story had broken in Kingston that Christine King, a former secretary in the Rhode Island basketball office who recently dropped a sexual harassment lawsuit against Harrick in exchange for a $45,000 settlement from the university, had accused Harrick of falsifying hotel and meal reports for recruits. Harrick claimed ignorance.

That set him off—he claimed that he had talked to the AD Ron Petro for about 10 minutes a month ago and that Petro told him they had taken care of all her complaints. He stated it was in the middle of the season and he didn't learn about it again until he read it in the papers. He said, "That was the first time I heard of it."

I then came back at him and said, "If what you're saying is factual, why should you allow yourself to be punished and not let people know what you're telling me?"

He said, "You know what? Let's do the interview. All I ask is that you give me a chance to express myself on the issues."

I assured him there would be no sneak questions and we would discuss only the things we'd spoken about in his office.

We did the interview early that evening. I gave him a chance to talk about Cole's accusations that Harrick let him use his credit card. "For him to have my credit card, that's ludicrous," Jim said. I let him address the kid's claims that he didn't go to class and got As without showing up. I gave him a chance to address the Rhode Island situation.

"It's all a bunch of crap," he told me. "Maybe we tried to build the program too quickly, Maybe we made poor recruiting decisions, but we don't do academic work for our players; we don't give them money. Those are the issues that are important to me.

"Jarvis Hayes and his brother live in the dorms. He doesn't have a car, doesn't have clothes, doesn't have money. He's one of the top three players in the SEC. If you were going to give out money, wouldn't you start there? I rest my case.

"I'm immensely confident everything will work out."

We got done, shook hands, and he thanked me. That night before the Georgia-Florida game, he presented me with the International Spirit Award for promoting intercollegiate athletics. Then he gave me a Bulldog hat to wear, and the crowd went crazy.

I thought he was in a pretty good mood because he felt relieved he'd had a chance to share his feelings. Afterward, he was all excited because he won a huge game on Senior Night—his team scored on the last five possessions and upset the highly rated Gators, 82-81.

The sad part was the fact that as soon as the interview ended, the phones began ringing off the hooks at ESPN. Reports immediately surfaced that Rhode Island and UCLA administrators disagreed with the graduation rates Harrick had mentioned.

ESPN, which had been all over this story, carried a report from an assistant AD at Rhode Island on *SportsCenter* who claimed Harrick—who told me he'd graduated 31 of 32 players at Pepperdine, 23 of 27 at UCLA and all eight during his two years at URI—had bad figures.

According to URI, the number was actually one of eight. None of the other players Harrick recruited are still in school. Five of the seven players Harrick inherited from Al Skinner graduated.

Ron Petro also differed with Harrick's version of the sexual harassment suit, suggesting he'd told Harrick the details of the lawsuit during their conversation and told Harrick he would call if he needed him.

There was also a story in *The Atlanta Constitution* in which Harrick was quoted as saying that Dale Brown, who runs a non-profit foundation to help needy kids, had sent a check to pay for Cole's phone bill. Harrick claimed he was misquoted after Brown told ESPN he'd never sent any money to the Harricks.

ESPN conducted a poll after my interview with Harrick, asking viewers whether they believed Harrick or Cole. The network got over 40,000 responses. More than 70 percent backed Cole.

The next day, there was an announcement from Georgia. Jim Harrick Jr. was stepping down. Basically, he was fired after Chris Daniels, another player on the team, said he'd never seen Tony Cole in class.

The sad part is that Harrick could really coach. He took four different programs—Pepperdine, UCLA, Rhode Island and Georgia— to the NCAA Tournament.

But he couldn't avoid controversy.

At UCLA, it was a falsified expense report that got him fired in 1996, the year after he had won an NCAA championship. "That was an internal thing that should have been handled behind closed doors," Harrick said. "But they chose not to do that."

At Rhode Island, it was Lamar Odom—a gifted 6'9" talent but a questionable recruit. He had been turned down for admission at UNLV the year before when he failed to complete the required summer school courses and allegations surfaced that he had accepted money from a Las Vegas booster.

Administrators put pressure on coaches to win, yet they are the same guys who scream about academics. Then we read the transactions column in March and April in the local papers and see all these coaches getting fired—many of whom never had a problem. In fact, many of them graduated all their players.

But when your record is 7-20, you get the ziggy. Do you think maybe that pressure inspires a coach to take a chance on kids who haven't done it academically but have great potential athletically?

Harrick had a history of recruiting suspect kids. He recruited Kenny Brunner, a transfer from Fresno State who had been involved in an alleged assault case, and 6'11" center Larry Turner, a high school star at the time, who had his board scores nullified—in fairness to Turner, he persevered until he received a legit score and is now a part of Kelvin Sampson's successful program in Oklahoma. And Harrick must take the ultimate responsibility for signing Cole.

In explaining the reasons why they ended up with Cole, Harrick recalled, "We recruited Gerald Jones out of South Carolina. Come June, July, he calls and tells us he didn't pass the test. His father was a high school coach and he was certain his son would make it. Well, he didn't. And now we have to find a backup point guard and it's so late. We tried everywhere—Europe—looking for backup. We couldn't find any. We finally found Cole, so we were willing to take a chance.

"Any time you take a kid late, it's a risk. But I didn't think it would end up like this. The student body, the players, our 60 Hoop Girls all know who he is. Our players didn't want him back on the team."

But it was too late.

President Michael Adams had played a major role in the hiring of Harrick four years ago. The two had worked together at Pepperdine and were friends. Adams also allowed the athletic department to work around the nepotism rule to hire Jim's son as a part-time coach, part-time development employee. Adams was the final person to sign off on Cole's admission.

But Adams felt he had no choice in this case. He and Dooley agreed to put Harrick on paid leave. Eventually, Harrick was dismissed. He's retired now, back in Southern California where he and Sally can visit with their seven grandchildren. Man, I'm hoping to see the transactions that say Jim Harrick has been hired by an NBA team as a coach or a member of the administration, because this guy knows his hoops.

The players he left behind, though, weren't so lucky.

Georgia also suspended Daniels and starting guard Rashad Wright, declaring them academically ineligible in March after an investigation showed they were given preferential treatment in the same class taught by Harrick Jr. They banned the remaining members of the team from playing in the SEC and the NCAA Tournament.

I felt really sorry for those kids. They were an afterthought in the process. They were victims in the university's attempts to show it was trying to move in a positive direction.

Innocent kids who were never involved in any shenanigans—like the Hayes brothers, Jarvis and Jonas—should have been allowed to play.

It was mind-boggling. I knew Georgia was going to have a limited roster, but the punishment was totally unfair.

I did Tim Brando's radio show on *Sporting News* right after that, and he said to me, "I don't know if you remember this, but a few years back, you did another interview like that."

I started scratching my head.

"Don't you remember? Jimmy V. It was right after the book *Personal Fouls* came out in August, 1989, and the author made all kinds of accusations about Chris Washburn's academics."

ESPN had asked me to do the interview.

Man, it was tough. Here was a guy I really liked and had a super time with socially. And I had to present to him many of the issues that were listed in Peter Golenbock's book. It really bothered me, but I've got a job to do and I have to do it professionally. The only thing I ask myself is, "Am I being fair?"

In November 1988, I was in Springfield to do the Hall of Fame Classic. Kentucky was the marquee team on the bill, but nobody wanted to talk about their chances.

The NCAA was investigating allegations that a Kentucky assistant, Dwane Casey, had sent $1,000 to the father of forward Chris Mills—a high school star in L.A.—in an Emory Air Freight package in March of that year. They were also looking into allegations that forward Eric Manuel had cheated on his college entrance exams by copying answers from the test of another student in Lexington.

The whole thing was a mess—and it was getting worse.

During the opening of the show, I stated that it was time for Eddie Sutton and his staff to step down before the whole thing got even more out of hand.

I said it because I believed it at the time, but as I look back, the timing probably wasn't right. I should not have opened that show with such a strong statement. I could have waited to voice it on *SportsCenter*. Obviously, some people at Kentucky weren't happy with my statement. But the bottom line is, a change was made after the NCAA dropped the hammer the next spring, claiming the stories were true. They prohibited Kentucky from postseason play for the next two years, barred the school from live TV during the 1989-90 season, restricted the program to three scholarships the following two years, and ordered the school to return the money it had made during the 1988 NCAA Tournament.

Casey, who still claimed he was innocent, was put on conditional probation for five years, meaning he couldn't coach at another NCAA school. Mills, who also said he was not guilty, transferred to Arizona. The only reason the program wasn't given the death penalty was because Kentucky's president convinced AD Cliff Hagan to step down, and Sutton and his staff resigned.

Sutton got caught in a difficult situation, but I'm glad he was able to bounce back. He has done a phenomenal job at Oklahoma State in a league where it is difficult to compete.

He handled it with class with me, too. He said that he was unhappy with what I'd said but that I was entitled to my opinion.

But I'm all about compassion, too.

We've remained friends since.

Man, if you're ever caught breaking the rules, the NCAA can make you pay.

The NCAA Infractions Committee banned the Wolverines from this year's postseason and put the program on three and a half years' probation because of a booster's payments to players that dated back to the Fab Five era. The team also will lose one of its 13 scholarships annually for four years, beginning in 2004-05.

The case stemmed from an investigation involving a Michigan booster, Ed Martin, who pleaded guilty in 2002 to conspiracy to launder money. He'd told the feds that he gave hundreds of thousands of dollars to former players, including current Sacramento Kings star Chris Webber, while they were in high school and college. Martin died in February—on the same day Michigan officials met with the Infractions Committee.

"This is one of the most egregious violations of the NCAA laws in the history of the organization," NCAA Infractions Committee chairman Thomas Yeager said. "The reputations of the university, the student athletes and the coach as a result of the basketball team's accomplishments from 1992 through 1998 were a sham."

Come on. The school punished the team by not allowing it to play in the 2003 NCAA or NIT Tournament. They removed four banners from Crisler Arena and any pictures, words or records in printed materials involving Webber, Maurice Taylor, Robert Traylor and Louis Bullock, forfeited 112 regular-season games and tournament victories from five seasons, plus its victory in the 1992 NCAA semifinals, and returned $450,000 to the NCAA from tarnished postseason appearances.

That was severe enough. But then to come back a year later and hit them again was overkill, man. I felt that if the NCAA hit Michigan with scholarship reductions, made them take the banners down and hit them with a financial penalty, it would have been sufficient.

I really believe coaches who were part of that situation warrant some punishment. But what did Tommy Amaker ever do? What did those kids who wear that uniform now do? They weren't involved with Chris Webber and the kids from that Fab Five era.

I have a major problem with a society that wants to penalize innocent people.

I was embarrassed when this stuff first came out because I'd praised that 1992 team to the skies. I said, "We will never, ever in college basketball see five freshmen assemble as a unit and reach the national championship game again." And they not only did it once—they went to the Final Four twice, and I certainly applauded it then. But I don't applaud it now. I'm being facetious when I say this, but, heck, they may have had a better payroll than some NBA teams. In fact, when you hear the numbers involved, it seems to me that Webber and the others probably had to take pay cuts when they left Michigan for the NBA. Only joking, guys. Only joking.

Their coach, Steve Fisher, who has since moved on to San Diego State University, had to have had some idea that things were getting out of control from simply seeing a guy like Ed Martin regularly visiting with the Michigan players. In all fairness to Fisher, I'm sure he had no idea his guys were getting those kind of dollars. I mean, it truly blew his mind when the reports surfaced and he read about the cash they'd received. But stating all that, a coach has to be accountable for what happens in his program. There are some who ask, and rightly so, why Amaker should be paying for what happened during Fisher's regime. Maybe Fisher should be getting the heat.

There are a lot of alums who want to be Charlie Tuna, who want to be the big fish. They want to be able to stroll around and let all the other alumni and fans know that they're in with the players. But the only reason they get in with the player is that they are stuffing loads of cash into his pocket. Usually, their message to the player is very simple—"Keep your mouth shut and I'll take care of you while you are on our campus. You'll be my guy." And many of these players buy into the scheme.

There are a lot of guys who are jock chasers. They end up destroying the reputation of their university. They can have such a passion for their school, but they also, because of their greedy actions and hunger in recruiting, ruin the lives of innocent coaches who are unaware of many of the transactions that take place. But no matter what, a coach must work diligently to make it clear to his players that they need to be careful about the kind of people they associate with.

In the end, the coach is the leader of the pack. It's like what's happening in the business world at places like Enron, where the CEOs can't dodge the bullet. They've got to take the hit because they're the guys in charge. They're the ones signing off on things, man.

But I will say this. The kids—Chris Webber and that group—have to be accountable, too. They know right from wrong. I don't want to hear, "Well, they're making so much money off my jersey." That doesn't give a player the right to do anything that's illegal. They may have a right to complain about it; they may have a legitimate argument—in fact, I would love to see the players get something from that $6 billion CBS TV contract; they deserve it—but don't tell me they don't know right from wrong when somebody's trying to lay cash on them.

I've often stated that players in the revenue sports—basketball and football—deserve at least $200 per month for spending money. However, it's easy to see the dilemma that this would create, as the big question would be, "What about all the other programs such as swimming, tennis, baseball and so on?" It would be a costly proposition.

I can already hear my girls Terri and Sherri screaming, "Hey, what about us? When we were playing tennis, we were working just as hard as the football and basketball players." And let me tell you, they have a legitimate argument. But when you think about the dollars that the basketball and football programs are bringing in and the pressure that it has now created for the student athlete, you just might begin to understand why I feel the way I do.

Saying all of that, in this day and age, these players are not little babies. They know right from wrong. They know they have no right to take cash from anyone. It starts in the home where kids get the right values. It starts with Mom and Dad or whoever is raising that youngster and their involvement in helping to shape that child's character from his earliest days to adulthood. I tell players all the time when speaking at various functions at which athletes are present, they simply have to make a decision. "Do you want to be a prostitute and have your body bought?" I ask. "Because the bottom line is that when someone is springing cash on you, they are simply saying that they want to own you during your days on this campus. Be a man. Look in the mirror, and tell yourself, 'I don't need it; I don't want it. I'm still gonna get my three meals a day, live in my dorm room, get an opportunity for an education, and get a chance to show my athletic skills— and then I'll move on with my life in a positive way without feeling obligated to anyone.'" That's what the winner does—guys like David Robinson, Tim Duncan, Grant Hill, and company. They have values, my friends. They have values.

I'm still on the side of Tommy Amaker and his kids. My problem with the punishment handed down to Michigan is the fact that the process just took forever.

Louisville got a harsh taste of that same reality in February, 2003, when the NCAA began snooping around, looking into Marvin Stone's eligibility over allegations of extra benefits that occurred five years earlier when the Cardinals' starting center was playing AAU ball in Huntsville, Alabama. Dan Wetzel, who co-wrote the best seller *Sole Influence* with Don Yaeger, was penning stories about a Ford Explorer Stone was driving three years ago.

The NCAA was all over Stone, who'd transferred to Louisville from Kentucky the year before, checking into wire transfers of money sent to Stone from his mom and two sisters in Alabama. Man, it was no secret these problems involving Stone took place. But that was three years ago. What about the timing—coming up late in his senior year? Give me a break.

It was a mess, but Stone was eventually cleared to play in March.

It didn't take long for Iowa State to whack its coach, Larry Eustachy, last spring. Eustachy was one of the better game-day minds in the country. He coached Iowa State to back-to-back Big 12 titles. I was hoping one day I'd get a chance to do one of his games in Ames.

But he lost a big-time $1.1-million-per-year deal after the *Des Moines Register* published pictures of him partying with students and hanging out with coeds at an apartment party in Columbia, Missouri, following a loss to Missouri in February.

It didn't take long for the paper to call for his dismissal. Eustachy apologized. Then he admitted he had an alcohol problem, said he had started counseling, and pleaded for a second chance.

He was brutally honest.

He even talked about the fact that his wife, Stacy, wrote him a letter in January after she'd found him lying drunk on the kitchen floor. She'd urged him to change before he wound up ruining his 15-year marriage.

But it was too late. In the previous year, six of Iowa State's players had been arrested and eight players had left. There was also the indictment of Randy Brown, an assistant coach, who was fired after the school discovered he had child pornography on his university computer. This latest incident was the last straw. AD Bruce Van De Velde had had enough and invoked a morals clause to fire Eustachy.

Eustachy, who admits he drank every day for the last 30 years, was known for his violent mood swings. Who can forget the NCAA Regional title against Michigan State when he went into total meltdown and was hit with two Ts at the end of the game and tossed?

Over the years, Larry Eustachy has given a lot of chances to kids. Not every school is Duke. Not every coach is going to be in a situation where he's getting the blue chip, crème de la crème academically and athletically.

But Eustachy was totally wrong in going to a party on or near a college campus after his team had just lost to Missouri and drinking with a bunch of kids and hanging out until 3:00, 4:00 in the morning. That's an absolute no-no. There's no way to explain that.

Alcoholism is a sickness, and in order to solve the problem, you have to admit that you have one. Eustachy says he has addressed the situation and says he is going to rehab. One of the things he said after this was, "Some of my heroes are Rudy Tomjanovich and Jerry Sloan, people who have bounced back." It's great that he can identify with those guys.

He'll get another opportunity. We have a country that's very forgiving when people are up-front about what their problems are.

But it's hard to know whether the country will be as forgiving with Mike Price.

The 57-year-old Price was the head football coach at Alabama. But the school fired him before he ever coached a game. There were reports that Price had spent hundreds of dollars on drinks for himself and friends and had paid for private dances at a Pensacola, Florida, strip club while in town for a Pro-Am golf tournament in March. In addition, an unidentified woman in the hotel room registered to Price had reportedly ordered more than $1,000 in food and drink and charged it to his room bill while he was on the golf course. The school investigated and found the reports to be true.

Price had just agreed to a seven-year, $10 million deal in January after coaching Washington State to a Pac-10 title and a second trip to the Rose Bowl in the last six years.

Alabama's new president, Robert Witt, on the job since January 27, informed the Board of Trustees of his decision, just four days after he said no disciplinary action was planned.

Price said at his press conference he didn't think the punishment fit the crime. "I asked President Witt for a second chance. He declined. Whatever happened to second chances in life? But President Witt did not give me that opportunity. I wanted to make something positive out of this negative. I really, truly believe the University of Alabama is bigger and better than this. We could have overcome this . . . I feel I was the man who could have put this behind us."

Sports Illustrated didn't think so, however. *SI* ran a story about the firing the next week. Among other things, *SI* quoted one woman from the club who claimed she and two others went back to Price's room that night. The magazine also quoted two Alabama students who claimed Price, who had apparently been chastised twice by AD Mal Moore for spending time buying drinks for students and hanging out in too many bars, went to a local bar a few weeks after he was hired and, after four hours of drinking, propositioned some female students.

Price, who has been married for 35 years and has two sons, Aaron and Eric, on his coaching staff, has since denied everything and is suing *SI* for $20 million. The magazine stands by its story.

In January, 2003, I was in Tuscaloosa to do the Alabama-Kentucky game, and I was going over the box score at halftime when they introduced Price to the crowd. He absolutely blew me away with his speech and incredible enthusiasm. I turned to my buddy Tom Niedenfuer, who pitched for the Dodgers and was a former Washington State athlete, and said, "Alabama has a winner."

Well, let me tell you, Niedenfuer, who knew Price from his days at Washington State, said, "This guy has the whole package."

We agreed they had made a great hire. Man, were we really fooled.

I mean, to think he threw it all away is absolutely wacky. What's really interesting, though, was that there was never a hint of a problem ever in Pullman, Washington. You just wonder what happened that caused him to go so wrong.

I don't know what his thinking process was—going to a strip joint, then carrying on in that fashion. I have no idea what a guy in his position could have been thinking—especially in this day and age, where everybody in the public eye is scrutinized. When you are a public figure, you have to be careful about things the average guy doesn't have to worry about.

I read a quote the other day from former Cowboys superstar Michael Irvin, who has had troubles in the past with drug abuse. By the way, Irvin has bounced back beautifully from the problems that he had during his NFL career and has now become a member of our ESPN family. He claimed Alabama should have given Mike Price a second chance because the greatest role models are those who have learned from their mistakes.

Huh?

I respect anyone who battles back from adversity. But to me, the greatest role models are those who have done things the right way and made good decisions their entire lives—baseball stars like Derek Jeter and Alex Rodriguez, basketball supers like Grant Hill, David Robinson, Tim Duncan—who have always understood the difference between right and wrong.

Along those lines, Washington got rid of Rick Neuheisel, its bright young football coach, for participating in college basketball betting pools and then lying to school officials about it.

You could say he gambled—and lost.

The 42-year-old Neuheisel admitted to NCAA investigators that he was part of a four-member team that had the overall winner for both years in what he called "a pizza and beer gathering with neighborhood buddies." Neuheisel and his friends reportedly bet $6,400 on the last two NCAA basketball tournaments and won $12,123 the year that Maryland won the title, according to the *Seattle Post Intelligencer*—which is now saying earlier reports of $20,000 in winnings were wrong. He said his group split the winnings. Under the format, participants bid on each team and the highest bid got that team in the tournament. The kind of pool Neuheisel described is not against state law unless a bookie is involved. Neuheisel claims an e-mail from the athletic department's compliance officer gave him permission to participate.

But the NCAA manual clearly says coaches, staff members and athletes may not knowingly solicit or accept a bet on any intercollegiate competition for any item that has tangible value.

At a news conference, Washington AD Barbara Hedges said she had little choice but to make a change.

Hedges had already put Neuheisel on notice in January after she found out that he'd lied about interviewing for an NFL job with the San Francisco 49ers. "At that time, he was told that further acts of dishonesty would not be tolerated by the University of Washington," she said.

Neuheisel was considered a rising young star when he arrived at Washington from Colorado in 1998. He was considered a players' coach who took his Buffs teams on rafting trips and played guitar in the locker room. Neuheisel was 33-16 in four years at Washington, coaching the Huskies to a 2000 Rose Bowl victory over Purdue. But last fall, the NCAA banned Neuheisel from off-campus recruiting this spring as punishment for 51 rules infractions while he was at Colorado.

I don't know Rick, but I am a college football fan, and to me he has always been walking on the edge. When you think about some of the problems that occurred at Colorado and Washington, he's been walking that thin line. He's a coach; he's got to know that by betting $5,000 and winning $12,000, he's headed in the wrong direction. I felt the school might reprimand him severely for betting, but, as it turns out, the gambling was simply the culmination of a lot of other little problems.

An office pool is one thing, but I don't participate in them, either. I just feel I would be sending the wrong message.

Bill Saum of the NCAA office sent letters out, constantly, trying to make sure certain guys don't send the wrong message. I remember him calling me and asking me to publicize the fact that gambling is against NCAA rules. Now, I do interviews on certain radio shows, and I don't know their sponsors. I guess I was on one that was taking ads from gambling services. They advertised something like, "If you want to make the right picks, call this number."

Saum just let me know about that. He basically said, "Dick, I know you can't scrutinize every show you're going to be on, but if you are aware of any show that's promoting gambling, think twice about being a guest."

I know the NCAA is working around the clock to combat gambling on college games. It's a major concern on campuses. You hear stories. We don't need anything like what happened in the '50s or the '60s when I was at Seton Hall and the betting scandals almost ruined the college game.

But history has a tendency to repeat itself, it seems.

In 1984, four Tulane starters and a backup, including future NBA forward Hot Rod Williams, were accused of shaving points. Two of the players turned state's evidence and testified that the others shaved points in exchange for cash and cocaine. Williams was acquitted, and nobody served jail time.

While I've been at ESPN, this is the only program that I've seen actually shut down by its school because the university president had had enough.

But it showed point shaving was still out there. And it happened again in the '90s at Northwestern and Arizona State.

So we've learned how gambling and drinking and sex have brought down some prominent coaches, guys who had great jobs and made some bad decisions that have hurt them professionally.

Nothing shocks me any more—wait, I take that back.

I was stunned when the players at St. Bonaventure voted to boycott their final two regular-season games. The team was protesting because the NCAA had forced them to forfeit six Atlantic 10 victories, and they were banned by Atlantic-10 presidents from participating in the conference tournament and could ultimately get hit with NCAA sanctions. The school got hit for knowingly using Jamil Terrell, a 6'7" transfer from Coastal Georgia CC in Brunswick, Georgia, who was declared ineligible for violating NCAA junior college guidelines because he had a welding certificate and not the required associate's degree.

The move cost the school $120,000 in fines.

It eventually cost Jan van Breda Kolff, the head coach, and school president Robert Wickenheiser their jobs. Two other athletic department employees—AD Gothard Lane and assistant coach Kort Wickenheiser, Robert's son—resigned after the school discovered three NCAA violations and released a report describing the men's program as being "in turmoil." Glad to hear van Breda Kolff will be back on hardwood in the NBA. He was just hired as an assistant by Tim Floyd of the New Orleans Hornets.

Van Breda Kolff made one major mistake at St. Bonaventure. When those players came in, upset that their teammate had been declared ineligible, and told their coach they were going to forfeit the final two games, van Breda Kolff should have looked those kids in the eye and said, "I respect your feelings. I feel for you. But I'm telling you guys—we've got practice today. We've got games coming up, and you either play or I'm getting 15 guys from the intramural league to wear the uniform and we're going to honor our conference commitments to UMass and Dayton."

A lot happened because he didn't do that.

Can you imagine kids walking in and telling Bobby Knight or John Chaney that they're not going to play? I mean, are you serious?

Some schools—and coaches—just can't seem to stay out of hot water.

The NCAA began chasing Jerry Tarkanian when he was starting out at Long Beach State, but they really got after him big time when he was at the University of Nevada-Las Vegas. He was at odds with the NCAA for 26 years.

Tark's been nominated for the Hall of Fame—and justifiably so, man. He certainly built up Hall of Fame numbers when he was at Vegas and later at Fresno State. He retired in March 2002, with 771 victories, one national title in 1990, four trips to the Final Four, a .794 winning percentage and 20 20-plus-win seasons in 29 years.

Tark is the Pete Rose of basketball. Rose had more than 4,000 hits and belongs in the Hall of Fame. When you look at his Ws and winning percentage, they just blow away the accomplishments of some of those who have already been enshrined. Vegas was eligible to play during Tark's time, so how could you not give him credit for those Ws? But his battles with the NCAA over the years have been legendary, too, and have cost him a chance to get into Springfield.

Tark could go on for hours and hours about how he felt that he was the guy the NCAA was always coming after and how it was deliberately trying to make life miserable for him. I don't know who's right, who's wrong, or what went on—obviously, the NCAA felt warranted in many of the complaints they had—but what amazed me throughout that whole chapter was how Tark could go to that gym, put it all aside, and coach, teach and make his players better.

There aren't many guys in America who could get players to play as hard as he did, night after night. They attacked you, man. That was all set up in practice. His practices were many times tougher than the actual games.

He was in the news again in the spring of 2003 when a former academic adviser for the Fresno State basketball team allegedly participated in the cheating scandal that has prompted an NCAA investigation, according to documents obtained by the *Fresno Bee.*

In February, the paper reported that former team statistician Stephen Mintz said he wrote 17 pieces of coursework for three former players—Courtney Alexander, Dennis Nathan and Terance Roberson—in 2000. Mintz claimed he was paid more than $1,000 for his service—and that Katie Fellen, an academic adviser to coach Jerry Tarkanian's team, organized some of the cheating.

Fellen has denied any involvement, but, according to the *Bee,* a letter from president John Welty to Mintz indicates the NCAA and the school believe Fellen was involved. If the NCAA finds out Fellen was connected, the school could face harsh penalties.

Tarkanian said he has not seen any evidence and will continue to support Fellen.

Fresno State banned itself from the postseason last year because of the violations. The school also imposed a two-year probation and cut three scholarships from the program for other violations that included players eating free food and accepting money from a representative of a sports agent and an overall lack of institutional control. I felt bad for the new coach, Ray Lopes, and the kids. They were challenging for an NCAA bid, and then this all came down.

Now Rick Majerus has run afoul of the NCAA Infractions Committee. Majerus has had a reputation for being a solid citizen in college basketball for the past 33 years.

The University of Utah coach has won big, coaching his Mountain West team to 10 NCAA Tournament appearances in 14 years and the 1998 NCAA finals; his players constantly excel in the classroom. He has an 85 percent graduation rate for his players.

But in the summer of 2003, the NCAA Infractions Committee painted both Majerus and the program in a troubling light, putting the Utes on three years' probation. The NCAA and the university have agreed to reduce the number of scholarships to 12 in each of the next three years and limit the number of official visits to 13 total over the next two years.

The two-year investigation was prompted by allegations about the entire athletic program made by a former ski coach who had been fired for altering an application for a waiver for initial eligibility.

The NCAA did not impose any penalties on Majerus, but cited him for buying most, if not all, his players what it considered impermissible meals from 1996 through 2001, observing three prospects during pickup games in official visits, entrusting an assistant to buy $20 worth of groceries for two players who had no money when they arrived on campus a few days before their financial aid kicked in, and purchasing tickets for his team to watch the movie *Remember the Titans* to promote interracial bonding while they were in town, a benefit that would have been legal if they had been on a road trip.

The committee also cited a former player for failing to reimburse the university in a timely fashion the cost of a $510 airline ticket to return home for the funeral of his best friend and said the program sometimes exceeded the 20-hour per week practice rule.

"This isn't about pizza and cookies," said Tom Yeager, the chairman of the NCAA Infractions Committee and the commissioner of the Colonial Athletic Conference. "It's about a dysfunctional relationship between a coach and the compliance director."

The committee figured Majerus should have listened to the compliance director when he was informed about the rules for impermissible meals. Majerus figured the rules fell into a gray area because of his unusual living arrangement.

He lives in a hotel.

If the same meals—which are legal now—were held at Majerus's home and catered by a restaurant, they would have been allowable. But Majerus did not have that alternative. So he invited players to join him for conversational lunches held over a sandwich at a restaurant on or near campus. The general purpose of those meetings was to discuss personal problems the players were having or general academic or team-related issues.

Majerus figures the meals in question to be no more than 22 over 14 years, with an approximate price of $10 per meal.

"When I took these guys out, we didn't go to fancy restaurants," Majerus said. "We went to pizza places, bagel places, hamburger places. You couldn't spend $10 in those places if you wanted to. I could have gotten those guys catered goose and duck. This was more about compassion."

One of the allegations in this Foodgate scandal involved forward Keith Van Horn, who is now with the Knicks. During Van Horn's freshman year at Utah in 1994, his mother called Majerus to inform him that her husband and Keith's father, Ken, had died unexpectedly from a heart attack and asked Majerus to be the one to break the news to Keith. Van Horn was devastated because he was close to his father. Majerus stayed with Van Horn throughout the night and into the next morning until he could leave town and return home. During their time together, the two shared a meal at Bill and Nada's at 3 A.M. When the bill arrived, Majerus paid for both. The cost was less than $10.

"I guess that night before I put him on the plane, I should have reached over to Keith and said, 'You owe me $9 for your steak and ham and eggs,'" Majerus said.

Majerus can counter other allegations with similar stories—like the player whose brother just attempted suicide or the player from a mixed marriage whose father had just filed for bankruptcy or counseling a player who was thinking about medical school.

"I thought with my heart instead of my head," Majerus said. "The rules require you to think with your head."

Majerus, who has never been involved in any major NCAA violation, certainly doesn't fit the profile of your common criminal. He was selected Muscular Dystrophy Man of the Year and Multiple Sclerosis Man of the Year in Utah. He builds homes for Habitat for Humanity as well as being active in numerous national and local charities.

"I told the NCAA, 'Find a player who said he got some money, find a player who said he got a ride,'" Majerus said. "There is none of that."

Majerus did admit to watching three prospects—Tim Frost, Cameron Goettsche and Jamal Scott—play for a few minutes in pickup games during a 10-day period in April, 2001 and not leaving the gym promptly once he discovered they were there. He had been away from the team for six months following heart surgery and had just returned from Milwaukee, where he had spent three months helping his 74-year-old mother, who was undergoing treatment for breast cancer, and wanted to reacquaint himself with his team. In all three instances, he claimed he was not in the gym to evaluate.

A person needs a doctorate of law to be able to interpret many of the rules within the NCAA's rulebook. How wacky is it that schools are reprimanded for various rules infractions such as those incurred by Majerus? When will people develop good judgment and use better reasoning?

Give me a break—a kid having dinner with a coach and talking about the passing of his dad and you're penalized? Are you serious? What is the advantage of recruiting in that scenario? Think about several of the rules. Eating pizza in his hotel room is a violation. Yet if he lived in a house, it's permissible for players to visit and eat. Where is the sense in this? I don't even want to go on about this, because there's no logic in it at all. It's totally insane. That's my take on the situation.

Hey, Majerus's story is trivial compared to what happened at Baylor. They're night and day.

Baylor is still reeling from an enormous tragedy that occurred at that Big 12 school in the summer of 2003 when Waco, Texas, police discovered the body of 6'9" forward Patrick Dennehy, who had been missing for six weeks, in a field near a rock quarry four miles from campus. Dennehy had been shot twice in the head. Carlton Dotson, who played for Baylor in 2003 and had lived in Dennehy's apartment for a few months, was arrested and charged with the crime on July 21, after telling FBI agents he shot Dennehy after the player tried to shoot him, according to an arrest affidavit.

Wow. What a shock. It doesn't get any worse than the loss of a life. Just think of the locker room—oh, yes, there are battles about playing time, and jealousies occur—but, man, the locker room is usually one place where there is so much respect for one another. How did it get so out of control that Dotson would *allegedly*—as of the publication of this book, the investigation is not yet complete—put a gun to the head of his teammate?

What we do know is that Baylor was a program out of control. The NCAA was on campus after a university investigation revealed major violations by the program. President Robert Sloan said they had uncovered improper financial aid and failure to adequately report a number of drug test results. There were also reports that a booster allegedly paid tuition for freshman Corey Herring and Dennehy, a transfer from New Mexico, because Baylor coach Dave Bliss had run out of scholarships due to the NCAA's five-eight scholarship rule.

Bliss wound up resigning on August 8, 2003, one day after Dennehy's funeral. AD Tom Stanton also resigned, and the school put the program on at least two years' probation. The Bears will not participate in any postseason play, including the Big 12 Tournament, next spring.

Fortunately for the Baylor players, they are now eligible to transfer without sitting out a one-year penalty.

It's all about a program that was a doormat in the Big 12 trying to get to the top of the mountain.

Then came word that Bliss tried to cover up alleged NCAA violations by telling assistant coaches and players to lie and say that Dennehy had been dealing drugs to pay for school, according to secretly recorded audiotapes. The recordings were made by assistant coach Abar Rouse.

Baylor's review committee found no evidence that Dennehy was involved in drug dealing.

I've known Dave Bliss for a long time, from the time when he was a graduate assistant on the General's staff at Indiana, during his days at Cornell and over the years at places like Oklahoma, SMU,

New Mexico and Baylor. He was trying to put the pieces together. But he obviously took the wrong route.

Nobody could blame Sloan for asking for the resignation of Bliss and Stanton. The head coach has to be accountable for the things that go on in his program. How in the world of recruiting—which is the heartbeat of any collegiate program—would Dave Bliss and his staff now be able to convince any blue-chip prospect to wear the Baylor uniform? It would be totally impossible, and therefore someone had to request that Bliss and Stanton be relieved of their duties.

How sad to see this case reach the point where the coach was so desperate to survive that he would even suggest that the staff make up stories. In essence, he committed coaching suicide. In no way, shape, or form can he resurface on the collegiate level again.

But one sobering fact will remain constant—Dennehy was robbed of his life. My heart just breaks for the Dennehy family. They sent their youngster to college to get an education and play some hoops in preparation for his future. How tragic that this dream was taken away from them all. I cannot begin to imagine what Dennehy's family must have felt when they learned that their son was a victim of such a horrible and bizarre incident.

Is there an answer to all these problems and rules violations?

Duke coach Mike Krzyzewski thinks the solution might be a separate governing body for college basketball that could legislate rules and act like its own police force. It may not stop all the problems, but he thinks it could put a dent in them.

"Coaches think about basketball every day of their lives," Krzyzewski said. "College basketball is a billion-dollar business—wouldn't you want somebody running a billion-dollar business to be thinking about it every day? Have you ever heard of a 3-5 year plan for basketball? We need somebody who could talk to the NBA and the NCAA and bring the high school federations under one roof.

"We have so many experts out there. John Wooden has been out of the sport since 1975. How has the NCAA used Coach Wooden? The same with Pete Newell, Dean Smith, John Thompson, Vic Bubas—these are enormous resources. If this were the Far East, people would be making pilgrimages up the mountain just to talk with them."

I agree with Mike on this—it would be great to have somebody with phenomenal experience in college basketball working hand in hand with the NCAA. We need somebody who understands the recruiting problems college coaches face and all the dilemmas that take place in that locker room.

Many of us criticize the NCAA, but let me tell you—they don't make the rules. The rules are made by committee members from the various universities. They vote on the legislation. The NCAA just enforces it.

If you have a person like John Thompson, Dave Gavitt or C.M. Newton working with the organization as a commissioner who represents the interests of intercollegiate basketball, coaches would feel comfortable going into that office and sharing ideas, sharing some of the problems they have—and, who knows?—maybe even some solutions.

10

THE PILLARS OF THE SPORT

You think those soap operas like *General Hospital* and *All My Children* are filled with drama? They're nothing compared to what occurred when word leaked out that North Carolina was about to make a coaching change and Roy Williams of Kansas was at the top of the list.

The college basketball world was going crazy with anticipation.

Williams was in Anaheim at the time, trying to prepare for an NCAA Sweet 16 showdown with the Dukies when the story broke. He did his best to dodge the question for the next two weeks, all the way through the NCAA Tournament. He finally blew up when Bonnie Bernstein of CBS tried to pin him down immediately after Kansas lost to Syracuse in the title game.

She asked him if he was headed for Chapel Hill. He responded tersely, "I don't give a *bleep* about North Carolina right now. I got 13 kids in the locker room crying their eyes out."

My heart goes out to Bonnie, because if a producer's in your ear and they want you to get the story, man, you're just trying to do your job. But I can also understand where Roy was coming from. This was not the moment when he wanted to talk about the Carolina job.

A week later, Williams finally made the decision to go home again, to leave Lawrence after 15 years, to take the head coaching job at North Carolina. He had won 80 percent of his games at Kansas, taken them to four Final Fours and coached them to nine conference championships. Man, they should be proud of what he added to the history of that program.

But Williams has always had strong feelings about his alma mater, ever since he spent a decade as Dean Smith's assistant. He has plenty of friends on Tobacco Road. He has a strong relationship with Dean Smith and Bill Guthridge. His son, Scott, played JV basketball at UNC, and his daughter, Kim, was a cheerleader while on the Carolina campus. The family really bleeds Carolina Blue. They're diehard fans, man—kinda like my guy Tommy Lasorda, who, as we all know, bleeds Dodger Blue.

It didn't take long for Williams to become emotional at his homecoming. He was obviously torn over this decision and began his press conference with an open letter to the fans and players of Kansas, telling them how much he treasured his experience there. "I'm a Tar Heel born. When I die, I'll be a Tar Heel dead," Williams said. "But, in the middle, I'm both Tar Heel and Jayhawk bred. Today was a difficult day for me. Two great places—and I wanted to coach both. Last time, I decided to stay because it was the right thing to do. This time, I decided to leave because it was the right thing."

Smith sat just to the right of the podium with Williams's wife. This was a show of solidarity that had seemed to be missing from the Matt Doherty era.

That period had lasted for three years but ended after Doherty—another former North Carolina player and one of Williams's former assistants at Kansas—was forced to resign after a 19-15 NIT season. Reports had surfaced that four of his players were ready to transfer and another—gifted freshman point guard Raymond Felton—was ready to declare for the NBA.

The Carolina job is in the right guy's hands now. It's in the hands of a guy who should have been there several years ago. Roy Williams has the whole resume. He's got instant credibility.

But it's not like he's inheriting a rebuilding job, either. Matt Doherty got slammed for a lot of things during his tenure at UNC, but one thing he did do was fill up the cupboard with goodies—blue chippers like Raymond Felton, Sean May, Rashad McCants, Jawad Williams and Jackie Manuel who could take Carolina back into the top 10.

I can't wait. It will be just like old times when Lefty Driesell, Dean Smith, Mike Krzyzewski and Jimmy Valvano were patrolling the sidelines and the ACC ruled the basketball world.

The ACC was starting to get away from the big names for a while. Now they've got giants like Duke's Coach K and Gary Williams of Maryland, in addition to Roy Williams. Wow, there are going to be some outstanding coaching matchups.

Williams is a disciplinarian. He told his players at the press conference that he would be demanding. I doubt if you'll see any of them running to the AD's office this year, though.

Kansas fans should be proud of what Williams accomplished, but Roy has taken a lot of unfair rips for leaving. When Williams announced he was going to pack up his bags, Kansas fans began to squawk. They didn't want to see him go, especially after Carolina had come after Williams once before, three years ago, and he turned them down. At that time, Williams met with Kansas fans at the 50-yard line of the football stadium and told them he'd never leave.

But times change. It's a job, not a marriage, man. Several members of the media treated it that way, though. One guy wrote that it was like Roy had cheated on his wife with his lover.

Some fans felt totally betrayed, too. One of them auctioned off on eBay a "Roy Williams is my coach" survival kit, which included a tissue and a Roy Williams family tree to plant in tar. It also included a certificate of loyalty, "signed in disappearing ink."

The same kind of sentiment was expressed by some of his players, too—particularly forward Wayne Simien, who underwent surgery after separating his right shoulder during the season.

"I gave my right arm for that man. Literally," Simien said.

I'll tell you this, though—Williams didn't arrive at his decision easily. North Carolina AD Dick Baddour asked Kansas for permission to speak to Williams two days after the Final Four. Williams agonized and agonized over it and claimed he almost pulled his name out on two different occasions over four days.

I know for a fact that Williams was upset leaving the kids he had recruited this year. He said he was sitting in his study one morning looking at a picture of one of them—Omar Wilkes, whose father, Jamaal, was silky smooth and had a velvet touch when he played for UCLA—and he picked up the phone to tell Baddour he wasn't coming. But he put the phone back down without calling.

And after he flew to L.A. to attend the Wooden Awards dinner and receive the Legends of Coaching Award, he almost did the same thing. He'd run into his senior All-American forward Nick Collison—one of his favorite all-time players—in the hallway of a Los Angeles hotel after a round-table discussion before the dinner. But he didn't do it then either. Instead, he decided to wait until he flew home to Lawrence to make his final decision.

In the end, he said he couldn't say no to a Hall of Famer like Dean Smith a second time.

In my mind, there's only one person to blame for the fact that Roy Williams is no longer at Kansas—the president of that university. He got rid of Bob Frederick, the former AD, who is a close friend of Williams. Things changed drastically when Frederick was no longer part of the equation.

I will never understand that. Bob Frederick had had the foresight to hire Williams in 1988, even though he had never been a head coach. Williams had been an assistant under Dean Smith at North Carolina for 10 years. When Williams applied for the KU job, Frederick already had a stack of applications of successful head coaches on his desk. But because of Dean Smith's recommendation, Frederick was curious enough to call Williams in for an interview. After the interview, he was positive Williams was his guy.

If Frederick had remained there, I honestly believe Roy would have stayed at Kansas. Williams was on cloud nine three years ago when he told that crowd at the football stadium he was not leaving. He was happy, content, but then things began to change administratively with the hiring of Al Bohl as AD. It affected Roy big time.

I'll tell you, man, Williams gets an A from me for having the guts to go back to that team banquet in Lawrence three days after his press conference at North Carolina. There aren't many guys who would have gone back after what he went through. Roy got to spend time with his players, too, trying to soothe some hurt feelings.

Most of those in attendance were supportive, but one person in the back staged a personal protest by screaming "traitor!" when Roy got up to speak. The guy was shouted down big time by Dave Collison, Nick's father, who retorted, "You ought to be ashamed of yourself."

Now, back to Matt Doherty, who came to North Carolina after just one year of head coaching experience at Notre Dame. He had created excitement at Notre Dame his first year in 1999, got them into the NIT and also posted two big victories over highly rated Connecticut. In fact, I felt that year Notre Dame, Virginia and Vanderbilt deserved to be in the NCAA Tournament. And believe me, I screamed it out big time.

Then he went to North Carolina as the second choice. I remember speaking to Doherty and saying, "Hey, Matt, you've seen the scrutiny Bob Davie is under in Notre Dame football. And North Carolina basketball is just like Notre Dame football. I hope you realize the pressure cooker you're stepping into."

Hey, here's a story that I haven't shared with many until now. North Carolina had just beaten a previously undefeated Wake Forest team at the Smith Center. Doherty is going absolutely wacko. I mean, he's crying with the crowd, he's pouring his heart out. It was beautiful to see, a coach filled with pride, bursting with emotion. He's standing off to the side while I'm getting ready to do a remote broadcast back to the studio. Then I hear the voice of Matt Doherty in the background saying, "Now you understand why I came here, Dickie V."

I turned back to him without breaking stride and said, "See me in a couple of years, baby."

Everything was going great, but in every game he was under the gun. And during the 2003 season, the roof caved in.

Doherty had his moments at Carolina, however, winning 26 games, beating Duke, Maryland and Wake on the road and advancing to the second round of the NCAA Tournament his first year. The Tar Heels looked absolutely sensational at the start of the 2002-03 season, winning the Preseason NIT. I couldn't believe the way they dominated Kansas and Stanford. In fact, their young trio—Raymond Felton, center Sean May and the MVP Rashad McCants—played like veterans. Then Sean May went down in the Holiday Festival with a foot injury, and it became an uphill battle from then on. The Tar Heels didn't have enough help up front to weather the storm.

That may be why there were so many crazy rumors appearing on Carolina's multiple fan websites. Among other things, there were anonymous reports about unhappy players meeting with the chancellor, James Moeser. There were reports that all kinds of players were ready to transfer.

It was a lot to absorb.

I came in and told him, "Matt, I'm hearing this, this and this." Matt told me I was about a month behind. He said, "It's not like anybody has to sign their name on the Internet. It could be a Duke fan or a State fan making it up."

The local papers, which cover Carolina basketball like it's the White House, were vigilant in checking out all these reports but never found anything substantial.

North Carolina fans started to vent their frustrations on the talk shows. They were still fuming over the fact that the school chose not to admit powerful 6'8" Jason Parker—who could have been a star under the right conditions—because of a transcript snafu. He wound up at Kentucky. They were also living with the recruiting disappointments of two years previously, when Doherty tried for Tyson Chandler, Eddy Curry, and DeSagana Diop—they all went pro. David Harrison, a seven-footer from Nashville, followed his older brother to Colorado, and then underestimated 6'10" shot blocker Emeka Okafor from Houston wanted to come but signed at UConn instead. In fairness to Doherty, he didn't believe Okafor was ready for prime time—and believe me, he was not the only major college coach to feel that way. Calhoun has done wonders with Okafor, who's now my preseason choice to be the 2003-04 national Player of the Year. And in the cases of Chandler, Curry and Diop, he was dealing with the megabucks of the NBA.

Carolina didn't make the Tournament, losing to Georgetown in the quarterfinals of the NIT.

What was Doherty fired for? Not for his Xs and Os, baby. He was fired because he got in kids' faces. He was unbelievably emotional.

I've often said when you win and you're Rick Pitino, Mike Krzyzewski, Bobby Knight, John Chaney, or John Thompson and you get in kids' faces, they say you're a motivational genius. But if you do that and you're a coach who's fighting for survival, most critics will claim that since you haven't earned credibility, you're unstable and just an emotional wreck. It amazes me how your Ws and Ls can change the whole equation of what people think about your actions on the sideline.

Come on. Matt Doherty was emotional because he had such pride, he wanted to do well, and he wanted his players to play well.

That brings back a story from years ago, back in the '60s when I was coaching at East Rutherford High School. Today when you're screaming at players and you're in their faces, many of them feel so affronted, they usually end up crying to their family, to the media, to whomever, and complaining about such demanding attention. I will never forget a player I coached at East Rutherford by the name of Duffy Alberta, who's now very successful in the business world.

One day, Alberta was waiting outside the locker room for me. He had tears in his eyes, and as I approached, he said to me, "Coach, I want to talk to you."

"What's your problem?" I simply asked him.

"My problem is that you haven't yelled at me in over a week. You've always said that if you're not yelling at us, you're not concerned about us."

Just like all great players, he wanted that discipline because he knew that meant his coach cared about him.

UCLA is another great program.

The good news is that UCLA is in L.A., but the bad news is that UCLA is in L.A. Hollywood, baby, where the entertainment dollar is divided among so many activities—the Dodgers, the Lakers, the Kings, the Hollywood Bowl, and, of course, the movies. People have all sorts of places to spend their money. Fans here want their players and teams to be bigger than life. If you're mediocre, the fans disappear.

And that's just what happened. They disappeared.

Steve Lavin—it's his first head coaching job, and the guy gets fired. Jim Harrick had gotten axed in January, 1996, after an expense account scandal that involved dinner with two blue-chip recruits—Jason and Jarron Collins—who eventually went to Stanford. Lavin happened to be there at the right time. He was on the staff for the team that went on to win the national title in 1995. He wasn't even the No. 1 assistant, but he stepped in. Lavin didn't force UCLA to hire him. He didn't put a gun to their heads. And he busted his gut—he tried and tried. But he was never accepted by anyone involved as the guy who was the legitimate coach at UCLA.

The situation just snowballed out of control in 2003.

Lavin was always in crisis management mode, from the day he took over the program. But he was usually able to pull off a miracle.

Lavin went to the Sweet 16 five times in six years—the only other guy who's done that over the same span of time is Mike Krzyzewski—and then Lavin had one bad year. The bottom line is that those five times weren't enough. Why? Because at UCLA, the expectations are so high. They're not about Sweet 16s. They're about national championships. That's because John Wooden, the Wizard of Westwood, won 10 of them. The banners hanging from the ceiling of Pauley Pavilion are a constant reminder of the glory days, man.

In 2000, when the Bruins were down, they reeled off eight straight wins and beat Stanford in a big game up in Maples Pavilion and made an eventual trip to the Sweet 16. The next year, when those Rick Pitino-to-Westwood rumors were making the rounds, Lavin was as down as could be.

They had just gotten beat by Cal big time in Berkeley on a Thursday night. They were humiliated in a blowout. It was blowout city. I will never forget Steve sitting very lonely up in the seats at Maples the next day as he was getting ready for his team to take the practice floor. I was there with my buddy, Brent Musburger. I looked at Brent and he looked at me and we said, "Let's go talk to the young guy."

We went over and tried to give him a big-time pep talk. Brent and I told him that we knew he was in a difficult situation with all the rumors about Pitino, but that he simply had to keep fighting and fighting.

Well, I'm going to tell you—we were shocked. I don't know what happened, but UCLA went out and played brilliantly that Saturday and upset a well-coached Stanford team. I mean, Mike Montgomery, the Cardinal leader, is one of the most underrated coaches among the fans in America, but certainly not in the eyes of his peers. And then UCLA went on to make another one of their typical runs at the end of the season, ultimately finishing in the Elite Eight.

But this time, Lavin didn't have enough talent to turn it around. The Bruins had only one star—Jason Kapono—and teams were constantly going box and one to limit him.

Lavin's job security was always a major topic of discussion. When UCLA's new AD, Dan Guerrero, announced the firing of football coach Bob Toledo in December, the first question out of the box at the press conference was, "Is Lavin next?"

In L.A., the media has always treated SC football and UCLA basketball like pro franchises. You should have seen what was happening on the talk shows and the Internet.

Those fans were tough. After one particularly bad weekend that included losses to Southern California and St. John's at home, someone began circulating an unfounded rumor that Lavin had told his staff he was going to resign. There were 40 members of the media at his next press conference, waiting for him to raise the white flag.

It doesn't help that the Bruins are no longer the premier program out West, either. Arizona has taken over, and it hasn't helped that Luke Walton—the son of one of UCLA's all-time greats—is playing for Arizona. His father has called Hall of Fame coach Lute Olson "the John Wooden of his day."

And Bill should know.

When UCLA was on top, the Bruins won five of their titles with Kareem Abdul-Jabbar and Bill Walton wearing UCLA colors. Both players stayed all four years. Wooden never had a player leave early. Jim Harrick had only one. Lavin had four leave in six years. Times certainly have changed, as kids are so impatient and they all want that quick jump to the NBA.

In the end, the school said they had no choice but to make a change. In most situations, it's unprofessional on the collegiate level to give a guy the ax in the middle of the season unless something immoral has taken place. But this was one time things had gotten so out of control for the players and the university, it probably would have been better just to make a change and assign one of the assistants as an interim coach. Your heart had to go out to Lavin for the pounding he was taking every day.

I've never seen the pillars of college basketball shake this much. In my mind, there are seven elite programs in the country right now— Kentucky, North Carolina, Duke, Kansas, UCLA, Arizona and Indiana. Three more—Michigan State, Maryland and Connecticut—are on the verge of breaking through.

The first time I saw this kind of upheaval was back in 1988 when Larry Brown left Kansas after the Jayhawks had won the NCAA title. He joined the San Antonio Spurs in the NBA. At the same time, UCLA, which had just fired Walt Hazzard, made pitches for Larry Brown, Mike Krzyzewski, and Jimmy Valvano during the Final Four before finally deciding on Jim Harrick, a former UCLA assistant who was head coach at Pepperdine.

I never thought Mike could leave Duke. But I thought Jimmy V would go. I felt he would have loved that whole Rodeo Drive scene. I believe he would have been right at home in that Hollywood atmosphere. But when it came down to making that final decision, he just didn't feel comfortable—especially after having seen the prices of homes in the Beverly Hills area.

I remember being on the phone with him, trying to get the story for ESPN, and he said, "Dick, I love the sunshine here, but you can't believe some of these little homes going for $3-$4 million."

And his wife, Pam, said there was no way she was heading for Hollywood. She said there was no way Jimmy would ever be home. He'd be out sharing times with all the stars like John Travolta, Tom Cruise, Denzel Washington, and Dustin Hoffman. He'd have been out with all the stars of stars. And, let me tell you, in only a matter of time, he would have been as big as any of them. He would have been the only coach in America to have his own sitcom—I can just imagine it, *The Jimmy V Show*—before UCLA would take the floor.

As for Larry Brown, I once had some fun with him on ESPN. I said, "He is gone. Get the U-Haul out. He's going to San Antonio. Come October 15, Midnight Madness, if Larry Brown is still at Kansas, I will get down on my hands and knees and scrub Allen Field House."

Well, Larry came on ESPN and presented me with a big brush that had *Kansas* written on it—I've still got it at home in my trophy case. He said, "Get ready to brush, 'cause I'm not going anywhere."

"Uh-uh, Larry," I said. "You're going to the NBA, baby."

I got a little nervous because he started to hesitate. I said, "My God, I'm going to have to get on my hands and knees and scrub that arena in front of all those students."

But in the end, he was out of there, and Kansas had to find a new cleaning company as well as a new coach.

Then, in 1997, Rick Pitino left Kentucky for the Boston Celtics.

I wasn't surprised when Pitino left, because his name was always being bandied about whenever NBA jobs opened. I think he felt once he'd won that national title at Kentucky in 1996, he wanted to find out whether he could do it on the NBA level again. He thought he could resurrect the Celtics.

Who could blame him?

When you think of programs that are the best in their respective sports, you think of the Yankees in baseball, Notre Dame in college football, and the Boston Celtics in basketball.

It didn't happen, though, and Rick is back in college, coaching Louisville. I think deep down—and I don't know if Rick would ever admit it—if he could do it over again, he would have stayed at Kentucky and built a dynasty similar to what's been done at Duke.

Of course, the Celtics had offered him $5 million a year—I wouldn't have thought twice, either.

And Dean Smith shocked the world when he resigned that same October, just before the start of the season. I was stunned when he made that announcement because he looked like he still had a lot left in the gas tank. I thought he was just as sharp as ever. But it shows you the kind of guy he is—he wanted to give Bill Guthridge, his longtime assistant, a chance to coach great players. Bill took advantage of it, taking North Carolina to the Final Four two of the three years he coached there.

Three years ago, Bill Guthridge resigned at North Carolina, opening the door for Matt Doherty.

But the biggest upheaval occurred when Indiana fired Bob Knight in September 2000. To me, Bobby Knight should have been a lifer at Indiana, just like Lou Holtz should have finished his career at Notre Dame. Just like Mike Krzyzewski doesn't belong anywhere but Duke. In certain places, you just expect the coach to be there forever.

I think of Bobby Knight and I think of that red sweater; I think of Hoosier basketball. Obviously, Bobby could coach anywhere and be a success. He's like Vince Lombardi.

The General won three national championships, dominated the Big Ten in his 29 years at Indiana. But he was very unhappy the last five years in Bloomington. Many a time, I'd felt that Bobby should have left earlier. He was not happy with the administration.

It had become a real problem, especially after he'd agreed to a zero tolerance policy after videotapes of him allegedly choking one of his players, Neil Reed, in practice became public in March, 2000.

Indiana president Myles Brand set off a firestorm. There were protests on campus when he axed Bobby the following fall. This happened after Bobby had purportedly taken hold of a student outside Assembly Hall. Bobby felt the undergraduate had insulted him by calling him "Knight" instead of "Coach" or "Mr. Knight."

Bobby spent the rest of the year in limbo, out of work and looking for ways to spin his side of the story to people like ESPN's Digger Phelps and the "sympathetic seven," a handpicked group of reporters he invited to campus.

I was still surprised. I'd thought that—somehow—there would have been a solution, a meeting of the minds. But sometimes a divorce is good for both parties. At the end, it was becoming a real problem as to who was right and who was wrong. There was so much controversy, so much notoriety.

Bobby and his wife came down to Sarasota and visited with my wife and me. We had some super conversations and also spent time talking about his situation. I had no doubt that he wanted to coach again. He flat-out loves the gym.

Everybody needs a second chance, even a Hall of Famer like Bobby Knight. After the General had sat out a year, Gerald Myers, the AD at Texas Tech, approached him about moving to Lubbock.

The two had always been friends, and that was a comfort zone for Bobby. Now he's back creating a winning atmosphere and a new basketball tradition. He's a very happy guy these days.

I know he is. Texas Tech finished 22-13 and was third in the 2002 NIT. But Knight told Myers to keep his base salary—all $250,000 of it—because he felt he didn't do a very good job coaching.

I've told him he is absolutely too tough on himself, as he didn't have anywhere near the personnel of Kansas, Texas, Oklahoma or Missouri.

I did a one-on-one with him after he went to Texas Tech. When I pulled up to the United Spirit Arena in Lubbock, I saw that it was located on—get this—Indiana Avenue. That drove me wild.

I said to him, "What's this? This can't be true. They didn't do this because of you, did they?"

He said, "No. It's been there forever."

But Bill Self and Ben Howland are still adjusting to their new addresses. They are two of the rising stars in coaching.

Certainly they're not there yet with Roy Williams and Mike Krzyzewski, and they'll be the first to tell you that. But they are guys who have been on the fast track and have gotten results wherever they've been.

They come from similar backgrounds. Each did a great job at the mid-major level—Self at Tulsa and Howland at Northern Arizona. Then they each went to a major school in a major conference and did well. Self won the Big Ten title at Illinois. Howland won the Big East title at Pitt. Now they've moved on to the elite programs—Self to Kansas and Howland to UCLA.

People could ask, if you're in a great program, you love it, you're making great money, and you've got things rolling, why would you go someplace where you're always going to be compared to the previous coach? But both these guys were very comfortable with their decisions.

Bill Self has a Big 12 background. He played at Oklahoma State and coached as an assistant to Larry Brown at Kansas. He was familiar with Lawrence. It was close to his family's home.

The same type of deal with Ben Howland—he was a California kid, dreamed about being at UCLA, and loved following the John Wooden teams. When he was growing up in Santa Barbara, he would stay up late and study videotapes of old UCLA games. Now he has a chance to go back home.

I heard Illinois and Pitt were ready to match the dollars to keep both guys, but it's hard to turn down a chance to coach at one of the shrines.

"I know," Bill Self said to me, "following a guy like Roy Williams is not going to be easy. Eyes are going to be glued to everything you do. But think about the success ratio—Ted Owens went to the Final Four, Larry Brown won a national championship, Roy Williams got to four Final Fours. The program has always been able to move on because of its reputation, its great fan following and the tradition it has."

Same with Ben Howland—he doesn't want to hear about the failures. He believes he can change things at UCLA.

And I agree with him.

I told the staff when I was an assistant at Rutgers that I wanted to go after the best players in the nation. I told our people, "I want to go and try to recruit Phil Sellers from Thomas Jefferson High in Brooklyn." I was going to go after the best. Sellers was the best prospect in the country. In fact, his senior year, he won the MVP of Sonny Vaccaro's Dapper Dan All-Star game. All I kept hearing was, "You can't do it; Rutgers plays in the Barn with only 2,500 seats." And I remember saying, "If you think you're mediocre, you're going to be mediocre. If you think you're special, you're going to be special."

All I have to point to now is the Final Four in 1976. Indiana, UCLA, Michigan and—ta da—this little school, Rutgers, led by Phil Sellers, Mike Dabney and the other great recruits that came along— Eddie Jordan, Hollis Copeland and James Bailey. Tom Young ultimately did a great job with those kids, but the foundation was established by previous head coach Dick Lloyd. I've always felt that Lloyd left the coaching profession too early—he moved on to administration—because, believe me, this guy knew how to organize, practice, and prepare for a game. He taught me so much about the Xs and Os.

Bill Self believes he's going to win at Kansas, and Ben Howland believes he's going to win at UCLA because the recruiting area is so fertile. But they'd better win 25, 26, 27 games at those places, because 19-12 is not going to get it done.

Both Self and Howland have come to these marquee programs as relatively young coaches. When you take on a program like Kansas or UCLA, you'd better expect to be under constant scrutiny and evaluation.

Guys like Pitino, Williams and Krzyzewski are not judged by every game. Unfortunately, for Matt Doherty and Steve Lavin—and I feel for those guys—every game was a final exam. Every day was a calculus test you'd forgotten to study for. Every time they stepped onto the hardwood, they would be thinking, "Do well here today or tomorrow the fans will be screaming and the players will be in an uproar, because they all think you're only as good as your most recent performance."

And guys like Doherty and Lavin want to get back to prove they can do the job.

Matt Doherty is a guy who just moved up too quickly. He should have stayed at Notre Dame. Even Matt says that. The AD there, Kevin White, wanted him badly, and he could have learned at Notre Dame because the pressure there in basketball is not the same as it is at North Carolina.

Somebody should give him another shot. The experiences he's had at Notre Dame and North Carolina have really prepared him for the next opportunity. I mean, this guy has the key elements that are important in making it in life. I've always believed in a very simple formula that I learned a long time ago and that I'll share with you now. It's very simple—Passion + A Good Work Ethic + Good Decisions in Your Personal Life = Success.

Matt Doherty has those things. So does Steve Lavin.

Steve Lavin will pop up again in coaching, too. In the meantime, he just signed a deal with ESPN to do 20 hours a week in the studio and work 30 games. My recommendation to him would be do some television, get some visibility, and then go back to coaching if that's what he wants. I know a lot of coaches feel they have to get back to prove what a mistake it was to fire them. I know I've always had that on my mind since my days of getting axed by the Pistons. It's something that's a little bit empty on my resume, something that I never got a chance to fill out.

Fortunately, television has given me 25 years, and you know what, baby? I hear about all the Ws Dean has, the 879 and all, but he can't touch my record, man. I'm undefeated, about 1,000-0 in the world of TV, where you never lose a game.

While we're on the subject of visibility—how about Notre Dame football? Bob Davie has a pretty good football mind and was doing a nice job with the Irish. Now he's with us at ESPN. Certainly, I hope and pray he gets another coaching opportunity, because he never had a shot from day one.

He was just like Doherty and Lavin. He took a team to the Fiesta Bowl three years ago. Notre Dame got ripped by Oregon State, and the talk started—and continued all year long. What happened? Well, he wasn't Lou Holtz. He didn't have the credibility. This was his first head coaching job.

Some coaches will always be on the hot seat.

They win enough so that they get the multiyear contracts and have the security mentally, but they never have the security from their boosters and the media.

Look at Indiana coach Mike Davis. He got a long-term deal after leading his team to the NCAA championship game in 2002. He deserved that.

But it seems that today, people can't accept a loss and move on. That's why Mike will be the first to tell you he's got to control what he says after games.

That's the learning curve that goes into coaching.

After several games, he's come out and made comments that he wanted to retract the next day. After the Hoosiers lost to Pitt, 74-52, in the second round of the 2003 NCAA Tournament, he came out talking about the things the players didn't do and how they didn't produce. He ripped the veterans big time.

Davis said his philosophy was "just fine. The players just didn't listen to me."

Talk about walking away from the wreckage.

"This team has been selfish from the time we were 8-0," he said. "Once we got to 8-0, everyone is in their ear. They get 10 phone calls a night, telling them how good they are, saying they should play more—and that's my fault. Last year, I had a team that started trusting me and believing in me and that was because people were criticizing them. This year, people are talking good about them and they believe everything they hear."

Davis was specifically critical of center George Leach, whom he claimed wanted to play only one end of the floor.

It's a shame. A lot of those players—like guards Tom Coverdale, Kyle Hornsby, and A.J. Moye, forward Jeff Newton, and Leach— helped Davis get to the Final Four only a year earlier.

You just can't do that; you can't criticize players in public. That's got to be a private, one-on-one, behind-closed-doors conversation.

It's great to be honest, but sometimes you've got to learn in the world of coaching that you have to be a little political and discreet about how you handle team matters. That comes with experience.

That's the incredible pressure that exists in the world of college coaching. People don't understand that. Everybody relates the pressure to the money; and that certainly is there. But what people don't understand is that when coaches get fired from one of those big-time jobs, most don't get back to the same level.

Mike Krzyzewski was lucky at Duke because he had an AD, Tom Butters, who hung in there with him in the early years when things were shaky. Hey, let's not forget that Duke was 10-17 in Krzyzewski's second year and 11-17 in his third year. There were calls for his head on a platter, but Butters's support for the coach remained strong. And then, in his fourth year, Krzyzewski turned things around, leading his team to an NCAA Tournament appearance and a 24-10 record. By the end of the 2002-03 season, he had racked up 590 wins, nine Final Four appearances, and three national championships in 23 seasons at Duke. If Mike were in the same situation today, who knows? He may not have survived that start at Duke. The whole climate has changed. It's all about today, today, today.

Tom Butters had the vision to watch Mike Krzyzewski, to understand he was a future star of coaching. He was patient and didn't pull the trigger—like so many guys do because of the pressures of the alumni and the media. Ultimately, Mike has become the star of the coaching community.

Butters, Frederick and Gerald Myers are all charter members of my All-Spielberg team. Hey, Steven Spielberg is one of the great directors of all time. He knows how to put a project together. Well, these ADs knew how to make the right call in their basketball program. They took a chance on untested coaches and then hit the jack-pot. I also put Rick Taylor of Cincinnati, Ernie Casale of Temple, Myron Roderick of Oklahoma State, and Jeremy Foley of Florida in that club.

In all of these cases—with the possible exception of Temple—these ADs had stacks of resumes on their desks, but they rolled the dice and made the call.

Rick Taylor took a chance on a young coach from Walsh College and the University of Akron—Bob Huggins. Huggins came to Cincinnati prior to the 1990 season from Akron and immediately turned a stagnant program around, leading the Bearcats to postseason play in each of his 14 seasons there. UC has been ranked No. 1 several times during the Huggins era, making the Final Four in 1992 and winning seven straight Conference USA titles.

Ernie Casale was the AD at Temple in 1982, when that school made a controversial change, pushing out the popular Don Casey—who had won 19 games that year and went to the NIT—and replacing him with John Chaney from Cheyney State, a Division II school. Chaney, a Philly guy, went out and did a Hall of Fame job, taking the Owls to the NCAA Regional finals five times—in 1988, 1991, 1993, 1999, and 2002.

Myron Roderick of Oklahoma State was willing to take the heat by hiring Eddie Sutton in 1991. Sutton had been looking for a job after that huge 1989 NCAA scandal in Kentucky. He coached the Cowboys to a Sweet 16 his first year, a Final Four in 1995 and a Regional final in 2000.

Jeremy Foley of Florida gets credit for listening. Rick Pitino convinced him to bring in Billy Donovan. Billy was 31 years old, coming from Marshall University, where he really hadn't posted big-time numbers. But Rick sold Foley on Billy's personality, his work ethic as a recruiter, and his style of play. It has been a magnificent marriage. Florida reached the NCAA championship game in 2000.

Coaching can be addictive, man.

USA Today did a great story on the returning coaches, guys like Billy Tubbs, Dick Bennett, and Dr. Tom Davis. And people want to know about Rollie Massimino. He was at the top of the mountain, living like a king, after he got the national championship ring at Villanova in 1985. Then he went to Vegas. Next, he spent seven seasons with Cleveland State, where he remained until the end of the 2002-03 season.

Why? Why does he do it?

I'll tell you why.

It's not about the money. It's about the fact that he loves the locker room. He loves the basketball court. That court is part of his life—the teaching and the motivating—and he can't give it up.

That's what happens to a lot of coaches, and it would have happened to me—I know it. If I hadn't gotten into television, I would have gone nuts without coaching. I turned down opportunities in the corporate world because I knew I would be unhappy there.

That's what brings Billy Tubbs back to the sidelines at Lamar, Dick Bennett to Washington State, Dr. Tom Davis to Drake. I couldn't be happier for these guys, because they can't get it out of their systems. They can't get it out of their blood. It's been part of their lives for 40 years. I've got to believe they're totally excited about the challenges ahead of them.

And I'm happy for them, man.

Billy Tubbs, 68, is again coaching at Lamar, his alma mater, which he led to its first two NCAA Tournament appearances in 1979-80. He has won 595 games and coached Oklahoma to the 1988 national championship game. He said he got tired of playing chess and checkers on the Internet.

By the way, he's also the AD—"I talked to my AD the other day," he said, "and he told me I can coach as long as I want to."

Bennett, 60, another retired Final Four coach from Wisconsin, has taken on a rebuilding job at Washington State. He had won 453 games in 25 years and thought he was burned out. But then he went ballistic over a call in an Indiana women's game—the Hoosiers are coached by his daughter, Kathi—and he got the urge to try it again.

Davis, 64, who was 543-290 in a career that included stops at Lafayette, BC, Stanford and Iowa, was forced out at Iowa in 1999 after taking the Hawks to nine NCAA appearances. He never left Iowa City, where he remains extremely popular in the community.

Dr. Tom was happy reading books and taking golf trips to Florida and Scotland—until Drake AD Dave Blank called, looking for somebody to rekindle the fortunes at his school, which has not been to the NCAA Tournament since 1971. Drake is located in nearby Des Moines.

Some people have asked me if I would ever come back.

There is not a job in America—even if they offer me multimillions of dollars—good enough for me to give up what I'm doing now. Not one. Talking about basketball on ESPN and ABC is the greatest job in the world, and to receive a check for it makes it even that much sweeter.

Obviously, when I was coaching the Titans, there were nights when I would toss and turn in my bed, thinking about what it would have been like if I were coaching at the Golden Dome, if I were the head coach at Notre Dame.

I'm constantly telling Digger that at one time, I was always dreaming about getting his job coaching at the Golden Dome. But trust me, today I have no desire to step back out on the hardwood, because I absolutely love coaching Indiana on Monday, Kentucky on Wednesday, Duke on Thursday, North Carolina on Saturday—and always going home with a big W. Plus, I love the freedom that the off season brings, so that I can share quality time with my family.

Does this mean I've been cured?

11

THE GLOBAL GAME

I had a brief experience with royalty when I was over in Barcelona in 1992 filing reports on the summer Olympics for ABC radio—and I don't mean the king and queen of Spain.

I'm talking about the original Dream Team—Michael Jordan, Magic Johnson, Larry Bird, Charles Barkley, Patrick Ewing, Scottie Pippen, Karl Malone, David Robinson, John Stockton, Chris Mullin, Clyde Drexler—all NBA superstars—and Christian Laettner from Duke, who was added as the 12th man because of his contributions to USA Basketball when he was in college. Most of these guys have spots reserved for them at the Basketball Hall of Fame in Springfield.

This was the first year America sent NBA players to the summer games. They were so good that Isiah Thomas—the best player ever to play at Indiana—wasn't even invited to be on the roster.

At first, the idea of using NBA stars bothered me. I loved the idea of our premier college kids competing against the best of the rest of the world. But I changed my opinion after the Seoul Olympics. Our USA squad—coached by John Thompson—was a purely amateur team.

I will never forget the overseas phone call I got from Sonny Vaccaro the night before we played Arvydas Sabonis and the Russian team in the semifinals of that tournament.

He said to me, "Dickie V, forget about it. These teams have no chance. It's blowout city, baby."

I felt really good hearing that.

Then, all of a sudden, I come home and I see on the news that we were beaten, 82-76. Watching their players celebrate that big W, I realized, "Hey, man, it's time for us to send our best."

And, oh baby, did we send our best in 1992.

The rest of the world knew it, too.

By the time they arrived in Barcelona, they were being treated like rock stars. Members of the media were calling them the American Beatles, man. They were like superheroes to the people there. They were in a different class from the rest of the athletes in terms of recognition and the way people reacted to them. They were so ballyhooed.

They were so big and so visible that they couldn't stay in the Olympic village. They stayed in $900-per-night rooms at the Hotel Ambassador. Every day, there were mobs of autograph seekers outside the doors, which were guarded by armed policemen. When they went to practice and the games, their bus was accompanied by a military escort of tanks, helicopters, police cars and SWAT teams. And if they did try to go out to party at night, they were immediately devoured by the crowd.

Everybody wanted a piece of this team—except the countries they were playing.

Take a look at the scores.

• USA 116, Angola 48
• USA 103, Croatia 70
• USA 111, Germany 68

- USA 127, Brazil 83
- USA 122, Spain 81
- USA 115, Puerto Rico 77
- USA 127, Lithuania 76
- USA 117, Croatia 85

Team USA won by an average of 43.8 points, and the closest any opponent came was 32 points. Back then, it didn't matter which players were utilized. You could have gone to the bench—that's a nice feeling. You're winning by 20, and now you want to substitute and to give the starters a break, so you're turning and saying, "Hey Larry, can you go in for Jordan?"

No problem, man.

As great as this team was in its individual players, what made it extra special was that these players totally understood how to play the game. Often, when you have a collection of superstars, it just becomes a one-on-one, individual show. But Chuck Daly, the coach of that '92 team, did a good job of keeping them focused.

Nobody on Team USA apologized for running up the score, especially Charles Barkley, who led the team in scoring. Barkley got some heat from the world press when he stuck his elbow into the chest of a skinny little Angolan player in the midst of a 31-0 run in the first game. He had this advice for his critics—"If they don't like it, they can turn the TV off." Well, my friends, that was just Charles being Charles.

The only real crisis occurred just before the end of the carnage when the International Olympic Committee informed the players that anyone who wasn't wearing a Reebok uniform wouldn't be allowed on the medal stand. Reebok had paid $4 million to outfit every American gold medal winner, but the players—particularly Michael Jordan, who was getting $8 million from Nike—refused to go along.

In the end, a compromise was negotiated by NBA commissioner David Stern. Team USA wore Reebok sweat suits, but they were allowed to cover up the logo—Michael draped an American flag around himself to hide it.

Everybody thought this dominance would last forever.

After all, the only international players most Americans had heard of at that point were Arvydas Sabonis of Lithuania, Detlef Schrempf of Germany, Oscar Schmidt of Brazil and Toni Kukoc and the late Drazen Petrovic of Croatia. Sabonis, Schrempf and Petrovic played in the NBA. Schmidt made his reputation when he scored 46 on the USA during a 120-115 upset in the 1987 Pan Am games in Indianapolis. And Chicago GM Jerry Krause had just offered Kukoc $3 million to sign with the Bulls.

But the times, they are changing.

Marty Blake, the NBA's director of scouting, was the first person to look at international players, back when he was the GM of the Atlanta Hawks. He found Dino Meneghin in Italy. Meneghin was a 6'8", 260-pound, 18-year-old forward who played for Rio Madrid.

Marty drafted him with his 11th pick in the 1970 draft and wanted to sign him, but the owners thought it was a publicity stunt, so it never happened. Meneghin went on to play in four Olympics and was voted the best European player of all time. He was just inducted into the Basketball Hall of Fame in Springfield.

I never recruited any foreign prospects when I was at Detroit, although I once had a player from England on one of my teams. But times were different then.

When I started working for ESPN, international players were still pretty much an afterthought. Most of the ones who did make it to the NBA—guys like Leo Rautins of Canada, who played for Syracuse, Rik Smits of Marist, who played for Indiana, and Detlef Schrempf of Washington, who played for Seattle, among others—got noticed because they'd played college ball in the states.

But now, every NBA club has a full-time international scout. There are 5,000-6,000 foreign players. You're bound to find 15 to 20 who can really play.

The thing about the NBA is if there's a kid who can play—anywhere—Marty Blake and the NBA scouts will find him. I don't care where they are. Very few are looking to slip through the door.

In the 2003 season, there were 65 international players on NBA rosters. Four of them—7'5" Yao Ming of China and the Houston Rockets, guard Steve Nash of Canada and forward Dirk Nowitzki of Germany and the Dallas Mavericks, and guard Predrag Stojakovic of Yugoslavia and the Sacramento Kings—made the All-Star team. Six more played in the NBA rookie versus second-year players' game.

This year, the number on NBA rosters could reach 80.

The NBA had representatives from five different continents in the NBA semifinals. They were Mehmet Okur of Turkey and Zeljko Rebraca from Serbia-Montenegro from Detroit, Dikembe Mutombo of Congo from the Nets, Manu Ginobili of Argentina and Tony Parker of France from San Antonio, and Nowitzki and Nash, Eduardo Najera of Mexico and Tariq Abdul-Wahad of France from Dallas.

It's like having a United Nations on the court.

There were eight foreign players selected in the first round of the 2003 NBA draft, including 7', 245-pound Darko Milicic of Serbia, who went No. 2 to Detroit, and 6'6" guard Mickael Pietrus of France, who is known as "The French Jordan" and who went with the 11th pick to Golden State. There were 21 taken overall, easily eclipsing the previous record of 14 taken last year.

Maciej Lampe, a 7' forward from Poland, is only 18 and was the youngest player ever to play for the Rio Madrid first team. He might have gone in the lottery, too, but he still has two years remaining on his contract and was not cleared to play by the NBA prior to the draft. He finally went to the Knicks with the first pick in the second round.

Milicic is also only 18 years old, but he is considered the best young prospect in Europe, even though he averaged only 9.5 points and is still establishing himself on his team. Hemofarm Vrsac is in the first division of the Yugoslavian Professional League. He has never played on a European championship club—he is considered too young, but he's packed a lot into those few years.

He was born in Novi Sad, Montenegro, and grew up in a country that has been torn apart by war. His father is a policeman. His mother works for the pharmaceutical company that sponsors his team. He has been on his own since 14, living in an apartment provided by the team.

He practiced in the gym six to seven hours a day against older guys—the average age of his club team is 27.

Apparently, nothing gets in the way of practice. Once, when he was 14, a bomb shook the gym where his cadet team was working out.

The coach simply told them, "Keep practicing."

One thing about international players is that they don't have a lot of the luxuries that we have here. Many a time we spoil our athletes. Across the seas, though, they are absolutely hungry and have a thirst for knowledge that is unique.

Milicic plays in a gym that holds just 3,500, but the crowd can be rowdy. There are stories about fans throwing firecrackers onto the court when they're upset with a call.

Milicic is totally ambidextrous. He's a skilled, versatile big man who's cut along the same lines as Nowitzki, something this country has not been producing in big numbers these days. His agent, Mark Cornstein, brought Milicic and two of his countrymen—6'7" Alexsandar Pavlovic and 7'4" Slavko Vranes—along with Zoran

Planinic, a 6'7" guard from Croatia, to the United States for a month to work out at John Jay College prior to the draft. Planinic went to the Nets at 22. Vranes went in the second round to the Knicks.

The Pistons, who stayed in New York for the NBA Eastern Conference finals, had a shoot-around in the same place where Milicic was working out one day.

Some of them wandered in to watch, and jaws started dropping everywhere—even GM Joe Dumars had his mouth wide open.

There was only one American center—Chris Kaman, a 7' junior from Central Michigan—taken in the first round. There were just two more—Wesley Wilson, who played just a half year at Georgetown, and Donald Little, who was thrown off Cincinnati and wound up becoming Rookie of the Year in Turkey—at the NBA pre-draft camp in Chicago. And there were none at the USA Basketball junior trials at Colorado Springs.

Marty Blake went with John Thompson when he was scouting the European championship for the 1988 Olympics. He asked John about coaching big men who could play with their backs to the basket. Having coached guys like Patrick Ewing and Alonzo Mourning, Thompson was familiar with that type of player.

John told him it was getting harder and harder to find guys like that because nowadays they all want to play facing the basket.

Conversely, there are supposedly 30 seven-footers in China. With two million people playing the game in that country, you're going to produce some great players just by osmosis.

The U.S. should be the favorite to win the gold medal in Athens in 2004 because of all the heavyweights they've assembled. USA Basketball received assurances that centers Tim Duncan of San Antonio, Elton Brand of the L.A. Clippers and Jermaine O'Neal of Indiana, forwards Karl Malone of the Lakers, Tracy McGrady of Orlando, Richard Jefferson of New Jersey, and guards Kobe Bryant of the Lakers (whose participation is now in doubt, due to his legal trouble), Allen Iverson of the Philadelphia 76ers, Jason Kidd of the Nets, Ray Allen of Milwaukee and Mike Bibby of the Sacramento Kings would all play. USA Basketball also added forward Nick Collison from Kansas as a reward for all his contributions to their age-group programs.

Larry Brown of Detroit, a Hall of Famer, will be the coach, and I really like our chances because everybody wants to be there. But this country is no longer a lock to win every international competition.

When Yugoslavia shows up in Athens, they will have Dejan Bodiroga, a 6'8" guard who was drafted by Sacramento in the second round in 1995 and who is arguably the best player in Europe, and 11 other NBA-caliber players.

Our '92 Olympic team set the standard. They were great inspiration and motivation to opposing international teams. Those countries have worked and worked and worked to improve.

I never, ever thought the players from Europe would become as skilled as they have. I mean, these players keep getting better and better. Take a look at Nowitzki—he's got some Larry Bird in him. Take a look at the kid Manu Ginobili—I saw him do a reverse slam in San Antonio that was unbelievable. Take a look at Stojakovic—years ago when you thought about a foreign player, he was either a stationary long-range shooter or a physical, block-out guy down inside. But now we're seeing mobility and agility.

The advancement of the game has been incredible. A lot of that is the result of the teaching that's going on—American coaches, like Hubie Brown from the Memphis Grizzlies, have been going abroad for years to put on clinics. And international players have really taken to the game.

The fact that players around the world can catch the NBA on TV has provided a lot of inspiration. David Stern has the game pumped into more than 200 countries. I think what has motivated a lot of young kids has been the sight of their fellow countrymen becoming success stories and loving to play here.

Years ago, the legendary Johnny Most, who called the action on the radio for the Boston Celtics for over three decades, was at the McDonald's Challenge on ESPN when the Celtics played abroad. It was an absolute riot listening to him. He'd say something like, "Hey, I don't know who these guys are." And then he'd go, "That's a jump shot by, ah, the guy with the hair on his chest."

Today, though, we do know these guys.

Other countries have closed the talent gap. Bob Ryan of *The Boston Globe* put it best when he said, "They got a barometer to measure themselves when they played against our Dream Team. They were able to study, analyze, look at their kids, realize the level they had to get to."

And they did it.

Lithuania almost beat the U.S. in the 2000 games at Sydney, and you know what happened at the 2002 world championships in Indianapolis. Our country got an absolute wake-up call—after winning 58 straight games in international competition, the roof collapsed on USA basketball. The team we sent to the world championships lost three times and did not win a medal.

International teams simply embarrassed us in Indianapolis.

The U.S. lost to Argentina 87-80 in pool play, lost again to Yugoslavia 81-78 in the quarterfinals of the medal round, and lost once more to Spain 81-76, in the fifth-place game.

We can say all we want about not having our superstars there. Shaquille O'Neal, Kevin Garnett and guards Jason Kidd, Kobe Bryant and Ray Allen didn't play. And maybe Jason Kidd or another shooter like Allen Iverson could have totally changed the chemistry and the outcome.

But the fact remains the USA got totally embarrassed on our home turf.

Listen, I know the NBA season goes on forever. And the world championships are a six-week commitment in the summer. Sometimes guys are rehabbing from injuries. They have their livelihoods to think about. However, I'm from the old school. I feel that, when Uncle Sam comes a'calling, you should go a'running.

But we had an NBA coach—George Karl, then of the Milwaukee Bucks—and 12 NBA players—Elton Brand of the Clippers and Andre Miller, at the time also of the Clippers and now with Denver, Antonio Davis of Toronto, Baron Davis of New Orleans, Michael Finley of Dallas, Raef LaFrentz of Dallas, Shawn Marion of Phoenix, Reggie Miller and Jermaine O'Neal of the Pacers, Paul Pierce of the Celtics, Ben Wallace of Detroit, and rookie Jason Williams of the Chicago Bulls—and we still couldn't hang in and beat those clubs because we didn't make the extra pass, we didn't do all the little things it takes to win.

We didn't have players with that kind of commitment. A lot of guys thought they could just step out onto our home turf and blow people away simply because they were all NBA guys. And they found out teams with one or two NBA guys on the roster were beating us. A lot of it came down to effort, attitude and desire.

And the other teams had more.

After we got beaten initially, it looked like we were just going through the motions. And it came down to some selfishness on the floor. Our shot selection was horrible.

I felt bad for George Karl and his staff.

I think it should be mandatory for each potential USA team player to write a statement, outlining why he wants to play and represent this country. I mean, who wants guys on the team who feel like they're being forced to play? I don't.

Argentina, which had played 44 games together, ran a clinic on the U.S. with point guard Pepe Sanchez, a street-smart, fundamentally sound marginal pro from Temple, schooling NBA All-Stars like Davis and Miller as his team ran their pick-and-roll offense flawlessly for back-door plays and layups. The Americans struggled from the beginning and fell behind by as many as 20 points in the second quarter. They never got any closer than six points.

Yugoslavia, which had two established NBA stars in center Vlade Divac and Stojakovic of the Sacramento Kings and has kept the nucleus of its team together for 10 years, exposed the Americans' lack of low post defense, rallying from 10 points down with 6:42 remaining. Stojakovic finished with a game-high 20 points, and Divac added 16 points and 11 rebounds.

Spain defeated the U.S. when the American team, which had led by as many as 16 points in the third quarter, struggled to score in the fourth quarter and made just three of 16 shots to be outscored, 25-10.

Yugoslavia defeated Argentina, 84-77, in OT to win the title. Dejan Bodiroga, a 6'8" guard who was drafted by Sacramento in the second round in 1995 and is arguably the best player in Europe, scored 27 points, including nine in a row at the end of regulation to rally his team from an eight-point deficit.

Germany, with Nowitzki, finished third.

The disappointing performance by the Americans in Indianapolis points to a larger problem. Most American kids spend the summer traveling the nation on the AAU circuit. They play and play and play, yet they don't develop the individual parts of their game.

And NCAA rules don't help—they put a 20-hour-per-week limit on practice, which reduces the amount of time a college athlete can work out with a coach. How dumb is that? Do you really think that in those hours where he isn't permitted to work with a coach, a player is going to run to the library to study? Give me a break.

What's better than having a player-coach relationship? Why not let the coaches work with the players as much as they want? If the purpose of reducing the time that a player works with a coach or limiting the time of practice to 20 hours per week is to improve the student athlete's academics—forget it. The bottom line is that if a kid is determined to graduate, he will—the time he spends on a basketball court is not going to stand in his way.

I remember Nick Collison saying, "Here I am in Kansas and I can't go to a guy like Roy Williams—a great teacher—to work with me in the summer."

That's one of the advantages Milicic and all these kids from Europe have. They're getting all the great individual coaching they want, all year long; they're getting unlimited input on their strengths and weaknesses.

That's not a recruiting advantage. That's not cheating. That's survival, man.

The NCAA ought to be more concerned about going after people who are buying players, who are giving out cars and money. They shouldn't be getting on a kid if he's going to work with a coach to develop his skills.

Normally, when an international player reaches the age of 22, he automatically becomes eligible for the NBA draft. However, a player's current contract with an international team must be bought out or played through. NBA rules permit a team to pay a buyout of up to $350,000. However, it can be done only every other year. The rest of the buyout must be paid by the player. A player under 22 must declare, and he must turn 18 before the draft to be eligible.

With so much international talent available, NBA GMs are changing the way they approach the draft because they have become intrigued with players in the rest of the world. There are 29 first-round picks, and it's becoming harder and harder for kids in this country to get guaranteed first-round money. There are only so many draft slots available, and there were 36 underclassmen, 32 international players and six high school players who originally filed for the draft in 2003—you do the math.

When it was all said and done, 12 college, one high school and 14 foreign players pulled out. They were all smart enough to understand they were not going to be late first-round choices.

Jason Kapono, a 6'8" forward from UCLA who was an All-Pac 10 player, kiddingly said that if he had to do it all over again, he would have played one year of intercollegiate basketball at UCLA, then gone to Europe and changed his name to Vladimir Kaponovich.

He said, "I would grow a beard, shoot my jumper and I would have been most likely an NBA first-rounder."

You know what, Jason, there's no doubt about it.

As it turned out, he went to Cleveland with the second pick in the second round.

That's what's happened in the world of globalization. Maybe we should change the name from the NBA to the GBA—the Global Basketball Association.

I was worried about college seniors like Kapono becoming dinosaurs in the draft. But there were nine who went in the first round. That's two more than in the previous year and seven more than 2001.

Sometimes, scouts watch these kids so often, there's a tendency at times to start to nitpick about their abilities and fail to consider their maturity. But I'll tell you, kids like Kirk Hinrich and Collison of Kansas don't have to apologize for staying four years. Those are four of the greatest years of your life. It didn't hurt Tim Duncan, David Robinson, Grant Hill or a host of other kids who stayed and enjoyed campus life.

And guess what? They can play. They will be able to contribute immediately. Hinrich is going to help the Bulls as a combination guard and play the point for the second guard slot, and he should help to alleviate some of the Bulls' problems resulting from the loss of Jay Williams. And Collison is fundamentally sound—I thought the Knicks made a mistake when they didn't take him at No. 9, even though Mike Sweetney of Georgetown, though smaller than advertised, was a solid choice.

Chicago and Seattle obviously saw something they loved with Hinrich and Collison. The Bulls took Hinrich at No. 7 and Seattle grabbed up Collison at No. 12. I can vouch for them. I got to see them on a regular basis for ESPN. I can also vouch for guys like 6'5" junior guard Dwyane Wade of Marquette, who went fifth in the first round to Miami, and sophomore point guard T.J. Ford of Texas, who was chosen by Milwaukee with the eighth pick.

I think in a few years, we'll look back at some flops, some real mistakes in teams taking all these international players over our U.S. guys.

The draft has gotten so wacky. It's an inexact science. I just heard that in the previous three years, of the 85 players who were first-round picks, only 17 averaged double figures in their first year.

There is such a pack mentality about NBA guys, a willingness to forget about what they saw a kid do for three, four years and base their evaluations on what they see in a pre-draft camp or an individual workout.

NBA teams bring all these players in, put them through all kinds of workouts, and the kids rise or fall based on these workouts. I remember the year Paul Pierce of Kansas kept sliding because they didn't like what they saw in the workouts.

He went 10th to the Celtics—and now he's an All-Star.

Well, let me tell you, it's a whole different ballgame playing five on five with the lights on. And to me, more evaluation should be based on what a kid does in front of a crowd, playing in a game situation. You can be fooled sometimes where guys look good in shooting drills or ball-handling drills.

I think workouts are fine if kept in the proper perspective. It should be a time to get to know the player on a personal level, to gain familiarity with his attitude and his desires. But the bottom line is it should not be the end-all when deciding this guy is going to take you to the promised land.

I want to see how kids respond when their teams are down and they've got to make the big play. So many times we hear about the quickness, jumping ability, or strength of the player—hey, man, this is not the Olympics that we're judging these guys for. You're not measuring guys by how fast they run in the 100 meters or by how they rank in a bodybuilding contest. If we did, Larry Bird might not have made the league, let alone the Hall of Fame. You're talking about basketball, about being a player.

NBA scouts were salivating over 7'5", 303-pound Pavel Podkolzine, an 18-year-old center from Siberia, when they saw him in a public workout held at the same time the pre-draft camp was going on in Chicago. Podkolzine, who is only 18, was a relative unknown until he put on a show in a one-on-one scenario against former UNLV coach Billy Bayno. He is originally from Novosibirsk and was a backup to former St. John's center Shawnelle Scott at Verese in the Italian League, but he finally got a chance to show a little of what he could do in the European Cup. He can block shots and rebound. And he is huge. He's already earned the nickname "The Siberian Shaq." But he withdrew from the draft, and now he's back home again after he couldn't be guaranteed a top 10 spot. Podkolzine will be back again next year, along with 7'3", 300-pound He Seung-Jin of South Korea.

Over the years, I've pleaded with kids to stay in school until they know they're ready to make that jump. The one player who comes to mind is Omar Cook of St. John's. He was a McDonald's All-American at Christ the King High School in New York City. He was supposed to be the next Kenny Anderson because of the way he passed the ball.

But he couldn't make a jump shot.

I did a game of his two years ago in the Coaches vs. Cancer Classic at the Garden.

I can still remember him leaving the layup line and coming over and tapping me on the shoulder. He says, "Mr. Vitale, I am so excited that you're here to call my first game as a college player."

Let me tell you, I was really touched when he made that comment. Later that year, St. John's was playing a game at Villanova. I was standing with his coach, Mike Jarvis, and my partner, Brent Musburger. I said, "You know, Mike, there are rumors the kid's thinking about going pro. Would you mind if I said a few words to him?"

And he said, "No, not at all."

So I said to Omar, "I don't know who you're listening to, but please, please come back to school. You need St. John's more than St. John's needs you. Don't listen to those people."

"Well," he said, "I might be a late first-rounder."

I told him, "Agents tell that to everybody. Don't give up your college eligibility."

When I was done conversing with Cook, Brent looked at me and said, "There's no shot he's coming back to St. John's. He was not listening to a word you said. His eyes were wandering, looking up at the rafters."

Cook announced for the draft. He went to the Chicago pre-draft camp and didn't make a jump shot. He was eventually drafted in the second round by Denver, who traded him to Orlando. He wound up playing the past two years in the NBA Developmental League.

It breaks my heart when I see Omar Cook, Rod Grizzard of Alabama and Marcus Taylor of Michigan State—who all could have been college stars—bounce around like nomads from one minor league team to another.

Here's a bunch of guys who, had they stayed in school, could have gotten better and better; they could have improved their stock. They would have been first-round draft choices and ultimately gotten three years of guaranteed money and then—who knows what might have happened?

I'm reminded of Erazem Lorbek, a 6'10" freshman forward from Michigan State. He wasn't even a starter. He was coming off the bench for limited minutes until March, and he threw his name into the draft. He came up to Tom Izzo and told him, "I've got an agent." So he couldn't come back even if he'd wanted to. Lorbek decided to go overseas to play the next season, after realizing he had no shot of being drafted.

It's absurd.

But the list just goes on.

That's why I was so ecstatic that Chris Thomas of Notre Dame, who thought about leaving after his sophomore year, decided to come back to school. He tested the waters, worked out individually for some teams, then realized the draft was just too loaded with point guards. Let me tell you, Thomas made a smart decision. Going into the 2003-04 season, he will be my preseason first-team All-American point guard, and his stock should go up, up, and up.

The NBA is a lot different now than when I was coaching in it. Basketball prominence in those days was determined by how effective you were in the three-second area. Back then, you needed a dominant low-post center like Kareem or Robert Parish if you wanted to make some noise. Now, you can survive without one. There's Shaq, of course, but take a look at the NBA finals. Kenyon Martin of the

Nets and Tim Duncan of the San Antonio Spurs are good, athletic big men.

You've got the greatest athletes in the world in the pros, although, with the 24-second clock, it seems like there's more coaching on every possession. Sometimes freedom of expression is taken away. All those patterns and executions restrict the great one-on-one ability of some of the players.

Make the right player personnel decision or win the NBA lottery for one of the first picks—and you have a shot. It's all a matter of timing.

Just ask Memphis GM Jerry West.

Back in 1995, the Memphis Grizzlies, formerly of Vancouver, traded away their first-round pick for Otis Thorpe, a 35-year-old forward. This year, it came back to bite them.

Jerry West knew that if the Grizzlies won the lottery, they could hold on to their pick. Otherwise, it would go to the Pistons. The Grizzlies were in the final two, along with Cleveland, for LeBron James.

But they didn't win.

It was Heartbreak Hotel. Are you kidding me? Do you think that Jerry West is shedding a little bit of a tear? And what about Hubie Brown? Wow. I can see Hubie salivating over the thought of possibly coaching LeBron. With his brilliant mind and the information that he could have passed on, the learning process would have been incredible. But they wound up empty.

If they make too many player personnel mistakes, coaches and GMs get that pink slip. When the NBA season ended last year, there were nine job openings for coaches.

Just look at what's happened. Look at Rick Carlisle and what he's done—back-to-back 50-win seasons and a trip to the Eastern Conference finals—and the Pistons still fired him, just because somebody else with a higher profile might be available.

Oh, sure, there were some rumblings and complaints about his inflexibility offensively and some decisions he made in player personnel—like not playing the younger players like Tayshaun Prince. Most of all, there was talk that Carlisle didn't communicate with anyone in the Pistons' front office. I think it was totally unprofessional to let a guy go who brought his kind of results. Somebody should have sat him down and told him, "You've got to change a little or else you'll not be back."

You can't blame Joe Dumars, though, when he was able to hire a Larry Brown. Larry's 62 and wants a shot at a championship ring. He might get one, too. The Pistons are a good club and they're going to get better with Milicic—even though I would have made Carmelo Anthony my choice at No. 2. Hey, do you think this could turn out to be like the 1984 draft, when Jordan was taken at No. 3 in the draft by Chicago, rather than being grabbed by Portland at No. 2?

And how about Paul Silas? He was fired by the New Orleans Hornets. Here was a guy who was a consummate pro. Silas has big-time credibility with the players because of his own success as a player and because of his strong leadership skills. Hey, think about it—he took the Hornets to the playoffs after playing a large part of the season without Baron Davis and part of the playoffs against Philly without Jamal Mashburn.

Then there's Doug Collins getting fired in Washington. Obviously, he's part of the Michael Jordan fiasco, but Collins has a brilliant mind and a feel for the game, as well as a drive to excel.

Coaching in the pros is so unstable. You can win NBA Coach of the Year one year, and the next year, you can be gone.

In the world of teaching, they give professors tenure; they give guys awards when they have experience and stay because they have so much more knowledge to offer. In coaching, if you don't win, you're gone. I find that mind-boggling. I remember that while I was coaching the Titans at the University of Detroit, Ray Scott had been voted the NBA Coach of the Year for the great job he did in guiding the Pistons. Then, only a year later, he got the axe. To me, that's like saying that coaches get dumber as they get older. Could it be that maybe the talent level dwindled a little and half the league's players didn't perform to their ability? It just goes to show you that in the NBA, the players rule. As Scott said so accurately years ago, "The inmates run the asylum." The coach is there for only a short time, and he'd better make the most of it.

But the coach has some decisions to make, too.

He's got to know when to move on. Larry Brown coached Philadelphia to the NBA Finals in 2001, but he left two years later when—even though Brown will deny this, I really believe it—he felt he'd gotten the maximum out of his 76ers team and had become frustrated with the antics of Allen Iverson off the court. But give Iverson his due—pound for pound, inch for inch, Iverson is the best in the game. He gets the most out of his ability.

Iverson had the opportunity to play for two Hall of Famers like John Thompson and Larry Brown. But I don't think you're ever going to win a world title when an Allen Iverson is taking 35 shots a night and four other guys are standing around taking pictures and making like the Kodak man.

There are other parts of the job—like being punctual and attending practice—that are just as much a part of the formula for a team's success. Last year, the Sixers were playing the biggest game of the year—Game 6 of the NBA Eastern Conference semifinals against Detroit in Philly. They lose and their season is over. And Iverson arrived a mere 32 minutes before game time, claiming he was tied up in traffic on a rainy night on the Expressway. Then, later on, he said he'd had a flat tire.

Iverson can talk all he wants about traffic and the problems he had getting to the arena, but the bottom line is that he has to be responsible for being punctual. I mean, he sets the tone in the locker room, and here it is the playoffs—where his team is playing for the right to be a champion—and the players are wondering, "Oh, my God, where's Iverson? He was supposed to be here an hour and a half, two hours ago, and he's not here."

What do you think that sets off? It sets off anger and gets coaches concerned and gets everybody upset. Sure, he goes out and gets 38 points, but he took more than 30 shots to do it, and they lost in overtime.

I'm from the old school, so I know it had to tear Larry Brown apart because he's a purist. I still remember when Iverson had that press conference one year at which he said he didn't think it was a big deal to miss practice. I remember the quote—"What are we talking about? It's practice. We're not talking about games. It's practice." He was always very nice to me when he played at Georgetown, but I don't think he gets it.

Same scenario in Orlando with Doc Rivers, who's one of my favorite coaches in the NBA. He was a star high school player in Illinois and a superstar with Marquette, and he had a solid career as an NBA player. Rivers understands people, and that's what makes him a success. I'm sure he will agree with me that you can't win when your team is one-dimensional. Remember, the Magic still couldn't get past the first round, even though they had Tracy McGrady, the league's leading scorer. They needed Grant Hill. He would be such a stabilizer for the Tracy McGrady show. There's no doubt that if the game were strictly one-on-one, you could not beat McGrady—but it isn't. Other people have to contribute. If the ultimate goal is to win a world title, those teams need more help.

Remember, the game of basketball is all about the team concept. You win championships when you play as a team. Did you see Syracuse in 2003? Did you see San Antonio?

12

GAZING INTO
THE CRYSTAL BALL

H ey, baby, this is supposed to be a book about hoops. We're talking about the game of round ball.

So why did college football and politics sneak onto these pages?

I'll tell you why.

The Atlantic Coast Conference, one of the most respected conferences in the country, decided earlier this year they wanted to expand from nine teams to 12.

I know what is driving this. It's the pigskin—football. Football, football, football. It's setting up the megaconferences. The ACC wants a championship game because they smell the $12 million-plus the SEC is getting. They've seen the Big 12 title game, and now they're saying they want a piece of that action, too. They also want to become more of a player in the Bowl Championship Series.

There is big money involved here.

The ACC, which currently guarantees its member schools $9 million, stood to make between $6-8 million from a conference title game, another $4 million if they got a second team into the BCS, and potential big cash from a new TV contract if they expanded their reach into the Northeast corridor.

So they raided the neighboring Big East for Miami and Virginia Tech. Originally, they had romanced Miami—who is a traditional national contender in football and is the second most marketable program in the country after Notre Dame—along with Boston College and Syracuse. That would have made the ACC much stronger, but would have torn the heart out of Big East football by reducing the number of football-playing schools to six—Pittsburgh, Virginia Tech, West Virginia, Rutgers, Temple, and newest football member Connecticut.

North Carolina and Duke stood up against the decision. The ACC couldn't get the seven votes necessary from the other school presidents to take in those three Big East schools. Hey, the University of Virginia was under pressure from the state legislature to make sure Virginia Tech—which played in the national championship in 1999 with the Great One, Mike Vick—remained part of a strong football conference.

When you look at the whole scenario, it was an embarrassment for the ACC. Any way you cut it, after all the publicity and notoriety the league received, what looked like a slam dunk—getting Miami, Boston College and Syracuse—has certainly backfired.

In the end, the ACC—which celebrated its 50th anniversary during the 2002-03 season—went in a completely different direction. They voted for a compromise, taking in Miami and Virginia Tech—a school whose admission they had previously voted against—which at least made sense geographically.

But they left BC and Syracuse, who had both really gone out on a limb for this, standing at the altar. I wonder how their presidents felt when they woke up the next morning?

As you might expect, those six remaining football-playing schools in the Big East, particularly Connecticut, which sank $90 million into a new football stadium outside Hartford, were mad—mad enough to sue the ACC for irreparable damages, mad enough to sue Miami, whose president, Donna Shalala, had reportedly told the Big East as late as March, 2003, that her school would stay in the league.

The whole thing is a mess.

It's a wacky world. There's no good reason for this situation to have occurred. They can talk about all the great matchups and the incredible pageantry it will produce, but all these realignments are taking place for one reason and one reason only, man—money. When a school does something like this, I just want an administrator to look into the camera and tell us the truth—rather than lay all kinds of spin on us—and simply say it's all about piles and piles of good old George Washingtons.

It hurts so many innocent programs. My heart goes out to programs like Connecticut. I was doing a speaking engagement on May 14 at the Greater Jewish Federation in Hartford when the news broke. There were 500 Husky fans there, getting ready to eat dinner, when a local TV guy came down and said, "Hey, we just got the word about the ACC presidents voting to expand."

I'm telling you, there was a buzz in that place like you couldn't believe. Everybody who loves Connecticut sports was in a panic. "Hey, what is going to happen?"

I replied immediately, "Relax, basketball will survive. Jim Calhoun and Geno Auriemma run first-class programs that have both won national championships."

"But what about football?" That was the big question among the fans.

The Huskies, under AD Lew Perkins, had done a fantastic job developing a great program in a short amount of time. Now what do they do? They've also lost their AD, who went out to Jayhawk country where he took over the program at Kansas. And where does Rutgers go?

Hey, if you're just talking basketball, baby, the Catholic schools can put together their own quality basketball conference. Think about it—Villanova, Seton Hall, St. John's, Georgetown, Providence and Notre Dame.

But without Miami and Virginia Tech, it's a huge blow to those Big East schools that play 1-A football. I know one thing, man. You're not going to see Big East commissioner Mike Tranghese and ACC commissioner John Swofford exchanging Christmas cards.

Everybody is wheeling and dealing. Everyone is thinking, "What's the best for us?" But what about the ramifications for the other sports? Does anybody talk about the tennis players, the swimmers, the baseball players? Does anybody talk about how those kids factor into this? Or don't they count because they're not the revenue producers, the big stars?

Well, let me tell you, they do count. I had two girls play tennis for Notre Dame. I know how important it was to the coach and the girls to compete, to be treated the same way in terms of travel. Those kids put in just as much practice time as any athlete who plays basketball or football. But let's get real—while the football and basketball teams fly in a chartered plane and get back to campus quickly, many of the non-revenue teams jump in the van and have to travel site to site.

I mean, let's face it, this is all about the playoffs, the magic playoffs on Saturday. The SEC, the Big 12—they're dreaming of those matchups. And the cash will be rolling in.

I want to make a point about the lack of loyalty.

I flat-out believe that Buzz Shaw and the Rev. William Leahy, the presidents of Syracuse and Boston College, should have stood tall a long time ago and simply said, "We will not entertain any interest at all from the ACC because we belong in the Northeast." That might have stopped it, because at the time, Miami was saying it would go to the ACC only if it could be accompanied by two other teams in the Northeast corridor.

Man, I would have loved to have seen Shaw and Rev. Leahy take the same stance as the president of Kentucky, Lee Todd Jr., who emphatically denied the suggestion that Kentucky might move to the ACC to give that conference its 12th team so that they could qualify for a football championship playoff. He stated without reservation, "Kentucky belongs in the SEC. It's a charter member, and we are going nowhere. We're remaining in the SEC." Salute, man. Let's give a tribute to president Lee Todd Jr. That, my friends, is a leader and a man who has strong character.

Hey, a coach with power who voiced his opposition strongly and publicly was Duke's Mike Krzyzewski. Can you imagine if big John Thompson was still in the Big East? Do you think he'd be screaming and yelling? You'd better believe it.

You wonder why I admire Mike Krzyzewski? It's because he is a guy who cares about people and who will speak what he believes. He could see the damage this was causing the rest of college athletics, not to mention his own conference, which had built its reputation over the years through its classy basketball tradition.

Let me tell you, I respect him because he said at a press conference, "There's a price to be paid for everything. When you make a change, you might move into a great house, but you have to sell the old house and your kids will be going to different schools. Obviously, we haven't distinguished ourselves in how we've gone about this. I know it's a business, but as a great university in a conference, we have to be sensitive to our brethren in other conferences.

"This isn't about big business swooping down and getting another company. The hidden cost here is the destruction of what, in essence, intercollegiate sports should be about.

"Before this, the ACC had done a great job of keeping alive the spirit of the game. But I think in this process, we've gone overboard to the other side of it.

"There's a reason why the United States doesn't have a state in France or Venezuela. It's because we don't belong there."

The addition of Miami and Virginia Tech is supposed to take place in 2004. Like many others, Krzyzewski has no idea how the ACC was going to come up with the TV money to fund this move and still be able to guarantee each of the 11 schools the same payout.

Still one school shy of the 12 teams needed to hold a conference championship football game, the ACC is lobbying for a rule change to allow leagues with only 10 teams to be eligible for such a game. They probably feel it would be easier to add another school—maybe Louisville—in the future. But the BCS numbers figure to escalate if the Big East is eliminated from the mix and the new-look ACC becomes a powerhouse football league. Five of their schools—Miami, Virginia Tech, NC State, Maryland and Virginia—are strong enough to be a factor.

Ironically, keeping Syracuse and BC could only help the Big East in basketball while the addition of Virginia Tech and Miami could actually water down ACC hoops.

But Krzyzewski seems more concerned about the bitterness this will cause than with strength of schedule. "Hopefully," he said, "we mend fences. When you've obviously gone into another person's yard with your tractor trailer or John Deere and knocked down a few trees, you need to mend some fences."

It's not over yet, either. The defections of Virginia Tech and Miami are bound to cause a domino effect that will be felt throughout the country. The Big East needs teams and may look to take them from the Atlantic 10 and Conference USA; Conference USA may go into the WAC, and so on.

The growth of these megaconferences will change the landscape of college sports.

I hear all this jazz about academic integrity—what is it they keep preaching? Myles Brand, the former president of Indiana who is now the executive director of the NCAA, is always talking about the importance of graduation rates—and I couldn't agree more with him.

Last summer I was able to engage in a brief conversation with Brand on this very topic. We were both in Indianapolis for an awards banquet, where I was thrilled to be honored along with Cedric Dempsey, the former executive director of the NCAA, and future Hall of Famer Dan Marino. We each received the Pathfinder Award for our contributions to young people.

I turned to Brand, who was sitting at the same table as I was, and I suggested to him that it could all be solved quickly if we just make freshmen ineligible. The big argument to the contrary, of course, is that many more high school kids would attempt to make the leap to the pros rather than going to a college campus. My feelings expressed to Mr. Brand were simple—if they really have no desire to go to college, so be it. The game would still go on and would be as competitive as ever. We would have kids in college uniforms who really want to be there and want to wear those uniforms. And, most of all, kids graduate. He agreed, but it would be so difficult to get that passed in legislation, and it would be a costly endeavor. Isn't it amazing how everything comes back to cash, cash, cash?

You tell me how these conferences make sense with some of these matchups. I mean, Penn State should be in the Big Ten? Notre Dame playing in the Big East in basketball? There's really no logic to it geographically. When you factor in all the travel, it just bums you out when you think about it.

We've gotten away from what college athletics should be all about—and that's simply to be competitive, have spirit and have some great matchups. What happened to the great local matchups? They have absolutely gone by the wayside.

This is what the future looks like when I gaze into my crystal ball. College athletics is getting bigger and bigger. At least, some of its games are.

Michigan State and Kentucky are looking to make history this season at Ford Field, home of the NFL Detroit Lions. The event, called "The Basket Bowl: Hoops on the 50," will be telecast live nationally by CBS. They're expecting a crowd of more than 75,000, which would be a new world record for basketball attendance.

The current world basketball attendance record is 75,000, and it was set on August 21, 1951, when the Harlem Globetrotters played an exhibition game in the Berlin Olympic Stadium. The largest crowd ever to attend an NCAA basketball game was when 68,112 fans watched LSU defeat Notre Dame, 87-64, on January 20, 1990, in the Louisiana Superdome in New Orleans.

For this latest game contending for the record, MSU will transport its playing floor to Ford Field and set it up at the 50-yard line.

The game is the brainchild of Michigan State AD Ron Mason, the former MSU hockey coach in "The Cold War" when a world-record crowd attended a Spartan-Michigan hockey game in Spartan Stadium.

I'm for anything that creates excitement for the game. I remember when I was at the University of Detroit, I was trying anything possible to get people to talk basketball. One idea I came up with was a 24-hour basketball marathon where we could have hoops hysteria all day long. Every two hours, we were playing a game—alumni games,

games between the police and fire department, games between women's teams—and it all culminated with our Red-White scrimmage.

Kentucky and Michigan State are going to get all kinds of positive ink and publicity galore with a game of that stature. The only thing that could have made this much more special would have been if the game were on ESPN and not CBS. Only kidding, Billy. Only kidding.

Kentucky has the best traveling fan base in America. From that standpoint, Michigan State couldn't have picked a better opponent. If you'd asked me 10 years ago, I'd have told you that Michigan State would never have been part of that matchup. You would have thought Michigan, Michigan, Michigan. At that point, the Wolverines were regarded as being on a higher plane. But this just shows you what Tom Izzo up in Spartanville has accomplished—taking three teams to the Final Four and winning the national title in 2000.

That ought to be a wild atmosphere.

I've been blessed to sit courtside for a lot of special teams playing in famous college arenas—places like Duke, North Carolina, Kentucky, Kansas, Syracuse and Michigan State. They are the great draws out there, and that's where my bosses are going to put me. But I would like to do something unique for ESPN's Silver Anniversary Season. I would love ESPN to assign me to places where I haven't been, places where I can walk in for the very first time and be part of a new environment.

Hey, we could call it, "Dickie V: The 2003-04 Tour." Wow, like Bruce Springsteen has his tour, why can't I have mine? Let's start printing the T-shirts and passing out the bobbleheads and some alarm clocks. That's right, you could have my alarm clock—Dickie V could wake you up in the morning. Are you kidding me? Wow, who would have ever thought this would happen to me when I was teaching the sixth grade back in 1965.

I remember several years ago—it was so flattering—ESPN's coordinating producer of basketball, Dave Miller, called me up and said, "You will not believe what happened. But there's a petition campaign going on by all the kids at Rice University for you to come down and do a game."

Unfortunately, it never worked out.

But I would love to take a little early-season journey, going back to back to back—to different places that I haven't been yet—whether it be Iowa State in Ames or Southern Illinois, the Salukis, someplace where I know they would really have a lot of fun with me down there.

Hey, Gonzaga, Butler, invite me.

I would even like to do a game at the University of Detroit.

I've never done one there since I've been at ESPN. The year I got out of coaching, I did a game in Titan territory with a local TV personality, Ray Lane, on an independent network that was televised locally. Dave "Smokey" Gaines, my former assistant, was coaching the Titans. Michigan State came to town with Magic Johnson, Greg Kelser and company—and oh, man, were they absolutely brilliant. They were incredible that day.

How could I not have fun watching the Magic Man do his thing even though I was trying to coach the Titans on TV?

I have to admit, I was a homer big time. I was Harry Caray or Phil Rizzuto at my best.

I love praising the talents of a lot of new coaches who will become the future of this game.

Tom Crean coached Marquette to the Final Four last year. Then there was a lot of speculation that Illinois was going to come after him hard when Bill Self took the Kansas job.

But the 38-year-old Crean wasn't interested.

He likes Milwaukee. He doesn't have to deal with football. Basketball's king up there. They've got the great new practice facility coming in named after Al McGuire. He must be up in heaven jump-ing for joy for Tom Crean.

Al knew the game, and he told me, "Dickie, Dickie, Dickie, the kid we hired is going to be special. He's got the whole package. He can recruit; he can fire people up. He's a workaholic. He's got it all."

I know a lot of people said Tom Crean was going to be a good one, but they didn't know he was going to be this good.

He's no one-year wonder.

Guys like Crean, Bill Self of Kansas, Quin Snyder of Missouri, Mike Brey of Notre Dame, Billy Donovan of Florida, Stan Heath of Arkansas, Steve Alford of Iowa, and Tom Amaker of Michigan are the future of the sport. They are young coaches who got their training in a big-time program under a big-time coach, just like Alford of Iowa did when he was learning as a player under Bob Knight at Indiana, who at one time had placed 15 assistants in head coaching jobs.

Donovan is only 37, but he's also been to the Final Four, in 2000. He's had five consecutive 20-win seasons, five straight trips to the big dance. He's accepted the fact that football is No. 1 at Florida and utilizes it as a positive in recruiting. Think about it—what's bet-ter than to bring a recruit in for a weekend in an atmosphere that's filled with excitement when the Gators and Florida State Seminoles kick it off? He's turned the Gators into an SEC power and made the O'Connell Center a sensational home-court advantage with the Rowdy Reptiles doing their best Cameron Crazies impersonations. He coaches a style of play kids love. He doesn't hold them back. He lets them run, press and shoot.

He's shown he can recruit anywhere—San Diego, New Hamp-shire, South Dakota. Just last year, he got guard Anthony Roberson, a McDonald's All-American, out of Saginaw, Michigan. If I'm Michi-gan and Michigan State, I don't let Donovan off the airplane.

Self has already been to a pair of Elite Eights with Tulsa and Illinois, and Snyder made a huge impact two years ago when he coached a Missouri team that was a 12 seed to the Regional finals.

Pedigree means a lot here.

Crean and Heath both came from the Tom Izzo stable at Michigan State. It's amazing what Izzo has done. He has not only produced a national championship team in 2000 and been to three Final Fours, but he's also turning out head coaches from his staff on a regular basis.

Five of his assistants have become head coaches since 1996. Stan Joplin went to Toledo. Then Crean left for Marquette in 1999. Two years later, after the title run was over, Heath got Kent State. And in 2003, after another Elite Eight run, Brian Gregory moved on to Dayton and Mike Garland was the choice at Cleveland State.

Izzo's name must be like gold on a resume.

It still helps to have a godfather. Who can forget Rick Pitino's staff at Kentucky in the early '90s—back when Tubby Smith, Ralph Willard, Herb Sendek and Billy Donovan were his lieutenants?

It was just a matter of time before they started climbing that coaching ladder.

When Pitino left, Tubby came over from Georgia to become the Kentucky coach in 1998. He already has one national championship to his credit. Ralph spent time at Western Kentucky and Pitt. He's now at Holy Cross and has coached his alma mater—which finally has scholarships again—to the NCAA Tournament three years in a row. The guy can really coach. He gave Kentucky, Kansas and Marquette all they wanted in first-round losses each year. Herb has turned the corner at NC State and coached the Pack to the Tournament the last two years. And then there's Billy. Rick made a call to Florida AD Jeremy Foley on his behalf when Billy was still at Marshall.

Pitino has gotten that assembly line going. When he went to Louisville in 2001, he hired Mick Cronin away from Cincinnati. Mick, who is only 31, is now the new head coach at Murray State.

Mike Krzyzewski has had the same influence at Duke.

Think of the guys who've worked for him since he became the trail boss of the Dukies—Brey, Amaker, Snyder, David Henderson of Delaware and Tim O'Toole of Fairfield.

Brey, Amaker and Snyder have a shot to get to the Final Four in these jobs before their careers are over. I'm thinking Quin might be the first, since his center, Arthur Johnson, and guard, Rickey Paulding—two Detroit kids—decided to stay on campus for their senior years instead of chasing pro dreams. Let me just tell you this, Mr. Snyder—if I were still coaching at the University of Detroit, those two Motor City stars would never, ever have gotten out of town. And what's more, I wouldn't have allowed you to come into my town. Only kidding around, man.

There are some other new faces at major programs to keep an eye on—guys like Jay Wright at Villanova, Paul Hewitt at Georgia Tech, Dennis Felton at Georgia, Bruce Weber at Illinois, Tim Welsh at Providence, and Mike Anderson at the University of Alabama-Birmingham.

Then there are some young head coaches at mid-major programs who are headed for the top, guys who don't have big jobs yet, but who are on the fast track.

Mark Few of Gonzaga continued what Dan Monson started before he left for Minnesota. He's a regular at the NCAA Tournament and is not afraid to play the big guys during the regular season, usually on the road, just to upgrade his RPI.

Bobby Gonzalez of Manhattan, a Howard Garfinkel favorite, became the Prince of the City. He coached the Jaspers to an NCAA Tournament bid and dominated the Metropolitan area by beating St.

John's and Iona to win the Holiday Festival championship. He also had a big W over Seton Hall, a Big East team.

Jeff Lebo of Tennessee-Chattanooga is a former North Carolina star guard who played for Dean Smith. He's starting to build his reputation, with success at Tennessee Tech and UT-Chattanooga. He turned down Iowa State last spring because he may have his eye on an ACC job.

Bruce Pearl of Wisconsin-Milwaukee is a former Tom Davis assistant at Iowa who made waves a few years back when he accused Illinois of cheating when they recruited Chicago prep star Deon Thomas. He became a wanted man in that state. But he has bounced back strong, building a national Division II power at Southern Indiana before moving to UWM, where he pushed Notre Dame to the limit in the first round of the NCAA Tournament.

Todd Lickliter of Butler is a former Bulldogs assistant who is the latest in a long line of coaching stars at this school. Barry Collier of Nebraska and Thad Matta of Xavier were previous head coaches here. Lickliter, son of an Indiana high school coach, just waited his turn and made a big splash in the NCAA Tournament, beating Mississippi State and Louisville to reach the Sweet 16.

I love that we're seeing more and more assistants getting their shot. Iowa State just hired former Syracuse assistant Wayne Morgan, who most recently served as head coach at Long Beach State. Western Kentucky hired Marquette assistant Darrin Horn. Dayton hired Michigan State assistant Brian Gregory. Pitt promoted Jamie Dixon and Southern Illinois promoted Matt Painter. Wright State hired Ohio State assistant Paul Biancardi. St. Bonaventure hired Notre Dame assistant Anthony Solomon. Columbia, looking to turn around years of losing, gave Villanova assistant Joe Jones a well-deserved shot, making him part of a unique combo in the Ivy League along with his older brother, James, who is at Yale.

There are some other guys ready to break out—I mean they are sleeping giants, man, just ready for that phone to ring. Yes, they can become the future Tom Crean or Bill Self—guys who have labored as assistant coaches. All they need, man, is an opportunity. Check 'em out:

• Johnny Dawkins and Steve Wojciechowski of Duke. Johnny brings that NBA background with him and does a lot of individual instruction. Wojo brings that relentless personality to the staff. He's a workaholic—just the way he was as a player under Coach K.

• Freddie Hill Jr. down at Villanova—Mr. Jersey. His dad, Fred Hill Sr., is a big-time baseball coach at Rutgers, which made the tournament last year. Freddie worked at Fairleigh Dickinson University and Seton Hall. No one knows the state better.

• Josh Pastner, Arizona. Here's a young guy who grew up coaching one of his dad's age-group teams in a powerful AAU program in Houston. He's so anxious to learn. Lute Olson raves about him.

• Dave Dickerson and Jimmy Patsos, Maryland. Gary Williams is a perfectionist and he's in your face and he's a competitor and he wants nothing but success, success, success. Guys have to be able to respond to that. These guys have learned so much there as his assistants.

• Sean Sutton, Oklahoma. Eddie's youngest son has been with his father ever since Eddie resurfaced at Oklahoma State. Sean has been head coaching material for a while.

• Orlando Early, Alabama. Mark Gottfried has turned him loose, and the Tide has dominated recruiting in that state with kids like Mo Williams and Edwin Dudley.

• Anthony Grant, Florida. The top lieutenant on Billy Donovan's staff has used his strong ties in the Miami area, where he grew up, and has helped the Gators control recruiting in the state.

• Scott Rigot, Kentucky. He's a former South Carolina junior college coach who spent five years on Riley Wallace's staff in Hawaii and has strong international contacts that should help keep Tubby Smith's Kentucky Wildcats strong.

• Barry Rohrssen, Pitt. He opened doors for Ben Howland in North Jersey and New York when he first arrived and stayed put when Howland went to UCLA—which should be a huge plus for new coach Jamie Dixon.

• Troy Weaver and Mike Hopkins, Syracuse. Senior assistant Bernie Fine has been at Syracuse so long that he seems set in stone there. But Weaver and Hopkins each played a great role on that staff, too. Weaver opened the doors for the Orange in Baltimore and played a major role in the recruiting of Carmelo Anthony. Hopkins played for Jim Boeheim, came back there as an assistant and turned down the St. Bonaventure job this spring.

• Doug Wojcik, Michigan State. He's a former Navy guard who played on the same team as David Robinson and coached with Matt Doherty at both Notre Dame and North Carolina. Then he joined Tom Izzo's staff. Pencil this in—within five years, he'll be a head coach.

• Tom Moore, UConn. Watch this guy. He did all the scouting work as a part-time assistant when the Huskies marched to the national championship in 1999. Now he's full-time and should get a lot of play if UConn makes another run in March.

• Donny Daniels, UCLA. He was a key guy on Rick Majerus's staff at Utah before taking the Cal-State Fullerton job. Now, he's joined Ben Howland's staff at UCLA and should help him big time on the Coast with recruits.

• Oh yeah, I almost forgot. There are two other guys—Chris Collins of Duke and Pat Knight of Texas Tech, the General's son. Talk about diaper dandies—from the time they were in their cribs, you knew they were headed for this profession. They're both gym rats and they carry a lot of the same competitive fierceness their dads carry.

Right now, Pat's a second lieutenant, but I believe he's got that same type of fire. The same with Chris Collins, who's got so many of the same qualities his dad Doug possessed as an NBA player with the Sixers and as a coach with the Bulls, the Pistons, and the Wizards.

Coaching today is so much more sophisticated than when I was on the sidelines in the '70s. Today, the scouting, the analyzing, and the evaluating of players have all become so scientific. You can't hide anything any more. Every team is on TV, so coaches can go out there and see them on a regular basis. Coaches' offices are filled with video equipment so they can break down every aspect of a player's game. They analyze every jump shot; every pass and every turnover is broken down. It's amazing.

They can break down players' strengths and weaknesses and show players immediately, on video, all their best moments and their worst moments.

The skills of the players today are better, too. You have guys who are 6'8", 6'9" playing on the perimeter and using their ball-handling skills. Years ago, man, if you were 6'9", you went down to the box and you posted up with your back to the basket. Today, that just doesn't happen.

Hey, the first guy I saw who really demonstrated the versatility that we see today on the collegiate level was former North Carolina star Bob McAdoo. McAdoo, a 6'10" center, came to Chapel Hill from Vincennes Junior College in Indiana. He played the wing and the perimeter and was an inside/outside force.

Current players are bigger and stronger than ever.

Today, when you go to the trainer's room, it's unbelievable what's available. The physical fitness equipment and the intense programs that have been developed are unique compared to years ago.

Everybody's always looking for the winning edge, and many schools are showing their commitment to their personnel by spending cash on new practice facilities.

Oklahoma has put a lot of money into their men's and women's programs by building multimillion-dollar practice facilities for both teams. The same has happened at Florida and Michigan State.

I was told by Dee Rowe, the former head coach at Connecticut who's now an assistant AD and valuable fundraiser there, that Jim Calhoun took a tour of Oklahoma's practice facility when the Huskies went out there to play in January. At Connecticut, they had just finished improvements to their practice facilities. When Calhoun came back to Storrs, he said, "Oh my God, I can't believe it; I can't believe what they have in Sooner Country."

Let me tell you, I know what Jim was talking about because I was blown away when I visited Norman for the Oklahoma-Texas game and Kelvin Sampson took me on a tour.

It was a Taj Mahal in terms of video room, conference rooms, practice facilities for men's and women's teams. I mean, it was a thing of beauty that cost millions.

I thought to myself, "If this is the basketball facility, what is it like in Sooner country for football?"

Can you imagine what they must feel like down at Kentucky? They feel they're Numero Uno in basketball. Well, the UK administrators took a tour of Florida's practice facility when they played down there. Take it to the bank—there is no way Kentucky is going to allow Florida to have better practice facilities than they have. I'm sure Tubby and his people are already planning something that will be as special as can be.

Hey, I have some advice for the next generation of coaches, players and TV guys.

To the coaches, I would just simply say the opportunities are great out there if you can land one of the prime-time jobs. But you can't spend every day wondering what it would be like to be at the big-time campuses. You should take each day and try to learn as much as you can about the game. Man, I would go to as many clinics as possible. I would recommend you study, network as much as you can, and stay involved in every aspect of the game. Also, I'd advise you to read about and study the great coaches of the past who were vital in weaving the fabric of today's game.

Try to understand that it starts with leadership. You've got to learn to delegate responsibility to your assistants and allow them to have the opportunity to go out and teach. Hire the right people to carry your concepts. Be organized, have goals, meet with your players on a regular basis. When I look back on my coaching career, if there's one thing I wish I had done better, it is getting to know players personally rather than just knowing about their basketball talents.

Many of us in the coaching world become one-dimensional, and I got that way. We see a player, and all we're asking him is, "Johnny, did you work on your game last night? Hey, how did you play in the summer league? Did you hit the weight room?" We don't get into "Hey, how's your girlfriend? What's going on in the classroom? How're Mom and Dad at home? Things going okay in the family?"

These kids have problems like everybody else. Remember, they are worried as well about what's happening at home with Mom and Dad. Heck, Dad might have lost his job. Know about that. As a coach, know a player inside out; know about his personal life. Get to know him so you can have a relationship that's more than just basketball.

From a personal standpoint, also get to know other coaches. I recently told Matt Doherty, "Give a buzz to Bobby Knight, speak to him, ask for some advice on what it was like when he was let go at

Indiana." I know for a fact that Bobby Knight sought advice about getting another job. This guy is a Hall of Famer—and he was reaching out. He went to the AD down at Florida. From what I understand, he had a great session when he visited Jeremy Foley. Jeremy gave him some tips and told him what it would take for somebody to hire him. That's the message I was conveying to Doherty. You must reach out and ask for help, and if you do, people will respond.

Reach out to veterans. They're there. A Mike Krzyzewski would be thrilled for a young coach to call him up and ask, "Coach, can I come to practice? Would you mind if I could join you some day and discuss some concepts and issues I have? I know you have wisdom you might be able to pass on to me." That's a thrill for a big-timer to get that phone call.

And to the next generation of players, I'd say, basically, develop what we call a positive attitude, where you are able to view the glass as half filled rather than half empty. Also work every day with a specific plan to get better in areas you would like to develop. Certainly work on your basic strengths, but you must also work diligently to improve upon your weaknesses. Remember that it is very easy to develop good habits as well as bad habits. The bottom line is to put your best foot forward to create all the good habits that you can. Also remember— and it is as simple as can be—to treat people the way you want to be treated and have respect for all. Use the basketball as a means to the end of making yourself the best person that you can possibly be. Don't let the basketball use you.

If you're a skilled athlete, you're going to have chances to meet some of the most prestigious people on campus. They love being around athletes. Make that a positive situation and take advantage of the golden opportunity that you have. Remember, the typical student doesn't have access to some of the key people that you are going to be able to share time with. Exchange ideas with them, get to know them and stay in touch, because they may be able to open a door for you when your basketball days are over.

And, most importantly, prepare for later in life, the biggest game you'll play.

No matter who you are, understand, there will be a press conference—whether you're Michael Jordan, Larry Bird, Magic Johnson, whoever. There will be a press conference to announce it's all over.

I'll never forget Willis Reed when he was in the prime of his career. He was Mr. New York. He was the NBA's best player, a great team player. I remember being at his camp. Some high school kid said, "Come on, Willis, I want to play you one on one."

Willis asked him, "You really want to play me one on one?"

"Yeah."

So Willis grabbed his sneakers, put them on and they went out and played—and Willis just absolutely tore him apart. It was like, game of 11; winner's ball; you keep the ball; bam, bop, dunk, layup. And the kid said, "Come on, man, take it easy. I'm only in high school."

And Willis said, "Excuse me? Take it easy? Son, let me tell you, when you've laced up your shoes and it's time to play, you'd better be ready to perform." And he said, "I'm showing you that I'm going to perform to my maximum whenever I step onto the court."

To me, that's the first commandment of competing. So many kids forget. They get what we call "the slide and the glide." They get what we call "the hot dog." They feel they're better than everyone else—and that's when they get to a point where they don't get any better. They stagnate. But a player must have that incredible desire to want to get better today than what he was yesterday. And the special ones have that great desire.

Don't be satisfied. Don't be content with where you're at. So many kids become fat cats and forget where they came from. In many cases, they forget all the little things they did to get to the top level in their profession. The bottom line is that you should never lose the work ethic that is so essential for success.

I just read in a column recently some quotes from juniors in high school—superstar players who were talking about LeBron James getting that cool $90 million. I got the feeling that they're thinking, "Man, I got to get my game to a level so I can go to the NBA and be a first-rounder when I'm done my senior year in high school."

And that, my friends, scares me.

There's only a handful of guys who are at that level. We can count them on one hand—Kobe, Kevin Garnett, Tracy McGrady, and LeBron. Too many other players think they're in that category, and they don't care about that classroom. Everything is basketball, basketball, basketball. And we don't hear enough about those who don't make it—kids who are chasing a dream and become one-dimensional in their lives. And they don't understand how to prepare and chase other goals.

If I have one regret, it's that I didn't try to be a better student in high school. But I did know I had to have the necessary credentials to move on from high school to college. Then once I got my undergraduate degree, I also pursued my master's so that I had options if my dream of being a college coach didn't become a reality. I wanted to be prepared to be an administrator on the elementary school or high school level if coaching wasn't going to be part of my future. Preparation is so important, and it's essential to have a Plan B.

I always tell youngsters in all my speeches that there's no substitute for knowledge. I constantly remind student athletes to read as much as possible, whether it be magazines, newspapers or books about their favorite sports heroes, but read, baby, read. As the late great Arthur Ashe, who was an excellent tennis player, but also a man with great vision, said so many times years ago, "Knowledge is power." It gives you options in life.

What scares me is there are too many youngsters playing today who are pounding the ball and playing on the pavement, and all they think about is basketball, basketball, basketball. They see many of the pro stars come back to the 'hood with their gold chains, shiny Rolexes and fly wheels, and they immediately think of them as "the bomb." Well, unfortunately, for many of these kids, that leap to the NBA is not going to happen for them. That's why it's essential that they take from the game an understanding of the art of competing and the ability to blend with others from various backgrounds, all the elements that are vital in making the transition to the real world—all the little things that are important and help make them a complete person.

And to the TV guys—well, I could go on and on. I have such respect for guys like Jim McKay, who made his name on ABC's *Wide World of Sports* and just keeps rolling on in his 80s. Think about Keith Jackson—when you hear his voice, you know it's going to be a great college football game. There are so many in the business, and I know I will leave some out, but people like McKay, Jackson, Vin Scully, Dick Enberg, Brent Musburger, and Marv Albert, who have such an enthusiasm for the game they call. I respect these people so much because they have stood the test of time, and that's a sign of greatness. Two others who are no longer with us, the late Harry Caray of the Cubs and the late Hall of Famer Chick Hearn of the Lakers, were special because of the sense of excitement and youth they conveyed with each word out of their mouths.

Man, I'm really a sports junkie. I watch a lot of sports on TV—baseball, basketball, football, tennis. But I tell you, I get turned off when I hear announcers trying to show me how much they know technically about the game.

Then they go overboard and put me in what I call Zzzville, sleepytime land, because they don't remember that we're in the world of entertainment. That's what TV is all about. Scotty Connal convinced me of that years ago. It's not just about trying to prove to all your buddies that you know everything about the game.

I watch a lot of baseball games, and sometimes I hear guys who turn every pitch into the most complex situation until it flat-out turns you off. Come on, there are people out there who want to just hear stories about the players. In baseball, there's a lot of dead time during a game. You've got a chance to share stories about players and things that happen in the clubhouse, things that we don't know as fans.

That's why I enjoyed Joe Garagiola and Phil Rizzuto. They told stories, man. Okay, I can hear some critics screaming, "Yeah, they're Italian, baby. That's why he loved them." But I'll tell you what, I also love the baseball play-by-play guys like Vin Scully, Marty Brennaman, Joe Buck, Harry Kalas, Ernie Harwell, John Miller, our own Dan Shulman, and analysts like Joe Morgan, Tim McCarver, Tony Gwynn, Rick Sutcliffe, and Harold Reynolds who have a special way of sharing their love for the little white ball. They'll give you the nuts and bolts of the game. Hey, as a baseball lover, I eat, sleep, and drink *Baseball Tonight*, hosted by Karl Ravech. And, man, that show has an encyclopedia of baseball knowledge in Peter Gammons, who can seemingly store a computer's worth of data in his head. He is certainly Mr. Baseball.

I just think that, in many cases, there's over-technicalization. Producers, by nature, are workaholics and do a fantastic job. However, sometimes they are trying to come up with creative concepts that are unique, but that just end up taking away from the telecast. Some of the graphics I see on the TV screen are simply too difficult to absorb. There are numbers running all over the place and you're thinking, "What is all that?"

The main thing is to just entertain the fan so the fan can have a great time. Simplicity, baby. Entertain and educate—those are the two big Es.

Do that and I think you'll have a lot of fun and you'll have a telecast that goes in the right direction.

What excites me about basketball today is that the coaching is getting better and better. There's no doubt about it. Guys have become so skilled in handling the game, understanding the flow of the game.

What's exciting to me is the athleticism of the players. What's disappointing is they don't work on the basic fundamentals—the art of the pass, moving without the basketball, blocking out. Those are three teachable areas, and it frustrates me when I see kids who don't execute them, kids who want to just get by on their natural athleticism—the ability to get that quick first step, to explode, move laterally north and south, have the great bounce off the floor like a ping pong ball—rather than do all the little things that will make them better.

Players don't understand this, but if you put a clock on a player, you'll find that maybe he has the ball for a minute or so in a game—total—maybe two minutes if he's a superstar. But he's got to play for the other 38-plus minutes. You've got to learn to play without the ball, to screen, cut, flash to the ball, and to get on loose balls as well. Too many guys become stationary players, and man, they're the easiest to guard.

In the future, I can just see the players getting bigger and bigger to a point where I think that the NCAA Rules Committee will have to think about increasing the size of the court from 94 by 50.

I can also see women's basketball continuing to grow.

Connecticut has had a lot to do with that.

They are the closest thing college basketball has to a dynasty right now. They've won three of the last four NCAA Tournaments. I was talking with Dee Rowe, and he told me Geno Auriemma could definitely make the transition and coach a men's team.

Geno's record was 501-99 heading into the 2003-04 season. He's won three national titles, and he had a 70-game win streak before his team was upset by Villanova in the Big East Tournament finals. Connecticut got right back on a roll after that and won it all again with a 37-1 record. Junior guard Diana Taurasi scored 28 points to lead the young Huskies, who'd lost four starters from the previous year's 39-0 team to the WNBA, to a 72-66 victory over archrival Tennessee before 28,218 at the Georgia Dome in Atlanta.

Come to think of it, this could be the first year the men's and women's national Players of the Year come from the same school. The University of Connecticut has two strong candidates in Taurasi and junior center Emeka Okafor. Isn't it great that Okafor, like Tim Duncan and David Robinson, is patient and values education?

Auriemma does an amazing job getting his team to play at a consistent level of intensity. He understands that everyone is taking their best shot at him. It's the same with Notre Dame in football or Duke or North Carolina in men's basketball—everybody gives you their best shot. If you slip a little, you will be in trouble. And Auriemma has his players ready to play at a high level.

Right now, UConn is one of only a dozen or so great programs out there. Teams like the Huskies, Tennessee and Duke get the bulk of the superstar prospects. But programs like Notre Dame, Oklahoma, Texas, Stanford, Louisiana Tech, North Carolina, LSU, Ohio State and Georgia are certainly knocking on the door.

But it's starting to change as there is more attention being placed on the women's game because the quality of play is getting better and better. How do I know women's basketball is closing the gap with the men's game? Take a look at the transactions in March. Man, do the ADs want to win or what? Give me a break. Women's coaches are getting fired right and left. That tells me the pressure to win is just the same as it is in the men's game.

Taurasi is the best women's player I've seen since Cheryl Miller of USC, the great star of the USA's 1984 gold medal team. After Annika Sorenstam played in a men's PGA event at the Colonial in Ft. Worth, Texas, last spring, a lot of people are curious as to whether or not I think women can compete with men in basketball.

Skillwise, there are a lot of female players who can handle and shoot the basketball. They're fundamentally solid in every aspect. But when we talk about the quickness and explosiveness that takes place in the men's game, that's where it becomes a problem. I haven't seen a woman yet who could endure the physical contact and the pace of the men's game. But you can never say never. And there could be someone who can change that down the road.

There might even be someone who's better than Michael.

I honestly believe that 10 years from now, when it's all said and done, we could be arguing whether or not Kobe Bryant is the best ever to play the game—that is, of course, if he's able to continue playing.

Hey, the middle of July 2003 was a good news, bad news situation for the Los Angeles Lakers. On July 16, the Lakers held a press conference to let their faithful fans know that they are moving in a big-time positive way to get back to the championship circle. Yes, that gold trophy is what they want, and they want it badly. So what did they do? Lakers GM Mitch Kupchak announced proudly that they've signed All-Pro Karl Malone and All-Pro Gary Payton. Yes, there was certainly lots of joy and enthusiasm shared among the Laker fans with the news that those two perennial All-Stars will join the best tandem in the game, Kobe Bryant and Shaquille O'Neal.

But hold it, my friends, there was bad news on July 18, when Eagle County, Colorado, district attorney Mark Hurlbert stood in front of a horde of news cameras to make his announcement, certainly one that would bring sadness to the Bryant family as well as to the Laker faithful, that Kobe Bryant would be charged with one count of felony sexual assault.

Let's remember that the one beauty of our court system is that the legal procedures will ultimately determine the truth. Yes, let's not rush to judgment in any way, shape or form. But the bottom line is that it's certainly scary times for Kobe Bryant and the Los Angeles Lakers. The big question is, will Kobe Bryant be back in a Laker uniform or will he be serving a prison sentence? Only time will tell.

If Kobe's cleared of the charge, though, he has a chance to become the greatest basketball player ever. I never thought I'd say that; but when you watch this kid play and look at his numbers, there's a valid case for him.

One of my sons-in-law, Thomas Krug, a former Notre Dame QB, got into it with me. You know what his first argument was? He said, "Hey, man. I don't want to hear that with Kobe and Jordan. Kobe's got Shaq."

I said, "Wait a minute. I know he's got Shaq, but look at the rest of that roster. Let's look at the other support people whom Michael had around him in Chicago with Scottie Pippen and company."

Kobe is a human highlight film, just like Michael was in his prime. I watch and my jaw absolutely drops when I see him reverse jam and knock down jumpers. I see his range as a shooter; I watch him on the defensive end. Then I sit there and marvel that he's only 24 years old. And he hasn't just been doing it for one season—he's been doing it for the last five and he's already got three world titles.

While we're on the subject of predictions, I have one that I would give anything to be a reality. I know it's a dream, man, but why not chase a dream? As they say, I might just catch one. I know it's a stretch, but I want to see It's Awesome, Baby—a two-year-old colt that I co-own along with a group headed by Rick Pitino—standing in that winner's circle at the Kentucky Derby.

That's right. It's Awesome, Baby.

The day after Louisville got beat by Butler in the second round of the Tournament last spring, you would have thought that Rick Pitino would have been so down—I mean, here it is, they were drilled by Butler. The Bulldogs knocking down threes like crazy. I'm having breakfast; the phone rings, and it's Mr. Pitino. The first thing I wanted to do is talk about the Butler game, so I said, "Rick, what happened, trying to defend their three-point game?"

And he said, "Like I really want to hear about the Butler game. Give me a break."

Pitino said that Butler's shooting exhibition was the best he'd seen in many a year. According to him, they were effective at spreading the court to get the wide-open looks and they just moved the ball exceptionally well. Pitino said they were brilliant.

But that's not why he called. He didn't want to talk basketball.

Pitino has a magic touch in the horseracing world after being part owner of AP Valentine in the 2001 derby. He knew I had always been intrigued by horses and that I always visited the horse farms whenever I'd go to 'Cats country to do a game.

"Well," he said, "I've got a horse—a two-year-old. Two of my buddies and I are involved and we've got one open share. If you're interested in buying a quarter interest, then come in and have a little fun." But he warned me—"Now if you think you're going to make a lot of cash," he said, "don't come in. Not every horse is a Secretariat."

When Rick asked me what I wanted to name him, I said, "Hey, what about It's Awesome, Baby?"

"Fine, we've got to get it approved."

Well, it was, and now this two-year-old has started his journey to the top.

The horse has good bloodlines from Danzig—one of the outstanding studs in Lexington, Kentucky—as well as connections to Secretariat and Alydar. He trains under the direction of Cam Gambolati, who saddled up Spend a Buck and rode to the 1985 Kentucky Derby championship.

I've already had plenty of fun with the horse. I've been to Ocala to watch the horse train and have sometimes brought along my granddaughter, Sydney, Chris Sforzo and Terri's child. I loved seeing that smile on her face as she spent time petting the horse and watching him work out.

And I will never forget July 4, 2003. That's when we made a trip as a family—my wife and I, along with our two daughters, their husbands and our three grandchildren, Sydney, two years of age, and twins Connor and Jake, who were seven months old at the time—to Miami. Why? Because Rick Pitino called to tell me that It's Awesome, Baby would make his debut at the Maiden Special at Calder Racetrack in Miami.

Wow, were we thrilled.

I don't know a thing about horses. I mean, I could not have told you, when I was sitting with Rick and his family and friends in the Turf Club watching some of the races, what a trifecta, exacta, and all that other terminology was about. But let me tell you, it was fun city.

Then we were invited to the paddock area because they were ready to put the saddle on the horse and get him ready for the race. My son-in-law Chris said to me, "Hey, Mr. V, I like the horse's attitude. He seems to be edgy."

Well, Cam Gambolati, our trainer, was like a typical coach, man. He was as nervous as anyone before game time. Rick and I were all smiles as we said a few words to It's Awesome, Baby before they took him to the track—I wonder if he could understand my Vitalese?

We went back to the box when the race was ready to start, and I sat with Michael Pitino, Rick's son, who went to Notre Dame—and, by the way, the colors for the horse were blue and gold, with a shamrock as well, for the Irish.

When the race started, we were stunned as It's Awesome, Baby staggered out of the gate and fell way behind. But then, with a burst of speed, he got back to the middle of the pack. Michael said to me, "We're in great shape." He obviously knew the horse, but I looked at him like, "What're you talking about?"

And then, all of a sudden, he was a gem, man. As he put it into high gear, it was amazing to hear the announcer say, "*It's Awesome, Baby on the outside! It's Awesome, Baby closing the gap!*" and at the finish, "*It's Awesome, Baby by a head!*" He had won his first race.

The purse was $28,000, but that wasn't the important thing. What was so exciting was going back to the barn after the race and seeing my granddaughter Sydney passing out carrots and getting our pictures taken with It's Awesome, Baby. If he doesn't win another race, it has certainly been a thrill already.

My life has been so much fun. Any of you fathers will understand what I am talking about when I say that I became a nervous wreck after my daughters told me that they had gotten engaged. Man, I was lucky. Let me tell you, they could not have picked two nicer guys than Chris and Thomas.

My daughters have married two great guys who were athletes at Notre Dame. Terri's married to Chris, who played lacrosse there and will be a hand surgeon with Gulf Coast Orthopedics in Sarasota. Sherri's married to Thomas, who played brilliantly when he took over for Ron Powlus after Ron suffered an injury. Thomas played a vital role in guiding the Irish to the Orange Bowl in 1995.

Thomas is a perfect example of an athlete who's used his athletic ability positively and has transferred it to the real world. After he threw three touchdown passes in the Orange Bowl, Thomas was getting ready for the Blue-Gold spring game when he suffered a neck injury. X-rays revealed a congenital vertebrae condition that would not allow him to play football any longer. It tore his heart out, because he had two years of eligibility remaining. Thomas put all of the energy that he had previously put into football into graduating from law school in two and a half years. He's now working in the prosecutor's office as an assistant state's attorney in Sarasota.

The last two years have allowed me to enter a special part of life. Yes, I've always said that life is filled with chapters. I am now heading into my last chapter, and I want to make it the best of the best.

Lorraine and I have now became grandparents during the last two years, as Terri gave birth to Sydney and Sherri just had twins Jake and Connor last year.

Man, I'd heard from so many friends how great it was to be a granddad. Now I know what they meant. It is so fantastic, as you share some golden moments with your grandkids, and you don't have all the other little problems such as changing diapers, man. You don't have to deal with all the little problems that you do in raising your own. It is fun city. And I just am having the time of my life.

I had the chance on Father's Day to take Sydney and my two little guys, Connor and Jake, out to Tropicana Field in St. Petersburg for their first major league baseball game. Man, I was so excited at 64 years of age and acting about 12, as our grandkids had their Devil Ray uniforms on and were smiling like you can't believe. My buddies Mike Greenberg and Mike Golic of ESPN radio, whom I share words with every Monday, screamed at me and said, "Dickie, you've got to take them to a real major league game."

I said, "Hold it, man. This was major league in every way." We had our photos taken with all the players. They got autographed baseballs and bats and just had an absolute blast. Personally, I probably enjoyed it more than they did.

I can't wait to put them in their Notre Dame uniforms, which are already hanging in the bedroom, and take them to the Golden Dome for their first Notre Dame football game. It will be a real blast.

It's hard to believe that I'm heading into my Silver Anniversary season at ESPN. So many people have been so great to me. Man, I just can't thank enough my partners whom I've worked with recently—guys like Mike Patrick, Brent Musburger, Brad Nessler, John Saunders, Dan Shulman, Chris Fowler, Digger Phelps and all the rest—for putting me in such a comfort zone. They've allowed me to do my thing.

Over the years I've been excited to be part of a stable of analysts that includes veterans such as Bill Raftery, Larry Conley, and Len Elmore. These guys have a great passion for, and are extremely knowledgeable about, the game. I'm just so proud to have been a little spoke in the big wheel of the ESPN/ABC analyst group.

Oh, along the way, I'm sure I've broken lots of rules in the broadcasting profession, but the one thing I have tried to do with each telecast is pour my heart out about the game I love. Man, I've been so fortunate. I've been able to coach at the scholastic, collegiate and professional levels. Believe me, nothing has given me as much joy, professionally, as sitting at courtside in the best seat in the house and talking about the game I love.

I have been blessed to be *Living a Dream*.

EPILOGUE

I'm on a roll now. I can't leave yet. So, hey, let's have some fun. I have named teams over the years, the top dunkers, shot blockers, point guards, innovators and creators, and glass eaters. Here are my best of the best in college, over the past 24 years, as I head into my Silver Anniversary at ESPN. Here we go, baby.

All-Dipsy Doo "Dunkaroos"

These are for the high risers, the elevator men, the guys who play up, up and away, the guys who are human highlight films and are always on *SportsCenter* because of their incredible athleticism and their amazing dunking ability.

- Darrell Griffith, Louisville
- Kenny Battle, Illinois
- Jerome Lane, Pitt
- Harold Miner, Southern California
- Len Bias, Maryland

All-AT & T Long Distance

Hey, in the game of basketball is there anything better than to see a player who's skilled and absolutely, fundamentally solid shooting the jump shot, squaring his body, getting that great look and tickling the twine? These guys represent the best. Nothing but nylon, baby, letting it fly and knocking down the trifecta.

- Chris Mullin, St. John's
- Steve Alford, Indiana

- Chris Jackson, LSU
- Calbert Cheaney, Indiana
- Reggie Miller, UCLA

All-Velcro Defensive Stoppers

Hey, to win on any level, you need guys who will sacrifice for a team, take a charge, make a defensive stop—and that's what these guys represent.
- Stacy Augmon, UNLV
- Gary Payton, Oregon State
- Shane Battier, Duke
- Eric Murdock, Providence
- Gene Smith, Georgetown

All-Human Erasers

Shot blockers deluxe. Guys who say, "Thou shall not enter the lane." They are absolutely human erasers. They take away and eliminate many of the defensive mistakes that happen out on the perimeter.
- Patrick Ewing, Georgetown
- David Robinson, Navy
- Alonzo Mourning, Georgetown
- Adonal Foyle, Colgate
- Dikembe Mutombo, Georgetown

All-Thomas Edison Point Guards

Creators, innovators, guys who are like extensions of their coaches, but when things break down, they simply take the rock, break down their defender and create opportunities.

- Bobby Hurley, Duke
- Pearl Washington, Syracuse
- Mark Price, Georgia Tech
- Kenny Smith, North Carolina
- Mark Jackson, St. John's

All-Frank Lloyd Wright Coaches

Coaches who are great builders, who have the unbelievable creative ability and the incredible leadership skills to be able to build programs that many people think are impossible to take to the winner's circle.

- Bobby Cremins, Georgia Tech
- Lute Olson, Arizona
- Mike Montgomery, Stanford
- John Chaney, Temple
- Jim Calhoun, Connecticut

All-Windex Glass Eaters

Rebounding machines, guys who absolutely go after every rebound like it's their last meal, who just absolutely love attacking the glass.

- Xavier McDaniel, Wichita State
- Hank Gathers, Loyola-Marymount

- La Salle Thompson, Texas
- Jerome Lane, Pitt
- Shaquille O'Neal, LSU

All-Bob Vila Team

These guys built themselves into stars. They were players who came out of nowhere. They were no McDonald's All-Americans, but they simply went to work and made themselves into the stars they became.

- David Robinson, Navy
- Tim Duncan, Wake Forest
- Juan Dixon, Maryland
- Hollis Price, Oklahoma
- Ron Harper, Miami of Ohio

IT'S AWESOME, BABY: THE DICKIE V DICTIONARY

All-Mystique: never know what to expect

Blender: fits in the team system

Cream puff delight: schedule an easy opponent

Cupcake city: game that is no contest

Diaper dandy: sensational freshman

Dipsy-doo dunkaroo: flashy slam dunk

Dishes the rock: passes the ball

Doughnut offense: team without a center

Dow Joneser: up-and-down, inconsistent player

Drillin' Reggies when they need Pete Roses: taking long shots when they need short shots

Engine: the player who leads the team

Getting the ziggy: getting fired

Glass eater: a rebounding machine, a player who loves attacking the glass

High riser: good leaper (*also* skywalker)

Human eraser: great shot blocker

Human space ship: big player

Indianapolis Raceway: up-tempo

Isolation man: great one-on-one player

Knee-knocker: close game

Maalox Masher: close, intense game that usually comes down to the last shot

Maestro man: like an orchestra leader; he makes the big play

M&Mer: a mismatch

Mr. Pac Man: eats you alive on defense

NBN: nothing but nylon

NC: no contest

Perimeter J: a jump shot

PT: playing time

PTPer: a prime-time player

Prime Time: good basketball, what people pay to see

QT: quality time

Shoots the area-code J: shoots from long distance

Skywalker: good leaper (*also* high riser)

Slam, Bam, Jam: an impressive slam dunk

Space eater: big guy

Strawberry shortcake: NCAA Tournament time, when the under-achievers get their just desserts

Surf and turfer: superstar

3-D man: he drives, he draws, he dishes

3-S man: he's super, scintillating, and sensational

Times Square: playing slow-tempo

TO baby: coach getting a timeout

Trifecta: three-point basket

Uncle Mo: momentum has arrived

Velvet touch: silky-smooth shooter

Wilson sandwich: what you get when your shot is rejected in your face

Xs and Os: coaching strategy

Vitale's Teams

All-Airport team: players who look good in airports but get no playing time

All-Alcatraz team: players expected to have breakout seasons

All-AT&T team: long-distance bombers

All-Cawood Ledford team: top local college basketball radio announcers

All-Diaper Dandies team: top freshman players

All-Frank Lloyd Wright team: coaches who are master architects building a program

All-GQ team: sharp-dressing coaches

All-Innovative team: great point guards

All-Marco Polo team: best transfer players

All-Michelangelo team: coaches who are brilliant artists at work

All-Potential team: players who need to start living up to the billing they received in high school

All-Rip Van Winkle team: players who are sleepers

All-Rolls Royce team: superstars at their positions

All-*SportsCenter* team: coaches who need PR

All-Thomas Edison team: innovative point guards

All-Windex team: players who clean the glass (i.e., great rebounders)

All-World B. Free team: players with the best names

All-Zebra team: outstanding referees